PERSONALITY THEORY IN ACTION

Handbook for the Objective-Analytic (O-A) Test Kit

Raymond B. Cattell
James M. Schuerger

INSTITUTE FOR PERSONALITY AND ABILITY TESTING
CHAMPAIGN, ILLINOIS

Library of Congress Catalog Card Number: 78-50146

ISBN 0-918296-11-0

Contents

Chapter   *Page*

Preface   1

1   Origin, Purpose, and Research Basis of the O-A Kit   9

2   The Main Utilities of the O-A Kit   21

3   Description of the Source Traits Measured   25

4   Design of Batteries: The Main Kit, the Extended Kit, and the
    Individual Test Supplement to the Main Kit   33

5   Psychometric Properties of the Source-Trait Batteries
    in the Main Kit   49

6   Test Administration: Detailed Instructions   59
    Instructions for administering U.I. 16   62
    Instructions for administering U.I. 19   69
    Instructions for administering U.I. 20   76
    Instructions for administering U.I. 21   81
    Instructions for administering U.I. 23   89
    Instructions for administering U.I. 24   95
    Instructions for administering U.I. 25   101
    Instructions for administering U.I. 28   108
    Instructions for administering U.I. 32   114
    Instructions for administering U.I. 33   123

7   Scoring: I. Principles for Scoring the O-A   129
    Approximate or exact standard scores for a single factor battery
    from the main kit   132
    The use of corrections for age, sex, and other population
    differences   148

8   Scoring: II. Mechanics for Obtaining Subtest Raw Scores   165
    Answer sheet and expendable booklet scoring details   166
    Using the score summary sheet   168

9   Second- and Third-Stratum Personality Factors and the Use
    of Depth Psychometry   211
    Scoring of second orders   217

10 Criterion Relations: I. Arranged Under Individual
    Source Traits   227
    Criterion relations for U.I. 16, ego standards   227
    Criterion relations for U.I. 19, independence   228
    Criterion relations for U.I. 20, evasiveness   229
    Criterion relations for U.I. 21, exuberance   230
    Criterion relations for U.I. 23, mobilization-vs-regression   231
    Criterion relations for U.I. 24, anxiety   232
    Criterion relations for U.I. 25, realism-vs-tensidia   235
    Criterion relations for U.I. 28, asthenia-vs-self-assurance   236
    Criterion relations for U.I. 32, exvia-vs-invia   236
    Criterion relations for U.I. 33, discouragement-vs-
    sanguineness   238

Contents (Continued)

11   Criterion Relations: II. The O-A Kit Organized Under Educational, Socio-Occupational, and Clinical Uses 241
         Application in educational psychology   242
         Application in occupational and social psychology   247
         Clinical pathology and delinquency   248

12   The Use of Personality Theory in Relation to the O-A Battery . 263
         Alertness to psychometric principles within
         personality theory   265

      Appendix A: The Extended Source-Trait Kit 277

      Appendix B: Supplementary Tests, Individual in
      Administration, for the Main Battery 283

      Appendix C: Instructions and Illustrations for
      Scoring of a Trait Battery 287

      Bibliography 293

      Author Index 313

      Subject Index 317

Tables

Number   *Page*

3.1   Titles and Brief Descriptions of the 10 Source Traits in the O-A Battery 28

4.1   Descriptive Titles, Index Numbers, and Direction of Contribution of Subtests for Each Factor Battery in the Main Kit 36

5.1   Psychometric Consistency: Dependability, stability, and trait constancy coefficients for each source trait 51

5.2   Dependability Coefficients Corrected to One Hour Length Per Factor Battery 52

5.3   Concept ("Construct") Validities of the 10 Main Battery Factors 53

5.4   Concept Validities Using Computer Synthesis ("Variance Allocation") Scoring 54

5.5   Validation of O-A Primaries for U.I. 17, 24, and 32 Against Questionnaire Secondaries 57

6.1   Administration of the O-A Main Kit 60

7.1   Transitions from Raw Scores: Weights to be applied to subtests to obtain factor scores when using single trait batteries of the O-A main kit 133

      U.I. 16, ego standards   133
      U.I. 19, independence   134
      U.I. 20, evasiveness   135
      U.I. 21, exuberance   136
      U.I. 23, mobilization-vs-regression   137
      U.I. 24, anxiety   138
      U.I. 25, realism-vs-tensidia   139
      U.I. 28, asthenia   140
      U.I. 32, exvia-vs-invia   141
      U.I. 33, discouragement-vs-sanguineness   142

7.2   Weight Matrix (V_w) Values for Computer Synthesis Scoring of the O-A Main Battery 144

7.3   Corrections of Standard Scores for Age Differences 162

8.1   Scoring Instructions: Score summary sheets, specimen answer sheets, and numerical calculations for each factor of the main kit 170

      U.I. 16, ego standards   171
      U.I. 19, independence   175
      U.I. 20, evasiveness   178
      U.I. 21, exuberance   185
      U.I. 23, mobilization-vs-regression   187
      U.I. 24, anxiety   191
      U.I. 25, realism-vs-tensidia   195
      U.I. 28, asthenia   199
      U.I. 32, exvia-vs-invia   203
      U.I. 33, discouragement-vs-sanguineness   207

Tables (Continued)

9.1 Matches of O-A Primaries with Second-Stratum Questionnaire Media Personality Factors 213

9.2 Correlations Among Pure Factors at Simple Structure 215

9.3 Second-Stratum Factor Patterns from the Largest (Male) Sample (N = 2522) 216

9.4 The Nature and Scoring of the O-A Secondaries 218

9.5 Correlations Among Higher Strata Factors and the Patterns of Third-Stratum Factors 220

9.6 Criterion Relations of Second-Stratum Traits to Clinical Diagnoses 224

11.1 School Performance Estimated from Individual Primary Personality Traits in the Kit 244

11.2 Multiple R's Predicting Scholastic Achievement from the Whole Kit, With and Without Intelligence 246

11.3 Significance of Source-Trait Differences of Neurotics and Psychotics (Schizophrenics) from Normal Controls 250

11.4 Discriminant Function Weights in Differentiating Seven Groups 253

11.5 Measurable Changes in U.I. 23, Mobilization-vs-Regression, and U.I. 24, Anxiety Produced by Therapy 258

11.6 Trait Score Differences of Convicted Adult Offenders and Nondelinquent Controls in a Uniform Environment 260

11.7 Agreement of Discriminant Function Placements by O-A Battery With Psychiatric Diagnoses 262

A.1 Answer Sheet for Scoring Example 288

A.2 Scoring Example Computation 290

Figures

Number		Page
7.1a	Age Development Curve, U.I. 16, Ego Standards	149
7.1b	Age Development Curve, U.I. 17, Superego	150
7.1c	Age Development Curve, U.I. 19, Independence-vs-Subduedness	151
7.1d	Age Development Curve, U.I. 20, Evasiveness	152
7.1e	Age Development Curve, U.I. 21, Exuberance	153
7.1f	Age Development Curve, U.I. 23, Capacity to Mobilize-vs-Regression	154
7.1g	Age Development Curve, U.I. 24, Anxiety	155
7.1h	Age Development Curve, U.I. 25, Realism-vs-Tensidia	156
7.1i	Age Development Curve, U.I. 26, Narcistic Ego	157
7.1j	Age Development Curve, U.I. 28, Asthenia-vs-Self-Assurance	158
7.1k	Age Development Curve, U.I. 32, Exvia-vs-Invia	159
7.1l	Age Development Curve, U.I. 33, Discouragement-vs-Sanguineness	160
7.2	Translation from Standard Scores to Stens and to Centile Ranks	163
11.1	Separation of Clinical Groups and Normals by Two Discriminant Functions	254

Preface

A touch of history—personal and general—in relation to objective personality test development, and some tribute to the hundreds of people involved in it, is appropriate in this preface. When the history of the half century of research on personality structure by objective measures and multivariate experiment is finally written, it will make surprising reading. It will surprise sober scientists in the same way that the real story of the Copernican revolution, or Harvey's concept of circulation of the blood, or the germ theory of disease, or the death of phlogiston does. And although these are greater examples, the degree of aptness of the present example is as great because it occurred in the century in which far more people were believed to be trained in scientific thinking.

To a methodologist, it would seem obvious that personality structure would be open to unraveling by the measurement of behavior and the application of multivariate analysis by flexible factor analysis and related methods. Clinical and everyday observations, by their natures, are but a crude, factually undependable and perceptually loose approach to the same principles and methods. Yet a good historical account from 1905, when Spearman introduced these methods, to about 1965 would show that the majority of psychologists either did not know what was going on or interpreted factors as strange "mathematical abstractions."

Equally lost from view—except for a minority of experimentalists with multivariate education—was the importance of having personality theory develop on objectively measured responses in defined and replicable situations, i.e., on underlying objective tests, rather than on questionnaires and vague ratings—sometimes contaminated more by the personality of the observer than reproducing the personality of the one being observed. It is no exaggeration to say that nine-tenths of books on personality assessment have dealt with ratings, questionnaires, interviews, and the like. One must not overlook that over and above the unreliability of a given particular "score" by these methods stood the weakness of the theoretical conceptual domain that tried to build on such a foundation.

The advent of a few objective test devices like the Rorschach and the Szondi could not remedy this situation since they did not provide the broad spectrum of personality behavior necessary for factoring of trait structures. Neither could the broader span of some four hundred miniature situational tests in *Objective Personality and Motivation Tests* (Cattell & Warburton, 1967) until basic research had structured them, though the fact that this became a Psychology Book-of-the-Month-Club choice showed that interest in objective devices was mounting.

1

Meanwhile, the basic programmatic factor-analytic research, moving on steadily and strategically from concept to inferred test development, to test findings, and to improved concepts, might have been in another world as far as the awareness or interest of practicing psychologists and clinicians was concerned. Yet, the research basis of the factors found, and the batteries for measuring them, was to a rational and empirical methodology far sounder than anything in the traditional stream of clinical practices.

To anyone, aware that even today scientific advance is dominated as much by social currents as by rational, methodological realities, it became evident that researchers in this area would do well to desist awhile from basic research and statistical discussions as in *Psychometrika* and *Multivariate Behavioral Research* and get the concepts and batteries into the hands of practicing psychologists. Only then would the instruments' value become recognized at a practical level, their powers of criterion prediction tested, and their conceptual development brought into clinical theory. As for clinical psychology itself, its quixotic retreat from meaningful diagnosis, occasioned in large part by the poor testing devices at its disposal, might be this aid be reversed sooner than would otherwise come about.[1]

Accordingly, considerable effort has been made to put a finished and practicable battery in the hands of psychologists as soon as the replication of factors (found over 20 or more researches) and the construct validation of subtests (on over 30 years of experiment) could be completed. Previous to this publication only research descriptions of tests and loadings in some 40 scattered articles had been available. Apart from a brief battery for a small group of researchers developed in 1955, this is the first time that a battery of *objective* tests, oriented to and validated against the chief defined personality factor source traits, has been available in psychology. To the psychometrist and psychologist with perspective over the last half century this is therefore a historical turning point in personality assessment, though the road may be rough with adversity for awhile, as in all pioneering moves. The solution to the hardships of this initial period is for actual practitioners to show how administration and scoring methods can be improved, and to enrich the predictive values by relating factor sources to a wider circle of educational, counseling, industrial, and clinical criteria. The aim of the Handbook, as the title, *Theory in Action*, indicates, is to

---

[1] The vulnerability of questionnaires to faking and the poor validities, which leading psychometrists like Vernon (1953), Cronbach (1946), Thurstone (1944), Jackson and Messick (1962), and many others have noted, left personality measurement, in the minds of many psychologists, as rather a poor relative of ability measurement. For in the latter, one can point to a history of reliable and valid intelligence tests, as well as to a recent important development of culture-fair intelligence tests (Horn, 1964, 1968) and to an increasing precision of measures of primary abilities, from Thurstone (1944) to Hakstian (1976). One is, therefore, surely building on no exaggerated hopes in foreseeing a new era of precision and power in personality diagnosis and prediction through this advent of objective batteries, comparable in objectivity to ability tests, appearing for defined source traits, in suitable form for all uses.

develop the practical measurements in relation to a general personality theory. Central to this theory is the assertion that the application of correlational factor-analytic methods to a truly broad personality sphere of behavior must encompass the main dimensions of temperament and dynamic structure. The 20 unitary factorial source traits now checked in this wide array of behavioral measures, and proven to predict an equally broad sample of educational, occupational, and clinical criteria, must be regarded as the main structures with which a scientific personality theory can seriously concern itself. Since these patterns unquestionably exist, and account for the larger part of the variance in a wide spectrum of personality behaviors, the psychologist, hitherto flirting with clinically generated (or even subjectively fabricated) concepts, must eventually turn to organizing his theories around them—if his theories are to keep touch with reality. There is enormous scope here for the researcher-practitioner for years to come.

Looking more closely and personally at the history of the whole research development itself, the authors would see the main creativity in the structural exploration as lying in the work of invention of miniature situations and responses, deliberately designed to (a) cover a wide spectrum of behavior and (b) test the hypotheses emerging with the new factor patterns. The experimental designs and factor-analytic techniques, as such, were relatively routine. The detailed story of the test design in response to covering theories in an inductive-hypothetico-deductive spiral, however, would make instructive reading. The essentials have been covered in biographical terms by Hall and Lindzey (1974) and Krawiec (1974), and in technical manner by Cartwright (1974), Cattell (1957a), Cattell and Kline (1977), Cattell and Scheier (1961), Cattell, Schmidt, and Bjerstedt (1972), Cattell and Warburton (1967), Damarin and Cattell (1968), Eysenck (1952, 1960, 1961, 1972), Hundleby, Pawlik, and Cattell (1965), Nesselroade and Delhees (1966), Pawlik (1968), Schmidt, Häcker, and Cattell (1975), and others.

A considerable array of testable theoretical concepts about these personality structures is now in the literature. One may mention "ego standards" (indexed as U.I. 16 in the standard series), regression (U.I. 23), anxiety (U.I. 24), psychotic tension and unrealism (U.I. 25), and exvia-invia (U.I. 32) as concepts from the above researches. Meanwhile, evidence is accumulating on their predictiveness in everyday life and psychological practice (Cartwright, 1974; Cattell, 1973b; Cattell & Scheier, 1958a, 1958b, 1959, 1961; Cattell, Schmidt, & Bjerstedt, 1971; Eysenck, 1961, 1972; Eysenck & Eysenck, 1968; Hundleby, 1973a, 1973b; Killian, 1960; Knapp, 1960, 1961a, 1961b, 1961c, 1962, 1963, 1965; Knapp & Most, 1960; Meredith, 1967; Nesselroade & Delhees, 1966; Schuerger, 1970; Tatro, 1966; Wardell & Yeudall, 1976). From such interlocking studies some 20 *factors* have each been replicated across from 4 to 20 researches (Hundleby, Pawlik, & Cattell, 1965), and the 10 that are best confirmed and

3

shown to have most relation to life criteria have been gathered into the present O-A Battery.

The choice of the 10 personality source traits which should thus be made available in the first objective personality test battery was also based on the degree to which the discovered factor patterns showed constancy and continuity across *age development levels* (Cattell & Coan, 1959; Cattell & Gruen, 1955; Damarin & Cattell, 1968; Hundleby, Pawlik, & Cattell, 1965) and across *cultures*. Recent work (Cattell, Schmidt, & Pawlik, 1973) with the same set of objective tests across American, German, and Japanese subjects gives ample proof that at least the 10 factors chosen for the O-A Battery have this constancy and universality of pattern in human nature. The source-trait measurements deal, in short, with *basic and stable dimensions of human nature*, which occur across ages and cultures and can be used for both developmental and cultural comparisons.

No matter how thorough, creative, and well-checked research may be, the reception of its results may be profitable or unprofitable depending on quite different, sometimes accidental, and always largely social circumstances. It has been said by students of scientific progress (Kuhn, 1962) that there can be very little relation between the intrinsic contribution of a new idea and the speed of its reception. Indeed, the greater the single stride made in some conception, the less it is likely to be readily applied. Historians point, for example, to about 40 years' delay between Faraday's discovery of the principle for constructing what later came to be known as a dynamo and the actual industrial application of the principle.[2] The psychology of personality has passed through three or four thousand years of literary humanistic insights, another hundred years of

---

[2]The strong research arguments for moving from questionnaires to objective tests (or, at least, supplementing questionnaires with objective tests) have so far been slighted in psychological practice for two reasons. First, there is the economic reason: the understandable unwillingness of test publishers to go to the far greater labor and expense in putting out complex objective test batteries. This becomes still more uneconomic by reason of the lesser demand to be expected for instruments which only the better trained professional psychologists can use. The lag in the application of the basic research findings to practice occurs also because of the disturbing demand on psychologists to learn new skills. (Actually, the O-A requires no more practice, however, than to administer, say, the Binet and its derivatives.) If the closed circle of teachers teaching only what their teachers taught them can be broken, and if research demonstrating actual effectiveness in psychological work properly takes precedence over immediate convenience, an accelerated use of objective personality measures is likely to yield a new harvest of psychological knowledge which will in turn raise still further the superiority of objective tests.

Undoubtedly, a third and major obstacle, until now, has been that the psychologist wishing to measure these source traits had to search out some 80 subtests in several dozen research articles and prepare and standardize them for himself. The present O-A test construction provides, after more than 30 years of relatively recondite and scattered research publication, the first readily accessible and standardized comprehensive personality trait battery for general use in applied psychology and personality research. Wherever researches on predictions from personality factors, measures of developmental change, effect of educational and therapeutic procedures, etc., are involved, the O-A offers the most factorially comprehensive source of measurement. An attempt has been made to make a choice of primary source traits that is central to personality in that it gives prediction of about two-thirds of the variance on any broadly chosen sample of one or two hundred behavioral measures.

4

deeper clinical insights, and is now well launched on a third phase of quantitative experimental personality research. This last phase has turned out to demand far more technical knowledge than the two preceding phases, particularly because the most effective experiment has turned out to be of the multivariate rather than the older bivariate design (Cattell, 1966c). Many clinicians—and in some universities even the bulk of students trained in psychology—lack the grounding in multivariate experimental methods that would enable their enquiring minds to study directly and judge for themselves the evidence of source traits as factors. Even the lesser aim of understanding how to use those measurements effectively in diagnosis and prediction is sometimes neglected.[3]

The result of this educational situation has been, first, that many practitioners do not understand the advantages of the psychometric properties and the scientific universality of meaning provided by source-trait batteries over arbitrary scales, and, secondly, through unfamiliarity with use of objective tests, they continue (even if with factored scales) with questionnaires where objective behavioral tests would be more powerful and dependable. Admittedly, the objective tsting requires more time and skill, but if the return to functioning of, say, a clinical patient is an important and humanitarian aim, then the more reliable diagnosis and direction of therapy to be gained surely justifies a decent allocation of time.

For the psychologist who does not have an extensive background related to understanding factorial source-trait findings, or familiarity with testing procedures, one can only suggest that he read into the subject on his own initiative. In the clinical field, for example, one may refer to the books of Freedman and Kaplan (1975), Mahrer (1970), Sankar (1969), Spielberger (1966), and Wolman (1973) as incorporating treatment of these source traits, while in general psychology one thinks particularly of the books by Cartwright (1974), Cattell and Kline (1977), Eysenck (1960), Hall and Lindzey (1965), Koch (1959), Pervin (1975), Wolman (1973), and others. Or one may attend workshops in which the newer concepts and methods are taught in relation to actual clinical, industrial, and educational needs. Nevertheless, as far as possible in the limited scope of a primarily practical, applied handbook, we have tried here to give some understanding of the research meaning of the personality factors and of the statistics of the specification equations in which they can be used.

---

[3]Statistical concepts being essential to any progress in psychology as a science, one might expect that in a faculty of, say, 20, some 10 would be especially competent in ANOVA and 10 more especially in CORAN (correlational analysis, including factor analysis and other multivariate methods), since all experimental work and evaluation of theories requires in the end ANOVA and CORAN methods. There are far more instances actually where 2, rather than 10, teach in a way to give understanding of these methods. In this respect, the equipment of most psychology departments is about as obsolete as that of the world's navies when Billy Mitchell pointed out that planes had made battleships obsolete—so many years before Pearl Harbor.

The user of the O-A has no need whatever to delve into factor-analytic technicalities as such, but he *should* understand the *logic* of factor analysis and what it means in guaranteeing that any one of these source traits is a real functional unity. Secondly, he should have as clear a conception as possible of the psychological meaning of each source trait. Thirdly, he should understand the statistical and psychological interaction of an individual's profile of source-trait scores, e.g., in the *specification equation*. Lastly, he needs to be familiar with the various criterion relations quantitatively expressed in research findings. As stated elsewhere, this book is not only the usual Handbook to a test battery, but is planned as a well-illustrated teaching aid for personality courses aiming at understanding of the above theoretical and substantive issues. To profit from an imaginative and exact use of these measurements, in relation to all kinds of criteria, therapeutic influences, physiological variables, developmental studies, and so forth, the psychologist *must* help to advance the research knowledge. At present, in some fields we must depend for theoretical understanding of the nature and development on a first relatively thin harvest of applied research. However, this research is advancing internationally. For example, the simultaneous publication by Schmidt and Hacker of a German version of the American O-A, as well as its use in England and Australia and translation for use in Japan, etc., should provide a guarantee of the broad scientific development of these concepts which the international character of science requires.

Finally, in giving credit for origins of the basic concepts which made the production of these O-A Batteries possible, one must go far beyond the immediate authors, and even the laboratories, such as the Laboratory of Personality Analysis at the University of Illinois and the Psychiatric Institute at the Maudsley Hospital in London, which have programmatically pursued this goal over 30 years or more. Just as in astronautic development the final small object that is put in orbit is apt to deceive one's estimate of all the forces and the preparation that went into the rocket thrust, so here it would be a mistake to overlook the individual work of an army of implicit co-workers. If we may be forgiven inadvertent omissions, we would name particularly Adcock, Anderson, Arnold, Baehr, Baggaley, Baltes, Bartlett, Barton, Bartsch, Beloff, Bjerstedt, Blewett, Brogden, Bolz, Brengelmann, Bucell, Burdsal, Buss, Butcher, Cable, A. K. S. Cattell, Coan, Cogan, Conner, Coulter, Cross, Crutcher, Curran, Damarin, Das, Delhees, Dermen, DeYoung, Dickman, Dielman, Digman, Dreger, Drevdahl, Dubin, Duffy, Eysenck, Fahrenberg, Finkbeiner, Fiske, French, Ford, Gibb, Gibbons, Goldberg, Gorsuch, Gray, Gruen, Hakstian, Hammond, Hargreaves, Haverland, Herrington, Hildebrand, Horn, Horowitz, Howarth, Hundleby, Husek, Ishikawa, Jaspars, Karson, Kawash, Killian, Klein, Kline, Knapp, Korth, Kristy, Krug, Lily, Luborsky, Laughlin, Lushene, Mayeske, McMichael, Meeland, Meredith,

Meschieri, Nesselroade, Nichols, Patrick, Pawlik, Peterson, Pichot, Pierson, Porter, Price, Radcliffe, Rethlingshafer, Rhymer, Rican, Rickels, Royce, Ryans, Saunders, Schaie, Scheier, Schmidt, Schneewind, Schoenemann, Schuerger, Sealy, Sells, Stice, Sullivan, Sweney, Tatro, Thornton, Thurstone, Tiner, Tollefson, Tsujioka, Uberla, Valley, Vaughan, Vidal, Wagner, Warburton, Wardell, Watterson, Wenger, Wenig, White, Wilde, Williams, Wiggins, Witkin, Winder, Wispe, Yee.

The authors wish to thank for their help in the actual preparation of this Handbook, particularly Dr. Samuel Krug and Dr. David Madsen whose checking of complex interrelation of the text and the tables has been a very great help.

Raymond B. Cattell

Distinguished Research Professor Emeritus
University of Illinois

1

Origin, Purpose and Research Basis
of the O-A Kit

The title *Personality Theory in Action* should orient the alert reader to the fact that he has in the O-A something very different from the majority of test constructions. The O-A construction belongs in the realm of *structured tests*, i.e., tests that are shaped to the structures that basic research has shown to be essential elements of human personality in our culture—indeed, in most cultures.

Structured tests are a necessary requirement for *functional* testing and assessment, i.e., diagnostic testing, where the natural history, the age curves, the degree of inheritance, and the response to therapy of the traits measured is understood. With many older tests, e.g., the Rorschach, one depends only on empirical statistical relations between some bit of test behavior and some diagnostic category, e.g., schizophrenia. With structured tests, by contrast, one gets an evaluation of the trait understood in a tested theory of personality action. For example, we know that the source trait indexed as Factor U.I. 23, mobilization-vs.-regression, is dependably and significantly lower in neurotics and psychotics than in normals; that its hereditary determination is relatively unimportant; that it rises with age in a curve very similar to intelligence; that it is high in people capable of meeting emergencies, such as airline pilots, business executives, and astronauts; that it is lowered by chronic conflict and fatigue; that it rises significantly in middle-class neurotic patients under tranquilizers and good individual psychotherapy; that it has some physiological association; and so on.

Along with measures on other factors, in a total profile, this means that the psychologist is able, with theoretical insight, to make predictions and take remedial steps that go beyond the mere statistical estimate he is normally able to make between a raw score and some criterion which is valid only for that day. Since these measures have been born out of the slow process, from 1940 to 1975, of adequate, programmatic, basic research, it is not surprising that the full scientific implications in applied psychology have yet to come. The several basic source-trait patterns are firm enough and, as the tables within the Handbook show, their batteries now reach reliabilities and validities close to those of intelligence tests. But they stand relatively stark in terms of theoretical embellishment because psychologists have been all too prone, in the past, to build theories around clinical entities, or from terms in a dictionary, rather than these admittedly truly strange and new—but real, replicable, and objectively measurable—broad source traits. They are strange because they emerge from sophisticated, multivariate experimental techniques—much as microbes emerged from microscopic and staining techniques in which most physicians, up to Koch's decade, were untrained. However, it is not necessary to get immersed in the theoretical origins in order to understand, logically and insightfully, the personality theory now growing from discovery of source traits.

For broader discussion of such theory, based on objective multivariate experiment, the reader must be referred to Cartwright's *Theories of Personality* (1977), Cattell's *Personality: A Systematic Theoretical and Factual Study* (1950), *Personality and Learning Theory* (1978), Cattell and Child's *Motivation and Dynamic Structure* (1975), Cattell and Dreger's *Handbook of Modern Personality Theory* (1977), Eysenck's *Structure of Human Personality* (1960), Guilford's *Personality* (1959), Karson and O'Dell's *Clinical Use of the 16 PF* (1976), Krug's *Psychological Assessment in Medicine* (1977), Hall and Lindzey's *Theories of Personality* (1974), Nesselroade and Reese's *Life Span Developmental Psychology* (1973), Pawlik's *Dimensionen des Verhaltens* (1968), Pervin's *Personality Theory, Assessment and Research* (1975), Royce's *Multivariate Analysis in Psychological Theory* (1973), Schmidt's *Objective Personlichkeits-messung in diagnostischer und klinischer Psychologie* (1975), Schuerger and Watterson's *Using Tests and Other Information in Counseling* (1977), Sells' *Essentials of Psychology* (1962), Spielberger's *Anxiety: Current Trends in Research and Theory* (1972), and Wiggins' *Personality and Prediction: Principles of Personality Assessment* (1973).[1]

In what follows, the theory will be illustrated in concrete applications and by descriptions of the characteristics of the various source traits. The central principle is that any specific behavior, school or job performance, or clinical symptom is the outcome of interaction of all traits in the personality and of the particular situation. This is expressed in the model of the specification equation as follows:

$$a_{hijk} = b_{hjk1}T_{1i} + b_{hjk2}T_{2i} + \ldots + b_{hjkp}T_{pi}$$

where a is a measurement in standard scores of the response or performance j in regard to the stimulus h taken in the ambient general situation k. The b's are *behavioral indices* (either correlations or factor loadings, with oblique factors) which express how much the particular stimulus—performance behavior—derives from the given trait. Since the values are peculiar to each trait, the b subscript finishes with a 1 for Trait T_1, a 2 for trait T_2, and a p for the pth Trait in the series, T_p. Since this is a prediction of the a_{hjk} performance for a particular individual i, we note this by writing a_{hijk}, T_{1i}, T_{2i}, etc.

---

[1]The more advanced explanation by some internationally leading writers is in Cattell and Dreger (1977). A general explanation adapted to students may be found in Cattell and Kline's *Scientific Analysis of Personality and Motivation* (1977).

Research gives us the situational b values for any given performance, while tests give us the T values for a given person. In what has been called "the two-file system" the psychologist will have files of b values —behavioral indices— for all kinds of performances and clinical prognostications, and he also will keep a file of T values for his patients, for company employees to be better placed, or for students advancing in school.

The traits—the T's—will be highly diverse in nature and action. Some will be of the ability modality, like intelligence, some general temperamental personality traits, like extraversion or ego strength, and some motivational traits of sentiment and ergic tension strengths, as studied in *Motivation and Dynamic Structure* (Cattell & Child, 1975). In, say, an estimate of school achievement, the b value for intelligence is known to be about $+ .50$, while the b value in the same situation for U.I. 16, ego standards, from the present O-A Battery, is about $+ 0.4$. The b's can, of course, be positive or negative, ranging from roughly $+ 1.0$ to $- 1.0$, and a negative weight for a behavioral index means that the trait in question *impedes* performance, as, say, introversion impedes performance as a salesman.

Discovery of behavior index values for an increasing number of clinical, industrial, social, and educational situations can be left to applied psychology, providing it measures traits well and meaningfully. It is the latter with which we are here concerned. Personality assessment and factorial delineation of the true structural unities suitable for assessment has proceeded through three media of observation: observers' ratings (L-data), subjects' answers to questionnaires (Q-data), and objective tests (T-data) measuring performance in miniature situations. The present book is concerned with the latter. Moreover, it is concerned with the general personality traits, recognizing that the ability modality has to be brought in additionally by the usual ability factors[2] and the motivation-interest aspects of personality by the Motivation Analysis Test (MAT) factors.

What makes the O-A Kit of factor batteries a unique contribution to psychological practice today is that it is both (a) based on replicated factorial evidence of personality structure across a wide sphere of human behavior and (b) based on measured actual behaviors rather than self-assessment by questionnaire. (Originally, many of the tests were of a laboratory nature, but ultimately all used have been modified for group administration and checked in their modified form. They are pencil and paper, but not scored as self-assessment. The laboratory tests are defined and available in works by Hundleby, Pawlik, and Cattell [1965] and Cattell and Warburton [1967] for those who wish to refer to the original batteries.)

By the *principle of indifference of indicator* (Cattell, 1973b), one concludes that L-, Q-, and T-data media are measuring the same personality source traits by different approaches. That is, the same personality

---

[2]For general intelligence we suggest the Culture Fair Intelligence Scales 1, 2, or 3 (Cattell, 1950; Cattell & Cattell, 1973) and for primary ability abilities, the Comprehensive Ability Battery (CAB) of Hakstian and Cattell (1975, 1976).

theory and the same research findings can be comprehensively applied across all and contribute to the meaning of all. However, (a) though L (life rating in situations) and Q (questionnaire-self-report) factors are matched one-to-one across the media (Cattell, Pierson, & Finkbeiner, 1976), it seems that the T-data factors are second-order[3] to Q- and L-data factors, and (b) questionnaires and ratings have problems of motivational distortion by the self-rater and the observer-rater, respectively, that do not exist in the T-data media.

Psychometry has developed some antidotes to motivational distortion, faking, and sabotage in questionnaires, notably MD (Motivational Distortion) scales and Trait-View Theory which, in the case of the 16 PF, CAQ, HSPQ, and other instruments, have been brought to some degree of accuracy. However, there are still situations, e.g., prison inmates seeking parole, court cases using psychiatric evidence, and uncooperative subjects where common sense forbids us to trust the questionnaires, where the objective test, T-data approach is indispensable. (By definition, an objective test is one "where the subject performs without knowing on which aspect of the behavior his personality is actually being evaluated.") Moreover, in any evaluation of the relative utility of Q- and T-data, it should be noted that present evidence shows the latter to be covering a wider span of behavior and, at least in the clinical field, achieving a higher degree of diagnostic degree of separation.

Objective tests have been developed and tried before, as in the Rorschach, the Downey (Cattell, 1946), Hartshorne and May's work, and so on, but *not* in a framework of multivariate experimental programmatic research leading to source-trait structures and a viable theoretical model. Developments are proceeding to extend the O-A Battery to other age groups, and special-purpose usage has begun in England, Germany, and Japan.[4]

To give fuller justification to the O-A (Objective-Analytic) title, let us point out that *objective* has sometimes been used in psychometry in the lesser sense that the *scoring* of some test is objective, as in multiple choice where a stencil key can be used—a procedure better designated *conspective*. By conspective ("seen together"), one means that two psychologists will write down the same score from a given answer sheet. This does not mean that the evaluation of the subject's personality from his score is

---

[3]For example, as will be illustrated later, extraversion comes out as a primary in T-data, namely, U.I. 32, but in questionnaires and ratings it is a second order, QI and LI, respectively, covering questionnaire primaries A, F, H, and Q_2.

[4]A first battery—admittedly in cumbersome form—was published by IPAT as early as 1955 and yielded some diverse criterion findings. The Japanese results are reported in Cattell, Schmidt, and Pawlik (1973). A kit which is close to a simple translation, with cultural adaptation, of the present O-A has already appeared in Germany through the work of Schmidt and Häcker (1975). The concern for cross-cultural precision of parallelism in the latter should greatly help natural use of clinical and other findings. Professor John Hundleby, of the University of Guelph, is meanwhile developing an O-A Kit of source traits for clinical settings.

objective: he may indeed have distorted his responses in answering the questions. By contrast, the objectivity of the O-A resides in the fact that the subject responds to a *miniature life situation, not knowing from what angle his behavior is being interpreted.* Additionally, in these tests the basis of scoring *does* remain conspective, so freedom from subjectivity in *both* respects is maintained. (Parenthetically, conspective scoring does not preclude "open-ended" tests, though multiple-choice tests are more easily adapted thereto.)

"Analytic" in this O-A title refers to factor analytic, and means that only those source traits that have been isolated, replicated and identified across diverse populations, and achieved psychological interpretation are used. The use of a single term and concept for any such source trait therefore rests on quantitative measurement followed by correlational proof of the trait being a functional unity, followed by demonstrated relevances to everyday life behavior. A gulf in scientific conception separates such new trait concepts from older notions based only on subjective hunches or intuitive clinical "insights." However, it is gratifying evidence of the consistency of methodologically different research approaches that several source traits, checked factor analytically, actually confirm and add precision to unitary structures previously perceived clinically, as in the case of *ego standards* (U.I. 16), *regression* (U.I. 23), *anxiety* (U.I. 24), *extraversion* (U.I. 32), *general inhibition* (U.I. 17), and other factors now uniquely defined by simple structure or con-factor rotation.

More than 20 first-order (primary) personality source traits are presently known, indexed by the universal index numbers U.I. 16 through U.I. 37. (Note the numbers U.I. 1 through U.I. 15 are kept for primary ability source traits, as listed by French, 1953.)

The present O-A Battery, however, confines itself in the Main Kit to the 10 best replicated and verified factors among those, as shown in Table 3.1. Furthermore, it confines itself to tests that have been adapted (from the individual "laboratory" tests as initially designed) so that they can be administered in a group-testing situation. They remain functional, however, as individual tests when the psychologist needs so to use them. Since the battery of subtests typically required for each factor takes about 28 minutes in all (or up to 35 minutes until the psychologist becomes well practiced), the total Kit or battery of 10 source traits requires from 4 to 6 hours for administration, depending on the experience of the examiner, the age of the subjects, etc. Naturally, this does not have to be in a single long session.

However, the idea of designing as a "Kit" saves the psychologist from having always to follow this onerous procedure. It means that the battery is so constructed that any single source trait, or combination of the 10 source traits, can be pulled out and administered separately, according to the psychologist's specific aim.

The administration of the *total* battery thus requires somewhat unusual time demands. The use of separate factors, though saving time, still requires more skill than in administering a questionnaire. The *scoring* of the great majority of the tests, however, requires no "artistic" skill, since it is done from standard answer sheets, arranged for machine scoring. This fact, together with the above-mentioned design as a Kit of 10 separately administrable parts, permits all kinds of flexible uses and makes the battery, in the end, scarcely more difficult to use than most questionnaires. Often a particular criterion can be predicted to the full degree psychometrically possible by as few as one, two, or three factors, and the testing time, thus, becomes reduced to an hour or so. In following discussions we shall assume that separate use of factors from the Kit will be the rule, though references will sometimes apply to using the full battery.

As stated in opening this chapter, the scope of the book is greater than would normally be covered by a routine handbook. It is greater in that it illustrates personality theory in action, showing the student that an elegant model (as contrasted with more verbal and vague theories still extant) can handle the practical problems he will meet in educational, counseling, and clinical psychology. The 10 concepts of personality structure chosen for more concentrated study here are tangible in subtest behavior and in battery scores of known psychometric validity. The Handbook is broader, however, in the technical sense of reference to a wider field of psychometric findings than are covered by the 10 source traits to which, for practicality, the Kit confines itself. In this matter we refer one specifically to Appendixes A and B that handle the needs of those who want to extend personality measurement beyond the core of the most frequently replicated 10 source traits to which we have restricted the present battery. The Appendixes do this in two directions: (1) by extending consideration of psychological meaning to 10 additional *factors*, and (2) by extending the number of *subtests* available for measuring any one of the present factors. It does the latter mainly by adding individual testing and apparatus-demanding subtests. These are such as the general group-testing user would commonly not want, but they add to the validity of measurement for someone concentrating on measuring a particular factor.

For the first purpose, the Extended Kit in Appendix A enlarges the Main Kit by 10 more factors (U.I. 17, 18, 22, 26, 27, 29, 30, 31, 34, and 35), completing the 20 best known to research. For the second purpose, the Supplementary Tests, in Appendix B, proceed to list for each factor some usefully valid extra subtests that need individual testing or apparatus not conveniently usable in the Main Kit. They are extended principally to give maximum validity and maximal attenuation of specifics, when one wishes to measure source traits of greatest importance to some particular research. For clarity of reference in what follows we shall refer to the tests extended to factors as the Extended Kit, and the factors, extended by additional tests for any factor, as the Supplemented Battery.

In regard to the aim of making the Handbook an illustration of theory in action there is no intention of making it a theoretical treatment as such, but only of designing it as an *adjunct* to a class text in personality. Whenever personality is taught as part of a scientific psychology, we have received enthusiastic response from teachers who have experimented with the *16 PF Handbook* (Cattell, Eber, & Tatsuoka, 1970) as such a supplementary text. With its rich illustrations of actual occupational and educational profiles and specification equations for clinical and social psychological criteria, it evidently can give such substance and concrete interest to the personality and developmental theories being discussed as satisfies more intellectually critical students. Although criterion relations are not yet equally extensive for the O-A Battery, the design of the present Handbook has nevertheless aimed to make its discussions of validity, criterion prediction, the measurement of developmental change, and the references to genetic behavior values applicable to classroom teaching in personality, in psychometry, and in social psychology. Hopefully, the design of segregating certain chapters has succeeded in doing this without diminishing the book's immediate convenience for the busy practicing psychologists concerned with actual administration and scoring. Indeed, this experiment in hybrid design might not only provide an enrichment for personality courses by its realistic applications, but will also be found to give to the practicing psychologist a degree of guidance in the use and background of measurements that in effect is often absent from test handbooks.

When we suggest that the descriptions of known trait patterns, along with the evidence on life-development curves, actions in the specification equation, clinical diagnostic findings, and educational predictive powers, can give substance to courses of personality and personality theory, we have to recognize that this depends on what text the instructor is using. Because of ease of reading, and the fact that complete myths can be made more entertaining than the laborious, half-built structures of science, publications of a certain kind have flooded the college market with texts deleterious to the advance of students aiming at becoming professional psychologists. (See Cattell, 1978, for a critical analysis of the educational issues.) Fortunately, just within the last decade a line of texts has appeared, turning a sharp corner from the old "drug" of diluted clinical concept and literary anecdotes. These new texts[5] promise to make a symbiosis of a theory text and "laboratory practice," as embodied in this Handbook, a real possibility.

---

[5]One thinks at once of Arndt (1974), Baughman (1972), Bischof (1964), Brody (1972), Byrne (1974), Cartwright (1977), Dreger (1962), Eysenck (1952, 1960, 1961), Levy (1970), Liebert and Spiegler (1970), Hall and Lindzey (1974), Maddi (1976), Pervin (1975), Sahakian (1965), Sarason (1966), Sells (1962), Stagner (1974), Wepman (1963), and Wiggins (1973), as well as the already mentioned companion volumes and the books by Cattell and Dreger (1977) and Cattell and Kline (1977). All of these integrate in greater or lesser degrees the experimental and correlational evidence on personality and dynamic structures, and incorporate quantitative evidence on development of these structures with sound theory.

With an eye to the substance of such texts, technical references to theory have been made in the interstices of test practice descriptions here. However, any more systematic excursions into personality theory are relegated to the later chapters (after Chapter 9), and it is there that the progressive teacher can give some assigned reading. Such reading will concern mainly general personality and temperament factors for, as indicated, the Handbook does not deal with motivation and interest measurement per se. However, as already indicated, it does—despite dealing with objective test (T-data) instruments—keep in focus the relation to trait concepts also from rating (L-data) and questionnaire (Q-data) approaches. Among the three media we have already stated that the *principle of indifference of indicators*, or of *instrument-transcending* personality factor structures (Cattell, 1973*b*), has recently been well supported (Cattell, Pierson, & Finkbeiner, 1976) as regards the alignment of factors from L- and Q-data, both in number and nature.[6]

A breakthough demonstrating that "transcendence of instrument" exists between the present T-data and the older Q- and L-data factor source traits was begun when it was found (Cattell, 1955) that the second-order factors exvia (QI) and anxiety (QII) in the questionnaire medium align, respectively, with Factors U.I. 32 (also called exvia) and U.I. 24 (likewise soon recognized as anxiety) in the T-data series. That *first* orders in T-data may consistently align with *second* orders in the questionnaire domain is suggested by a further instance—that of superego (QVIII) with U.I. 17—recently found by Wardell and Yeudall (1976), and the less proven but promising alignments of the questionnaire second order of general psychoticism (Cattell, 1973; Delhees & Cattell, 1971); Eysenck (1968) with U.I. 25, and of cortertia (QIII) and independence (QIV), respectively, with U.I. 22 and U.I. 19. It could well be that with a decade of systematic research on this problem we shall find all personality factors expressing themselves consistently across the three media—the same structures in different instrumental dress. Meanwhile, however, the U.I. objective test (T-data) factors have reached 20, but only 10 (Krug & Laughlin, 1977) to 15 (Cattell, 1973) second-strata factors in Q-data have been identified which suggests that at this point we are getting greater coverage of personality factors through objective tests at the first-order level than we are with questionnaires at the second-order level.

Initially, the personality factors—in any medium—are simply unitary, uniquely rotated factors, inferred to be personality structures

---

[6]There remain obscurities regarding the relation of L- and Q-data to T-data. In order to avoid the error that might arise from giving the same technical name, prematurely, to factors believed to be the same in T-data, on the one hand, and L- and Q- on the other, the listing of discovered source traits in each medium has initially been preserved in separate indexes. An alphabetic indexing system has been followed in L- and Q- domains, where fortunately a one-to-one matching soon permitted the economy of a single series (Cattell, Pierson, & Finkbeiner, 1976). In the T-data medium, on the other hand, U.I. (universal index) numbers have been the standardized form in many articles and books. Besides the identifying index numbers, names of a tentative descriptive or interpretive nature have additionally been given in L-Q and in T series.

responsible for response potential in a pattern of defined environments. The discoverer of a uniquely defined and replicated factor pattern, as in the experience of someone picking up a curiously shaped stone on a beach, does not immediately know what could have produced the pattern. Sometimes later research will show that a factor is a pattern due to common genetic, chromosomal influences, possessed more by some people than others, and expressed in maturation of a temperamental dimension. In other cases it is an acquired, learned pattern, the elements of which vary together as some people are exposed more than others to exact conditioning by a social institution.

The exact determinations of the "natural history" of source traits—their curves of growth, their nature-nurture ratios, their relation to life criteria—can come only after the factor pattern itself is discovered and psychometrically well measured. The "natural history" knowledge is patchy as yet for all but three or four of the source traits measured in the O-A Battery, but the ongoing work of many of the researchers named above is sure to extend our understanding of its origin, developmental changes, and criterion associations. Practicing psychologists, working with the newly available battery, are likely soon to enrich the criterion associations in clinical, educational, occupational, and social psychology in a way that will increase the predictive and diagnostic power of the instrument for all users.

Turning from these general questions of the research origin and theoretical understanding of source traits to the specific foundation for construction and design of this pioneer battery, we would point out: (a) that the decision as to the choice of the most soundly replicated factors rests on the wide collation of factor-loading patterns—typically some 10 researches for each factor (Hundleby, Pawlik, & Cattell, 1965). Continuing with the best subtests, these decisions have been confirmed by three more recent studies (Cattell & Kline, 1975; Cattell, Schmidt, & Pawlik, 1973; Cattell, Schuerger, Kline, & Finkbeiner, 1976), and (b) the choice of tests for each factor rests on higher average loading levels of a test across all researches, on the relative absence of loadings on other factors, and on the convenience of the test form.

Since the O-A is intended both for late high school and adult subjects, the test must retain validity across this age range, and this ideal has required keeping level of cognitive demand low enough to exclude ability variance as much as is practically possible.

In summary, the theoretical and research bases underlying this O-A Battery are:

1) That structure in personality can be shown to take the form of unitary common traits, i.e., meaningful functional unities such as general intelligence, ego strength, proneness to anxiety, and schizothyme temperament. They are factorial dimensions common to all subject samples on which any person can be assigned a particular score.

17

2) A battery yielding a 10- to 20-element profile of such scores is capable of accounting for a substantial fraction of interpersonal variance on a wide array of behavioral measures, and of predicting, psychometrically, much life criterion performance.

3) These traits are of quite diverse natures—ability and temperament dimensions, dynamic drives, and sentiment structures attached to social institutions—all due in varying degrees to heredity and environment. As our theoretical understanding and knowledge increase there will be a steady augmentation of our predictive and diagnostic power from their use. Meanwhile, they are confirmed as operating not only in the adult range but also at lower ages, thus maintaining a continuity of meaning from childhood through adult life. In another direction of consistency, they have been shown to be constant across at least three or four cultures so far compared, i.e., they are characteristic of human nature generally.

4) Although basically psychologically independent, source traits are somewhat correlated statistically through the organizing influence of higher order factors (to be explained later).

The central scientific and mathematical model that the personality theorist and the applied psychologist have to keep in mind is that expressed, among other places, in what has been called on page 10 the *specification equation*. As shown below, this states that any performance or act, a, is to be understood as due to all of a person's traits (T_i) acting together. They act with weights (b's in the following equation) peculiar to the environmental situation and performance j (and, of course, to each of the factor traits concerned)—and in some cases the b weights may be near zero. Knowing the weights or behavioral indices (b's below) from previous research, we can thus estimate any person's response or performance, a_{ij}, from his trait scores (T_i's) as follows:

$$a_{ij} = b_{j1}T_{1i} + b_{j2}T_{2i} + \ldots + b_{jq}T_{qi} + b_jT_{ji} + b_{js}S_{xi} + b_jE_j \qquad 1.1$$

The subscript j on each b means that the loading is specific to the situational performance, j. This differs from the usage on page 10 in that, to avoid cluttering the symbols we have let j stand here for hjk there, i.e., let it represent stimulus, performance, and ambient situation combined. The factor number ($1, 2, \ldots q$) means that the loading is also specific to the given factor. When the b values for any performance are known through previous research, and the present trait (T) scores of the individual are known through the O-A Battery, the predictive estimate can be made. (Note that here we have expanded on the specification on page 10

18

by recognizing that, in addition to the common broad traits, each performance involves a specific trait, T_j, a state, S_x, [actually representative of several states], and an error component, E_j, specific to the performance, a.)

If this equation should seem strange to any reader at first sight, he may note that it will be concretely illustrated later, as we proceed in the Handbook to describe scoring and diagnostic and prediction practices. Other numerous concepts that are pertinent to the O-A Battery, just presented in this chapter, will be developed later in this Handbook too.

2
The Main Utilities of the O-A Kit

It is usual in handbooks to point, at the outset, to the areas in which the test is intended to be used, though the substantiation of such use comes only later when estimates of criteria and diagnostic procedures are discussed in detail.

The broad utility of the O-A Kit, as a "general-purpose" personality test, is founded on: (a) its derivation from widely pursued research on general personality structure, which has produced a *comprehensive* array of source traits; (b) its shaping into a convenient form for both group and individual testing; (c) the flexibility of the "Kit" design, which permits the psychologist to take longer or shorter testing time according to his purposes and available time; (d) a moderate sufficiency of concrete validities, experimentally determined against life criteria; and (e) an adequate standardization.

The O-A's claims to utility rest on (a) an extremely broad basis of more than 400 kinds of explored behavior. The breadth of the behavior covered was directed by the *personality sphere* (Cattell, 1957a) concept of behaviors originally taken from the full scope of the dictionary. And on (b) the battery scores' having been demonstrated as substantially valid measures on the principal discovered unitary traits in personality structure. That is to say, this battery does not subjectively set up arbitrary trait definitions and make tests for these speculative targets. Instead, after a long period of research had first determined and confirmed some 20 factor dimensions, it has put together those of the 400 explored objective tests that show validity in measuring those factors. The argument for utility from the intrinsic construction of the battery rests further on (c) a functional relation of the measurements to research on growth and to concepts in developmental psychology in which these source traits are known to persist in recognizable forms over appreciable age ranges, and (d) the central position of these source traits as concepts in general personality theory (regardless of whether we measure them by objective test, questionnaires, or ratings). This last point makes them worthwhile reference traits about which pure and applied research can steadily accumulate evidence, e.g., on prediction of concrete criteria, age changes, physiological and genetic associations, and educational effects.

It should be pointed out at once in respect to utility that although for brevity the battery is called the O-A, it might be said to contain the HSO-A (*High School Objective-Analytic*) and an AO-A (*Adult Objective-Analytic*) since it is practically applicable over this whole range, though its greatest suitability is to younger adults. Unlike abilities, the temperament dimensions seem to alter relatively little in mode of expression with age after adolescence. Doubtless, personality psychologists appreciating the importance of personality factor batteries for testing the same dimensions with maximum accuracy at *all* levels will design O-A Batteries more apt to younger age ranges. But at present the O-A is certainly apt enough from 14 to 30, and is probably administrable well beyond the latter age, as shown in the work of Schmidt (1975).

As for practical administrative features, (*a*) although the clinician, for example, may prefer to administer the test batteries individually, they are fully "streamlined" for administration in large groups; (*b*) any one source trait battery, or any subset, can be taken out of the 10 and separately administered, which is useful when time is short or special purposes are involved; and (*c*) all but a few of the tests can be answered on answer sheets, which saves booklet expense and permits machine scoring or more rapid hand scoring (for details on scoring see Chapters 7 and 8).

So much for general utility as defined by the nature of the test construction. Evidence of usefulness in the following areas will briefly be given:

a) *Basic Research* needs primary source-trait measures in genetics, learning, age changes, physiological psychology, perception, social psychology, and wherever personality is either a dependent or an independent variable. Appreciable connections have already been established in these areas—e.g., with genetics Cattell & Klein, 1979; Cattell, Stice, & Kristy, 1957; Eysenck, 1960), with neurology (Pawlik & Cattell, 1964), with physiology (Barton, Cattell, & Conner, 1972; Cattell & Scheier, 1961), with school performance (Dielman, Barton, & Cattell, 1971), and with clinical concepts (Cattell & Scheier, 1961; Cattell, Schmidt, & Bjerstedt, 1972; Hundleby & Cattell, 1968; Killian, 1960; Knapp, 1961*a*) as discussed below.

b) *Vocational Guidance and Industrial Selection.* Due to the tendency in industry to use brief tests there has been little opportunity, prior to the appearance of the present condensed battery, for objective test battery results to be properly appraised. There have, however, been studies in the military area, e.g., by Cattell (1955*b*) in the Air Force, and by Knapp (1961*a*, 1961*b*, 1962) in the Navy. The important point is that in the future the availability of a battery which, unlike questionnaires, is largely unfakable, will be a boon in occupational selection situations where the dependability of less objective tests is questionable.

c) *Educational Prediction and Selection.* It has been abundantly shown, in four or five closely consistent replications (see bibliography in Cattell & Butcher, 1968) that the use of personality factor (source-trait) measures, even though gathered only by questionnaire, more than doubles the amount of prediction of school performance obtainable from ability tests alone.

More recently, the introduction of the O-A Batteries has shown that the measurement of the personality factor contributions as measured by the new objective batteries has equal or greater potency (relative to that of questionnaires) for predicting various school performance (Dielman, Barton, & Cattell, 1971; Dielman, Schuerger, & Cattell, 1970; King, 1977; Knapp, 1961b, 1962). In these applications in the field of educational psychology one must remember that this statistical potency in prediction of achievement implies also increased certainty in understanding the specific *personality* causes of backwardness in the individual case.

d) *Clinical Psychology.* The early work of Cattell and Scheier (1961), Eysenck (1952, 1961), Eysenck and Eysenck (1968), Scheier, Cattell, and Horn (1960), Swenson (in Cattell & Scheier, 1961), and others has shown that certain personality factors now measured in the O-A Battery very effectively distinguish neurotics from normals. Following this, the work of Tatro (1968), Killian (1960), and Schmidt (1972, 1975) showed that a profile of deviation on others of these factors also significantly distinguished various kinds of psychotics. Specific predictive values from this diagnostic work, as well as values brought out in the further discriminant function analyses of Cattell, Schmidt, & Bjerstedt (1972) are given in Chapter 11. Here it suffices to point out that the O-A Battery has high utility in clinical diagnosis and that, indeed, Schmidt has claimed that diagnostic psychiatric syndrome grouping can be more completely achieved by these factor profiles than by any other existing test instrument.

The usefulness of these factor measures to monitor therapy is indicated by the work of Rickels and Cattell (1965), Cattell, Rickels, and Yee (1966), and others showing significant reductions on regression (U.I. 23) and anxiety (U.I. 24) under therapy and chemotherapy. Other unpublished research also shows the source-trait measures to be sensitive enough to register changes under general therapeutic influences. The work of Hundleby (1973b) on adolescent behavior problems; of the Eysencks (1961, 1968) on the relation of U.I. 23, 24, and 25 to clinical diagnoses; of Wardell and Yeudall (1976) on neuropsychiatry; and of Wardell and Royce (1975) on relations to variables frequently clinically studied, has considerably extended the relevance of the trait measures to problems of adjustment.

The applications to all these fields will be studied in more detail in Chapter 11 on criterion relations. However, in viewing this utility it must be recognized that the O-A requires more time demands than that customarily required by questionnaires. Nevertheless, wherever maximally valid, reliable, and undistorted (by faking) measurement is vital, the objective test is indispensable. When one considers, on the one hand, the complexity of personality and, on the other, the important decisions made in schools, clinics, courtrooms, and personnel selection settings that depend on psychological measurement, it is surely not inappropriate to ask the psychologist for the greater skills and time expenditures that the new objective methods demand.

3

Description of the Source Traits Measured

So far only the general nature of the class of source traits has been discussed. The effective user of the O-A Kit, however, needs to familiarize himself with their specific psychological characters. Most attention will be given in this chapter to the 10 source traits in the O-A Main Kit, but briefer descriptions of the 10 traits in the Extended Kit, and the tests, which are named but not reproduced, may be found in Appendix A. Table 3.1 sets out the 10 source traits in the Main Kit, describing them by:

- a) A *universal index*, U.I. number, which is noncommittal as to interpretation but firmly aims to identify the reference to a well-replicated pattern, regardless of any debates over subsequent interpretation and naming.
- b) A *title* which is considered technically necessary and is the best available. Usually, each trait is accompanied by subtitles in more popular terms. Where research has advanced enough to permit largely unquestioned or widely accepted interpretation, e.g., as in anxiety (U.I. 24), regression (U.I. 23), or exvia (U.I. 32), the title will usually be familiar. In other cases, however, where the underlying cause of the pattern is still not established to everyone's satisfaction, a compromise has been made of settling on a term which is partly descriptive, e.g., *exuberance* (U.I. 21), *independence* (U.I. 19), or on an acronym which condenses a hypothesis into mnemonic form. Thus, *dissofrustance* (U.I. 30), from the Extended Kit, and *tensidia* (U.I. 25) mean, respectively, "tendency to use dissociation when in conflict from frustration," and being subject to "tense, rigid, inner ideation."
- c) A *description* of the nature of the source trait itself. The psychologist reading this will be aware that the location of unitary traits or dimensions in personality and ability has proceeded historically in two ways: (1) first by clinical experience and insight, as by Jung and Freud, and (2) by correlational, experimental, quantitative methods, as here. The former, useful in the hands of highly gifted men, has often degenerated into setting up concepts, almost as numerous as psychologists, based on attraction to some label, e.g., sensitivity, impulsivity, authoritarianism, etc. The latter, requiring patient and technically skillful collation of factors from extensively sampled behavior, accepts the unities experimentally confirmed, regardless of whether they happen to fit any fashionable term. Since correlation of observations by computer simply performs, in a more

accurate and systematic way, what clinicians do "by eye," one would expect continuity of the two phases of inquiry; and this is what actually happens, for factors were soon found by objective research to confirm, for example, the Freudian ego and superego and Jung's extraversion. But the greater precision and penetration from factor analysis, applied to objective behavior measures, has naturally led to the discovery of more subtle unities not easily picked up in a busy clinical practice. Some 20 such patterns are now well confirmed and available for measurement in the applied field of diagnosis and prediction, as well as in the basic research field of understanding the origin and development of personality structure.

In reaching an understanding of the nature of a source trait (factors are called *source traits* to distinguish from correlation clusters which are *surface traits*) we have two main approaches. First, we can look "internally" at the factor pattern, i.e., at the nature of the behaviors—the subtests of the O-A—which load on the factor: (*a*) positively, (*b*) negatively, and (*c*) not at all. Second, we can take the total factor score and by correlational and analysis of variance (ANOVA) methods, discover its relation to various life criteria, e.g., its "external" relations in clinical and educational performance, in age curves, in degree of genetic and environmental determination, in response to educational, social background and therapeutic influences, and so on. Both the internal and the external approaches are needed to support an adequate theory of the nature of a source trait.

As regards the first approach, greater skill is needed in interpreting personality factors in T-data, as in the O-A, than in the other two media—rating in life situation (L-data) and questionnaire (Q-data). For L- and Q-data the variables consist of behavior immediately described in words, so that an interpretation and naming is directly implied by the verbal variables (Pawlik [1974] aptly calls this an "inherent theory in the media"). But the performances in objective tests are behaviors to which one can only give "popular" terms with grave risk of misleading oneself and others, since alternative interpretations of what is behind specific behaviors are generally possible. Accordingly, we have in several cases carefully introduced neologisms which, as acronyms or Latin-derived terms, mainly express *descriptively* what is perceived as common to the subtests. Latin derivations give greater universality, and acronyms give immediate reference to the theory concerned, when there is no popular term that could be applied to what is seen in the common behavior, and which defines the concept. Only time and research alone can show how accurate these verbal, conceptual interpretations will be.

It will be noticed that the source traits in Table 3.1 are not numbered consecutively. The original consecutive numbering of objective test factors (Hundleby, Pawlik, & Cattell, 1965) was approximately in order of their variance size and frequency of replication in a dozen or more researches collated at that time. The numbering system ran from U.I. 16 to U.I. 35. However, as explained elsewhere, the present selection of 10 was made in terms of greatest usefulness and theoretical interest, which means that gaps occur in respect to the standard U.I. series.

Although, as indicated in introducing Table 3.1, some terms, e.g., exuberance, tensidia, and asthenia have to be novel; other concepts, e.g., anxiety, regression, extraversion (exvia), already are known by questionnaire and life criteria associations to be the measurable core of familiar concepts. Even so, familiar or unfamiliar, the theoretical definitions, as in any truly advancing science, cannot be final at this stage. The fact that theoretical meaning is in a process of emergence does not impair their usefulness as far as concrete validities or relevancies are concerned. The user may simply correlate the factor scores with the concrete criteria with which he is concerned and apply the appropriate regression weights. If existing experience with the O-A Kit, wherever the measures have been applied, is any guide, and the theory of the personality sphere is essentially sound, it is unlikely that any criterion will be encountered for which the battery as a whole will not give worthwhile prediction. For though the correlations of some criterion with individual factors may be low, the multiple correlation of the whole battery is likely to be significant and useful.

In obtaining such checked criterion results the psychologist will both improve his practice and add to the meaning of the factors in personality theory. Nevertheless, though the empirical determination of "relevance" weights provides an assured foundation, it is the aim of the personality specialist working with source traits to obtain such *psychological* knowledge of them that he can go well beyond a merely immediate statistical prediction, by adding insights and laws of a psychological nature, as discussed technically elsewhere (Cattell, 1973b). Indeed, the peculiar value of batteries based on the sure reference point of known structures is that a continuous growth of insight occurs as knowledge accumulates around these reference measures in both pure *and* applied research.[1]

---

[1]Parenthetically, let it be noted that findings on criterion and other interpretive relations for these factors are being pursued by other batteries, over and above the O-A itself. It is one of the advantages of structured tests, aimed at basic structures known to personality theory, that findings from other measures of the same source trait will be transferable, and will enrich their meaning and facilitative power. In this case, publications are proceeding in Germany from the O-A Kit of Schmidt and Häcker (1976) on the same 10 factors. Other results are appearing from the systematic work of Hundleby, in Canada, with an O-A Kit not yet published, with a choice of traits particularly adapted to clinical criteria. Several factors in that battery will eventually overlap with the 10 here, though all of Hundleby's are available here when the extension set in Appendix B are included.

Insofar as the primaries here coincide with the secondaries in the 16 PF and CAQ, the results can be incorporated from those sources as has been done in Table 9.1. There will also be available in the questionnaire domain a set of short scales validated directly to the O-A factors, for use in circumstances where a questionnaire might be appropriate or valuable as a check (Schuerger & Cattell, in preparation).

Table 3.1

**TITLES AND BRIEF DESCRIPTIONS OF THE 10 SOURCE TRAITS
IN THE O-A BATTERY**

Criterion relations are introduced only incidentally here, being more systematically handled in Chapter 11. The 10 factors in the O-A Extended Battery may be found in Appendix A.

Most factors are given bipolar labels since later interpretations may suggest a reversal to be more apt to common psychological meaning. The direction in which they are at present scored positive is that of the label on the left. For those factors having only a single label a high factor score is considered to be positive in nature.

1. U.I. 16: Ego Standards [or Competitiveness]

Many associations suggest this is ego strength in the classical psychoanalytic sense, and also in the sense of Factor C+ as ego strength in questionnaires. However, the title "hedges" on this identification deliberately because U.I. 16 has a stronger emphasis on self-assertion and achievement than is usual in ego strength. "Standards," suggesting a certain competitive assertiveness, is therefore added to avoid risk of premature historical interpretation with the common Freudian ego concept. The subtests show boldness, competitive assertiveness, speed of action and decision, some rejection of authority, and breadth (an "up-to-dateness") of interests and attitudes. It is lower than normal in psychotics, neurotics, delinquent gangs, in lower social status, in persons of small physique, and those showing poorer school performance.

2. U.I. 19: Independence-vs-Subduedness

This is a factor determining in its subtests independence, criticalness, accuracy, capacity for intensive concentration and perceptual "field independence" as studied by Witkin (1962) and others. It is a positive predictor of success in school and in some military (submarine) and scientific performances. There is quite a high hereditary component. There are consistent indications of the relation of the factor to the second-order factor of *independence* in the questionnaire realm, indexed Q IV, covering primaries E+, L+, M+, Q_1+, and Q_2+, i.e., the questionnaire dominance, protension, autism (internal values), radicalism, and self-sufficiency. Psychotics and neurotics are significantly lower than normals, and males significantly higher than females.

Table 3.1 (Continued)

3. U.I. 20: Evasiveness

This quite subtle trait has been the hardest to name, at least in any well-known single term. Descriptively close labels have been offered in "social, emotional evasiveness" (Hundleby, Pawlik, & Cattell, 1965), "dependent instability," and "posturing acceptance of social values," while interpretive labels have been given by psychiatrists as "bound anxiety" or "characterological anxiety" and "compensation for insecurity." The individual is superficially culturally conforming, but suggestible also to inconsistent (delinquent) values. He shows emotional instability (but not of the deep, C—, ego weakness form) and neurotic lack of objectivity, with some hostility and guilt proneness; but is sociable and dependent. Adult delinquents score high on the factor, but so, also, do involutional depressives, again suggesting conflicts in the area of guilt and antisocial or reality-evasive behavior. A literary instance might be Mr. Micawber—or even Dickens himself. Pending fuller research interpretations, the only suitable single term for it seems to be evasiveness—suggesting some dubiousness of character, a tendency to posture toward the immediate group style, and some emotional instability.

4. U.I. 21: Exuberance

Because this loads on some tests in the ability field it has sometimes been confounded with "ideational fluency" or "divergent thinking," but it is much broader than a purely cognitive pattern.

All manifestations are clearly those of high spontaneity, fluency, imaginativeness, speed of social and perceptual judgment, fast natural tempo, and sacrifice of accuracy to speed. In the questionnaire domain it shows some relations to surgency (F+), tension (Q4+), guilt proneness (O+), and imaginativeness (M+), and to ratings of energetic, forceful or dominant, and excitable behavior. It has a high hereditary determination, and some association with broad body build. It has sometimes been called the Winston Churchill factor.

A significantly subnormal score is found on this factor for both neurotic and psychotic patients, and particularly for all depressives. The most promising hypothesis is that it represents a physiological factor determining high metabolic rate in the brain (and perhaps the entire body). The alternative theory that it represents lack of inhibition, e.g., at the thalamus—should still be entertained.

Table 3.1 (Continued)

5. U.I. 23: Capacity to Mobilize-vs-Regression

Also called Mobilization-vs-Neurotic Regressive Debility and Neuroticism.

The measures are of flexibility, general competence (simulating intelligence at times), emotional balance (especially absence of depression), and endurance of stress. It appears to be about 50/50 hereditary and environmental. At the negative pole it is associated with neuroticism, and at an early stage was called Neuroticism by Eysenck (1961), though it is only one of half-a-dozen source traits equally or more strongly associated with neuroticism and is better called regression. This negative pole has some qualities of the psychoanalytic concept of regression, in showing a falling off of interest and vigor along with decline in capacity to organize one's thoughts. The fact that U.I. 23 is low in schizophrenics, depressives, and manics points to its association with disorganization as such. Competence in school, in stressful jobs, etc., is significantly related to the positive pole, as is freedom from "passing out" under stress (as found in the astronaut program). One hypothesis is that U.I. 23— represents an adrenal or other hormone deficiency following prolonged fatigue and impairing the whole dynamic organization.

6. U.I. 24: Anxiety

This well-defined factor, aligning also well with Q II, the second-order anxiety factor in questionnaires (C—, H—, L+, O+, Q3—, Q4+), has in some writings been called "emotionality." But it is *anxiety*, by every criterion—clinical, behavioral, situational, and physiological—that has ever been applied (Cattell & Scheier, 1961; Cattell, Schmidt, & Bjerstedt, 1972; Spielberger, 1966, 1972). It is high in neurotics and highest in anxiety neurotics, but not different from normals in schizophrenics (hence a diagnostic discriminator). However, high scores are not *invariably* pathological since "healthy" anxiety can be high situationally, as has been shown, for example, in measures during school examinations and dangerous military missions.

Table 3.1 (Continued)

7. U.I. 25: Realism-vs-Tensidia

Also called Normality-vs-Psychoticism by Eysenck and, more descriptively, Less-Imaginative, Task-Oriented Realism-vs-Tense, Inflexible Dissociation from Reality.

It loads accuracy, speed, rejection of disturbing, imaginative intrusions, and a realistic orientation to tasks. At the negative pole, which has been rated by some psychiatrists as a form of anxiety and correlates with O+, guilt proneness, and Q4+, tension, it shows emotional tension and a rigid, subjective inflexibility to reality indications. Tensidia is an acronym term attempting to capture this tense, inflexible, insensitiveness to reality. It has, by Eysenck's data, a fairly strong hereditary determination. At the tensidia pole it correlates significantly with *both* psychosis and neurosis and is particularly low in depressives. Realism (positive U.I. 25) is higher in normals relative to all pathological syndromes, in well-adjusted compared to delinquent adolescents, and (as a mean score) in more cohesive, better functioning groups than less cohesive groups.

8. U.I. 28: Asthenia-vs-Self-Assurance

Sometimes called Dependent, Negativistic Asthenia-vs-Undisciplined Self-Assurance.

This is a complex pattern believed to express ambivalence from a conflict between severe, demanding parental upbringing in socialization and the growing individual's own need for self-realization (Cattell, 1964a). There is conformity, but with resentment and a continual asthenia born of unresolved conflict. The questionnaire associations are with toughness (H+), imaginativeness (M+), lack of ambition, lack of agreeableness and cooperativeness, but also with some frustration (Q4+), jealousy (L+), and depression. It shows as more environmentally determined than hereditary. It has so far shown nothing but zero correlations with clinical data except in showing paranoid schizophrenics low (i.e., more self-assured, less asthenic) than nonparanoid, simple schizophrenics. Neurotics are above average, while delinquents, drug addicts, and some kinds of alcoholics are actually *below* normal, i.e., more self-assured and undisciplined.

31

Table 3.1 (Continued)

9. U.I. 32: Exvia-vs-Invia

The questionnaire correlations repeatedly found with QI (A+, E+, F+, H+, Q2—) demonstrate this to be the exvia-invia core of the popular "extraversion-introversion" notion. Schizophrenics, but also manics and depressives, are significantly below normal, i.e., more inviant, as are neurotics. It has no relation, or only a slightly negative relation (as found also in questionnaire, QI, exvia measures), to school grades. EEG activation measures, when subjects are active (calculating) are greater for exviants than inviants. Contingently, one can assume most proven extraversion-introversion criteria, e.g., in Eysenck (1961), to be related to this factor.

10. U.I. 33: Discouragement-vs-Sanguineness

This is clearly, from its content and associations, a factor of pessimism and discouragement of a lasting nature. Higher score is associated with lower socioeconomic status, poorer physique, lower self-ratings on confidence, cooperativeness, and calm objectivity. Schizophrenics tend to be above average and delinquents below average (both very significantly) on U.I. 33, discouragement.

4

Design of Batteries: The Main Kit, the Extended Kit, and the Individual Test Supplement to the Main Kit

As mentioned earlier, the Main Battery for these 10 source traits is designed in its entirety for *group* administration (though also *individually* usable, of course) and to involve a minimum of equipment. By the *Supplementary Battery* to the Main we mean a battery in which the validity of measurement of any particular factor as now reached by group tests alone can be augmented by some tests that are of good validity but can *only be given individually*, usually needing laboratory apparatus. Since the latter will be employed probably by less than 5% of test users (principally those in some aspect of basic research), we shall not impair the aptness of this account for the general user by interruptions, at this point, to digress into the supplementary tests and their apparatus needs. All of that Supplementary Battery of Individual Tests for the present O-A is relegated to Appendix B. Naturally, the regular group-administrable battery can also be administered to one subject at a time as an individual test, but the Supplementary Battery cannot, conversely, be group administered.

The *Supplementary Battery* should not be confused with the *Extended Battery*, by which we mean the battery extended as to *factors*, from a possible 10 in the Main Battery, listed in Table 3.1, to a possible 20 factors in all. However, in using the extra 10 factors of the Extended Battery, the reader will not be able to use already printed and standardized tests as in the Main Battery, but must build his own battery from the sources of test description in the Cattell-Warburton Compendium (1967).

Designing a personality test battery is a work of art in which the demands of various psychological and psychometric laws have to be ingeniously balanced. Consequently, considerably greater space than is appropriate in a working handbook would be needed to give the why's and wherefore's of every feature of design. However, a brief justification of choice, form, administration procedure, and scoring is called for in this still novel test domain.

The choice of factors is necessarily based first upon the *soundness of research definition* of the factors as independent, unitary traits. Here we have rested decision on cumulative evidence of steady replication (checked by adequate congruence coefficients of the pattern over at least 10 experiments with adequate samples). These evidences of the replicated pattern for each chosen factor will be found in the surveys of Hundleby, Pawlik, and Cattell (1965) and several articles in the last decade (Cattell & Klein, 1975; Cattell, Schmidt, & Pawlik, 1973; and Wardell & Yeudall, 1976).

The second basis of choice, after this primary concern for the reality of the pattern, has been the importance or relevance (sometimes called "concrete validity") of the source traits to everyday life predictions and diagnoses in educational, industrial, and clinical practice. Here, information is so recent—a matter of 15 years—that some mistakes in the choice of the "best 10" may have been made. For example, U.I. 17, general inhibition, and U.I. 18, hypomania, were omitted from our chosen first 10, but the work of Wardell and Yeudall (1976) shows the former related to important features of upbringing, while that of Tatro (1968) shows that in mental hospital samples the latter is the chief and most highly dependable indicator of manic diagnosis. But these results await replication. Meanwhile, the venturesome psychologist, prepared to put his own extended battery together using Appendix A, would do well to consider adding to the Main Battery U.I. 17 and 18 as well as U.I. 22, 29, and 30, all of which have interesting criterion relevances.[1]

After choosing the factors, the choice of *tests* for each factor derives from quite complex psychometric considerations. Most objective behavioral subtests load on two or more factors, though on one most highly. So, after choosing those with the highest correlation with a given factor, we had to look among them for pairs having mutual *suppressor action* (Cattell, 1973b) on unwanted factors. Occasionally, when a particular factor has proved short of good tests, we have taken a test which loads equally high on another factor that has a sufficient number of good tests, and used it to "round out" the weaker factor. Despite those features of design and the virtually complete avoidance of sharing of the same subtest by two factors, some slight correlation will arise between factor scores over and above that existing between the pure factors (due to some quite real resemblance in loading patterns). Parenthetically, this also has the convenience that it creates a self-contained battery for each factor (one does not have to borrow a test out of the file from another factor when testing just one). Naturally, this self-containedness of factor batteries means that a complete standardization for each factor is available when it is administered separately.

On the other hand, when the *complete* 10-factor battery is administered, one can, by using *computer synthesis scoring*, let every test in the battery lend its contribution to each factor. Computer synthesis scoring, which requires the whole battery, can thus raise reliability and validity of each single factor score appreciably.[2]

---

[1] The omission from the present group-administrable battery of U.I. 22, which is both well defined and important, is due to the impossibility of measuring it sufficiently well without predominantly individual tests.

[2] However, when using such computer synthesis scoring, using weights for each factor from all tests in the total battery, the user must note that the standardization will not be the same as when each factor is separately given and scored on its own subtests alone. The norm tables are thus for single factors: when the whole O-A Kit and computer synthesis scoring are used, the user must use his own sample to compute the standard score for each individual.

As to the number of tests per factor, although we are keenly aware of the desirability of bringing the O-A Battery total testing time down more closely to that of omnibus questionnaire factor scales, we calculate that seven or eight subtests per factor is a necessary minimum in terms of (a) reaching the desirable 0.85 validity, and (b) as many as seven or eight being needed to get a sufficient diversity of specific factors to rule out any powerful effect from a single specific. Incidentally, one sees this principle of attenuating specifics repeatedly ignored, e.g., in the Raven Matrices, and in the use of single objective tests of "personality," e.g., the Rorschach with its own "instrument factor," to the detriment of real psychometric dependability and validity. The subtests here are, therefore, deliberately chosen for diversity of content and style, and are typically brought to seven or eight per factor, as shown in Table 4.1.

If the experimenter wishes to concentrate on one factor, then he can, by using the individual tests, get as many as 12-14 subtests per factor and thus reach a very high validity for the given factor (see Supplementary Tests in Appendix B).

Much effort and regard for ingenuity in design has been brought to bear to reduce both the reading level required and the intrusion of intelligence variance into these personality tests. However, the age range of use—12 or 14 years to 30 years or more—forbids too great an adjustment of content to the extreme lower age limit, and it should be used with 12-year-olds only when good reading and general education levels are assured.

It was our intention to keep the testing time for the total battery to 3 or 4 hours—a not unreasonable time when one reflects that practitioners commonly give about half an hour for the objective testing of a single factor—intelligence. There turned out to be a rather marked difference, however, between the subject's actual time on test performance and the administrator's time in giving instructions, etc., since the instructions and material are more different from subtest to subtest than in intelligence tests. The subjects' actual time spent in performance for all 10 factors is 2 hours, 41 minutes, and 35 seconds, covering the whole battery. The total time *including* administration (set in standard form on audio cassette tape), however, is 4 hours, 27 minutes, and 55 seconds. The testing session can, of course, be broken up—into as many as 10 parts if necessary. As Table 4.1 shows, the time for the various separate factor batteries is very even, all being under half an hour, except for U.I. 16, which reaches 32 minutes. (The subject's time averages 16 minutes per factor, which is, by all evidence, as short as one can go and still retain the desirable psychometric properties demonstrated below.)

An appreciable influence in test unreliability in the past has undoubtedly been slips in oral instructions, variations in accent, emphasis in instructions, and accidental inattention to the stop watch. Freedom from these undeniably serious errors can be bought, but only at the cost of using

Table 4.1

DESCRIPTIVE TITLES, INDEX NUMBERS, AND DIRECTION OF CONTRIBUTION OF SUBTESTS
FOR
EACH FACTOR BATTERY IN THE MAIN KIT

Factor 1. *U.I. 16 Ego Standards*

Test No. in this Booklet	No. of[1] the Derived Performance Score on Scoring Sheet	Test (T) No.[2] in Encyclopedia of Objective Tests	Master Index[3] No. of Performance in Encyclopedia of Tests	Title on Test Form	Psychologist's Title Defining Performance[4]	Time in[5] Min. Sec.	Answered[6] on
1	1	361	244	Attitudes	Quicker social judgment	2:00	Answer Sheet
2	2	49a	6d	Coding	Higher coding speed	2:00	Answer Sheet
3	3	44a	307	Letter and Number Comparison	Quicker letter-number comparison	2:00	Answer Sheet
4	4	8a	288	Goodness of Work I	Quicker judgment, others' performance	1:30	Answer Sheet
5	5	20a	282	Modernistic Drawings	More seen in unstructured drawings	1:30	Answer Sheet
6	6	11a	2409	Assumptions I	More logical assumptions done	3:00	Answer Sheet
7	7	35a	199	Rapid Calculation	Greater simple numerical performance	2:00	Answer Sheet
8	8	43b	2410	My Interests	Greater fluency on objects (selective)	2:00	Answer Sheet
					Testing Time	16:00	
					Approximate Total Tape Time	30:00	

Footnotes are at end of table, on page 46.

Table 4.1 (Continued)

Factor 2. *U.I. 19 Independence-vs-Subduedness*

Test No. in this Booklet	No. of [1] the Derived Performance Score on Scoring Sheet	Test (T) No. [2] in Encyclopedia of Objective Tests	Master Index [3] No. of Performance in Encyclopedia of Tests	Title on Test Form	Psychologist's Title Defining Performance [4]	Time in [5] Min. Sec.	Answered [6] on
1	1	35b	120f	Problems	Higher accuracy/speed-numerical	2:00	Answer Sheet
2	2	37	206	Hidden Shapes	More hidden shapes correctly seen in Gottschaldt figures	2:00	Answer Sheet
3	3	6a	167c	Reading Comprehension	Better immediate memory from reading	2:15	Answer Sheet
4	4	422	2367	What Is the Right Design?	More orderly perceptual series seen	2:00	Answer Sheet
5	5	328	1387	Searching	More correct in searching task	2:30	Answer Sheet
6	6	242a	689	Picture Memory	Greater accuracy picture memory	2:00	Answer Sheet
7	7	114	51	Observation	Higher Index of carefulness	2:30	Answer Sheet

Testing Time   15:15

Approximate Total Tape Time   29:00

Table 4.1 (Continued)

Factor 3. U.I. 20 Evasiveness

Test No. in this Booklet	No. of[1] the Derived Performance Score on Scoring Sheet	Test (T) No.[2] in Encyclopedia of Objective Tests	Master Index[3] No. of Performance in Encyclopedia of Tests	Title on Test Form	Psychologist's Title Defining Performance[4]	Time in[5] Min. Sec.	Answered[6] on
1	1	10b(1)	34	Opinions I	Greater insecurity of opinion (Area one)	1:30	Answer Sheet
2	2	9g(1)	65	Opinions II	Less logical consistency of attitudes	3:30	Answer Sheet
3	3*	9bj(1)	38	Opinions III	Higher ratio dissonant to consonant recognition	2:30	Answer Sheet
4		9bj(2)	38	Memory		2:00	Answer Sheet
5	Used in score 1 above	10b(2)	34	Opinions IV	Greater insecurity of opinion (Part of performance 1 above)	1:30	Answer Sheet
6	4	38a	211a	Common Annoyances	More susceptibility to annoyances	2:00	Answer Sheet
7	5	16b	100b	Human Nature I	More pessimistic insecurity	2:00	Answer Sheet
	6**†	152b			Greater tendency to agree		
	7**	67a			Greater extremity of response		
					Testing Time	15:00	
					Approximate Total Tape Time	24:00	

*One personality performance score from two tests.

**These measures require no extra test time, being by-products. They yield independent scores from the opinions measures.

†This test will add to the correlation of U.I. 20 with U.I. 28 beyond what is permitted elsewhere in these batteries. However, since U.I. 20 is a psychologically important factor, which psychologists may want to measure just on its own with every available good test for it, 152b is included here (and in the scoring instructions) to make nine MI references in all.

Table 4.1 (Continued)

Factor 4. U.I. 21 Exuberance

Test No. in this Booklet	No. of the Derived Performance Score on Scoring Sheet[1]	Test (T) No.[2] in Encyclopedia of Objective Tests	Master Index[3] No. of Performance in Encyclopedia of Tests	Title on Test Form	Psychologist's Title Defining Performance[4]	Time in[5] Min. Sec.	Answered[6] on
1	1	411d	335b	Following Directions Quickly	Faster marking speed	1:00	Expendable Test Booklet
2	2 2	43a	271	Ideas	Higher ideational fluency	3:00	Expendable Test Booklet
3	3	88a	853	Drawings I	More concrete drawing completion	3:30	Expendable Test Booklet
4	4	164a	699	Can You Hear the Word? I	More garbled words guessed	4:20	Expendable Test Booklet
5	5	2d	7	Incomplete Pictures	Faster speed of closure	1:00	Expendable Test Booklet
6	6	3	8	"In and Out"	Higher frequency of alternating perspective	2:00	Expendable Test Booklet
7	7	51	28b	Listening and Writing	Greater dynamic momentum: Dictation	2:00	Expendable Test Booklet
8	8	136a	264	Tapping	Faster speed of tapping	1:00	Expendable Test Booklet
					Testing Time	17:50	
					Approximate Total Tape Time	29:00	

Table 4.1 (Continued)

Factor 5. U.I. 23 Capacity to Mobilize-vs-Regression

Test No. in this Booklet	No. of [1] the Derived Performance Score on Scoring Sheet	Test (T) No.[2] in Encyclopedia of Objective Tests	Master Index[3] No. of Performance in Encyclopedia of Tests	Title on Test Form	Psychologist's Title Defining Performance[4]	Time in[5] Min. Sec.	Answered[6] on
1	1	38b	242	Annoyances	Higher ratio social/nonsocial annoyances	2:00	Answer Sheet
2	2	44c	120b	Comparing Letters	Higher ratio accuracy/speed letter number	1:00	Answer Sheet
3	3	112	609	Where Do the Lines Cross?	Higher perceptual coordination	2:30	Answer Sheet
4	4	197	401	Which Would You Rather Do?	Less preference for competitive associations	2:30	Answer Sheet
5	5	11b	36	Assumptions II	Higher ability to state logical assumptions	3:00	Answer Sheet
6	6	20b	105	What Do You See?	Fewer threatening objects seen	1:30	Answer Sheet
7	7	224b	714	Matching Words	Fewer rhyming and alliterative words chosen	1:30	Answer Sheet
8	8	1a	2a(1)	How Fast Can You Write?	Lower perceptual-motor rigidity: backward writing	2:00	Expendable Test Booklet
					Testing Time	**16:00**	
					Approximate Total Tape Time	**27:00**	

Table 4.1

Factor 6.   U.I. 24 Anxiety

Test No. in this Booklet	No. of[1] the Derived Performance Score on Scoring Sheet	Test (T) No.[2] in encyclopedia of Objective Tests	Master Index[3] No. of Performance in Encyclopedia of Tests	Title on Test Form	Psychologist's Title Defining Performance[4]	Time in[5] Min. Sec.	Answered[6] on
1	1	430	2404	Humor Test	Preference for outright, rather than inhibited, humor	2:00	Answer Sheet
2	2	27b	117b	How Do You Like. . . ?	Less alertness to highbrow tastes	2:00	Answer Sheet
3	3	41a	219	Do You Sometimes. . . ?	More common frailties admitted	2:00	Answer Sheet
4	4	36	205	What's Your Comment?	More emotionality of comment	2:00	Answer Sheet
5	5	187a	218	Jokes and Tricks	More willingness to play practical jokes	2:00	Answer Sheet
6	6	163a	1370	Putting Up With Things	Less willing compliance in unpleasant tasks	2:30	Answer Sheet
7	7	38c	211b	What Bothers Me	Higher susceptibility to annoyance involving ego-threats	2:00	Answer Sheet
8	8	25	321	Favorite Titles	Book preferences: More questionable taste preferences	2:00	Answer Sheet
					Testing Time	16:30	
					Approximate Total Tape Time	25:25	

41

Table 4.1 (Continued)

Factor 7. *U.I. 25 Realism-vs-Tensidia*

Test No. in this Booklet	No. of the Derived Performance Score on Scoring Sheet[1]	Test (T) No.[2] in Encyclopedia of Objective Tests	Master Index[3] No. of Performance in Encyclopedia of Tests	Title on Test Form	Psychologist's Title Defining Performance[4]	Time in Min. Sec.[5]	Answered[6] on
1	1	16b	100b	Human Nature II	Lesser pessimistic insecurity	2:00	Answer Sheet
2	2	9bk	2411	Memory	Better immediate memory	2:00	Answer Sheet
3	3	431	2408	Memory for Numbers	Greater accuracy in digit span	6:00	Answer Sheet
4	4	31	144	Wise Statements	More agreement with homely wisdom	2:00	Answer Sheet
5	5	224a	714	Best Word to Fit	Fewer alliterative and rhyming	1:30	Answer Sheet
6	6	118a	249	Memory	Better memory proper nouns	2:00	Answer Sheet
7	7	49c	120h	Counting Letters and Numbers	Greater accuracy of ideomotor performance (Correct relative to number done)	1:20	Answer Sheet

Testing Time 16:50

Approximate Total Tape Time 27:00

Table 4.1 (Continued)

Factor 8. U.I. 28 Asthenia-vs-Self-Assurance

Test No. in this Booklet	No. of the Derived Performance Score on Scoring Sheet [1]	Test (T) No. [2] in Encyclopedia of Objective Tests	Master Index [3] No. of Performance in Encyclopedia of Tests	Title on Test Form	Psychologist's Title Defining Performance [4]	Time in Min. Sec. [5]	Answered [6] on
1	1	9c(1)	152b	Opinions V (Score 1, with Test 6)	More tendency to agree		
	2	9ek	116	Opinions V (Score 2)	Lower severity and guilt — These are three performances	5:00	Answer Sheet
	3	9d	125	Opinions V (Score 3)	More institutional values		
2	4	16a	100	Human Nature III	More cynical pessimism	2:00	Answer Sheet
3	5	19	192	How Long Would It Take You?	Longer estimates of time to do tasks	3:00	Answer Sheet
4	6	149	364	What Will Happen?	Preference for external control (indirect end to story)	2:00	Answer Sheet
5	7	96	1160(2)	What Does It Take?	More grudging skepticism re success	3:00	Answer Sheet
6		9c(2)	152b	Opinions VI	[No score for this on its own. It goes in with Test 1 to give Tendency to agree.	1:30	Answer Sheet
7	8	76	97	Longer or Shorter?	Longer estimate of waiting period real time	2:10	Answer Sheet

Testing Time 18:40

Approximate Total Tape Time 27:30

Table 4.1 (Continued)

Factor 9. *U.I. 32 Exvia-vs-Invia*

Test No. in this Booklet	No. of [1] the Derived Performance Score on Scoring Sheet	Test (T) No. [2] in Encyclopedia of Objective Tests	Master Index [3] No. of Performance in Encyclopedia of Tests	Title on Test Form	Psychologist's Title Defining Performance [4]	Time in [5] Min. Sec.	Answered [6] on
1	1	45	309	Judging Lines	Quicker line-length judgment	2:00	Answer Sheet
2	2	62b	737	Which Is More?	Greater willingness to decide on vague data	:40	Answer Sheet
3	3	142a	356a	Qualities	More correct attribute-naming responses	1:40	Answer Sheet
4	4	97	1169	Crime and Punishment	Less influenced by extenuating circumstances	2:30	Answer Sheet
5	5	13a	763a	What People Are Like	More fluency concerning people's characteristics	2:00	Expendable Test Booklet
6	6	164b	2412	Can You Hear the Word? II	More garbled words heard as family words	2:40	Expendable Test Booklet
7	7	121	15	Obstacles	CMS: more circles used	2:00	Expendable Test Booklet
8	8	1d	2a(2)	Writing Signatures	Lower motor rigidity	2:00	Expendable Test Booklet
					Testing Time	15:30	
					Approximate Total Tape Time	28:00	

Table 4.1 (Continued)

Factor 10. *U.I. 33 Discouragement-vs-Sanguineness*

Test No. in this Booklet	No. of [1] the Derived Performance Score on Scoring Sheet	Test (T) No. [2] in Encyclopedia of Objective Tests	Master Index[3] No. of Performance in Encyclopedia of Tests	Title on Test Form	Psychologist's Title Defining Performance[4]	Time in [5] Min. Sec.	Answered[6] on
1	1	22b	108	Performance Estimates	Less confidence in unfamiliar situations	1:30	Answer Sheet
2	2	64b	473	How Many Friends?	Fewer people who appreciate one as a friend	2:00	Answer Sheet
3	3	40c	2413	What Is Fun?	Less willingness to participate in activities	2:00	Answer Sheet
4	4	156b	1245	My Feelings	More depression	2:00	Answer Sheet
5	5	39	212	Chances of Success	Less belief in attainability of goals	2:30	Answer Sheet
6	6	9e1	116a	Opinions VII	More severe, pessimistic superego	2:00	Answer Sheet
7	7	24	112	How Would Events Affect You?	Greater expectation of unfavorable consequences	2:00	Answer Sheet
				Testing Time		14:00	
				Approximate Total Tape Time		21:00	

45

Table 4.1 (Continued)

In reading this table note:

1) The column of numbers on the extreme left gives the numbers of the subtests in the given factor battery, in order of administration in the booklet. The next column states the *scores* derived from them in the order used on the score summary sheet. Mostly Columns 1 and 2 have the same numbers.

2) As stated in the footnote commencing Table 4.1, the third column gives the numbers of these tests as they were defined for all kinds of research reference in the Cattell and Warburton Compendium (1967), where more may be read about their origins.

3) The fourth column is headed *Master Index* (or MI) number, also by the same list numbers as are adhered to in Cattell and Warburton (1967), Hundleby, Pawlik, and Cattell (1965), and elsewhere. This indexes a *particular measured performance*, not a physical test form, as in the T numbers. There *can* be more than one performance score extracted from a particular test, or two tests may occasionally give one performance score by a difference measure, etc.

4) Two titles are given for each test: the subject's title as printed on the test form, and the title conveying the meaning to the psychologist which is used throughout this Handbook and in reference to scoring procedures. The former is intended to be noncommittal as to what psychologically is being measured and merely fits the examinee's understanding of what instructions say he should do. The latter gives, as far as is possible in a phrase, an indication of what trait behavior is actually being measured. Note that there is always an adjective before the latter title, showing the *direction* in which the performance, scored as in the instructions, contributes to a higher (positive) trait score.

5) The time column gives for each subtest the actual time that the subject is engaged in his performance. The time for test administration is greater, because of time taken in listening to the instructions, etc. Consequently, what is labeled at the end of each factor, *Approximate Total Tape Time*, is longer than this summed actual testing time and represents the approximate time the psychologist must allow for completing the battery for the given factor.

6) The last column to the right indicates what material the psychologist needs to put before the subject besides the actual test booklet. This is generally just the appropriate *answer sheet*, but when Expendable Booklet is written it means that no answer sheet is required for that subtest and that the subject must mark on the expendable booklet itself. The booklets for this special use are so marked among the other booklets.

46

apparatus—the tape recorder and a sound system. It is a small cost to pay for escape from error through unstandardized conditions, and IPAT has increasingly advocated and introduced this technique, e.g., here and in the Early School Personality Questionnaire. Of course, if the psychologist happens to be bereft of his sound tape and speaker system he can still fall back on older methods, since IPAT has taken the trouble in this Handbook to provide a printed section setting out instructions and timing, as a facsimile of the tape, for the psychologist to use himself. A detailed account of how to proceed is given in Chapter 6.

The design of the O-A also employs, with rare exceptions, standard answer sheets rather than the procedure of answering on the actual test booklets. This has a double advantage: first, it has the economy of permitting the actual booklets to be used over and over again and, second, it brings an enormous saving in scoring time since the sheets can be machine scored. Machine-scorable standard answer sheets are not nearly so easy to design for objective tests as for questionnaires, since the former have responses very varied in nature. In the research and development on the O-A it was found that good subtests for a given factor sometimes lost sufficient validity of loading on the factor when cramped into the requirements of an answer sheet! However, these difficulties have been overcome, though it is good for the psychologist to recognize that the more complex design of certain tests is for purposes of adaptation to this need, and should be handled understandingly. The rare instances where a booklet *has* to be marked (occurring on Factors U.I. 21, 23, and 32) are shown in Table 4.1 by the note: "Expendable Booklets." (When ordering expendable test booklets, the psychologist should remember to order as many of these as he orders answer sheets.) It is *possible*, of course, to do the whole battery on booklets when the psychologist doubts that his subjects, e.g., deteriorated mental hospital patients, can handle answer sheets, but this will be uncommon.

The detailed particulars of administration and scoring for the *Main Battery* are given in Chapters 6 and 8. For sources of guidance regarding scoring of the *Extended Factor Kit* and the *Supplementary Tests* the reader is referred to Appendixes A and B, offering reference to research sources.

Our general experience with these objective tests suggests that the O-A Battery can safely be used again for a retest if the elapsed time is adequate. There has actually been no evidence, as yet, of significant gains or losses when the same battery has been readministered after the lapse even of only 2 or 3 days, but until further research results come in we would suggest that a retest to evaluate some intervening influence be delayed for a couple weeks or more. (Quite *specific* responses seem, in general, to be forgotten in anything from a few hours to a week.) In research on changes in personality traits it is in any case not to be expected that change from applicable influences will be brought about in less than 2 or 3 months (unless quite drastic happenings are involved), by which time recollections of the test itself are substantially lost. Cattell and Rickels (1964), studying therapy and control groups on certain weekly repeated retests on U.I. 24, found no sign of systematic testing effects as such in the controls, though changes occurred from drug and therapy effects in the experimental group.

5
Psychometric Properties of the Source-Trait Batteries in the Main Kit

A battery representing a modern advance in personality testing is appropriately evaluated by modern psychometric concepts. Basically, these deal with just two properties: (1) *consistency*, the agreement of a test with itself, and (2) *validity*, its prediction of that which it is designed to predict, in general behavior.

Consistency has three aspects: (1) *reliability:* the agreement ("test-retest") between two different *administrations* of the same test to the same people; (2) *homogeneity:* the agreement of the different *parts* of the same test, administered to the same people; and (3) *transferability:* the extent to which the test measures the same thing when applied to *different populations*. (See discussion of origins and statistical definitions of these logical concepts in Cattell, 1973b, Chapter 9.)

The *reliability* coefficient, in turn, has several subvarieties, according to whether the retest has the same or different administrators or scorers and a long or short interval, etc., but we shall report here the first main form of reliability—the *dependability* coefficient—when the test has the same administrators, scorers, and conditions, but is simply given *on two separate occasions*—which must be close together. As regards time separation, it is assumed in the test dependability coefficient that the testings are close enough together for no change to have occurred in the traits themselves, e.g., by learning or internal fluctuation.

If a retest occurs as long after as, say, 3 months, we are actually talking about a *stability* form of the reliability coefficient. It is important to distinguish the stability from the dependability coefficient because the stability coefficient falls short of unity due to the fact that it is always "suffering from" both the "undependability" of the *test* and the "undependability" of the *person* (trait fluctuation). Especially as we come to know more about the properties of traits as such, through using unitary, meaningful source traits rather than arbitrary "scales" in psychometric practice, distinctions such as this become important and informative.

Traits themselves fluctuate with time, and since they do so to different degrees it is helpful to know and allow for these trait property differences appropriately in psychometric prediction. Indeed, there is increasing evidence in recent research on traits, states, and trait-change factors (Bass, 1974; Cattell, 1957a, 1973b; Cattell & Nesselroade, 1976; Cattell, Schmidt, & Bjerstedt, 1972; Nesselroade & Bartsch, 1973; Nesselroade & Reese, 1973) telling us that the true oscillation of traits, even of intelligence itself, is greater than has been commonly supposed. If one knows the *dependability* coefficient, r_d, from *immediate* retest, and the *stability* coefficient, r_s, from retest after a month or two, one can calculate the constancy versus fluctuation property of the *trait* itself, as the *trait-constancy coefficient*, r_{tc}, thus:

$$r_{tc} = \frac{r_s}{r_d} \qquad (5.1)$$

(These and other relations are analyzed in Cattell, 1973*b*, Chapter 9.)

The *dependability* coefficients obtained here for the 10 source-trait batteries are set out in Table 5.1 along with the *stability* coefficients and *trait-constancy* coefficients. The last set of values have ideally to be calculated on r_d and r_s values from the *same* groups, which has not been possible at this stage of research, so the values must be considered rough at present. The trait-constancy values presented do not merely describe or belong to the *present battery* as such, but are statements in personality theory dealing with the situational constancy of the *traits* as personality structures. Inasmuch as we are concerned with theory, these pioneer estimates of functional constancy have been given, despite roughness.

As is well known, the quotation of numerical reliabilities in handbooks can be quite misleading to readers who do not keep an eye on such relevant matters as the length of the test. If objective personality batteries are to be thought of in comparison with intelligence tests, for example, then the values should be corrected to the same length. One hour has been suggested as a standard reference length of item-time for measurement of any one primary factor source trait, such as intelligence (gf or gc) or the personality factors here.[1] The results of such a correction from the less than half-hour lengths shown in Table 4.1 to the standard one hour, using the Spearman-Brown formula, assuming that in any test item numbers increase proportionally to time, is given in Table 5.2.

The validity of a test can be calculated as a *concept* (sometimes called "construct") *validity* or as a *concrete validity*, the latter being generally better thought of as a "relevance" rather than a validity, since there is no *single* concrete criterion in everyday life that is supposed to correspond exactly to any one personality factor. The concept validity is the correlation of the battery with the pure factor it is supposed to measure. The concept validities (Table 5.3) are calculated as a multiple correlation of the eight or so subtests in the battery with the pure factor. If $\mathbf{R}_v$ is the correlation matrix among the subtests and $\mathbf{V}_{fs}$ the factor structure matrix showing the correlation of each of these with the pure factor, then the first calculation we need to make yields the weights, $\mathbf{V}_{fe}$, for the best factor estimation of each factor from its seven or eight subtests, thus:

---

[1]This is longer than many practitioners are prepared to give, yet actually represents a reasonable and even ethically required standard when important decisions rest on the result. Cattell, Eber, and Tatsuoka (1970) have for this reason urged, for example, that all four forms (A, B, C, and D) of the 16 PF should be administered, instead of resting on about 3 minutes per factor as when a single form is used. But whether one hour is practicable or not, it is a useful standard reference time for comparing test consistencies and validities.

Table 5.1

PSYCHOMETRIC CONSISTENCY: Dependability, Stability, and Trait Constancy Coefficients for Each Source Trait (Calculated for scoring by separate factor method)

Universal Index No.	Factor Label	Dependability (2-24 hours)	Stability (3-6 weeks)	Trait Constancy
U.I. 16	Ego Standards	.75	.61	.81
U.I. 19	Independence	.75	.73	.97
U.I. 20	Evasiveness	.74	.64	.87
U.I. 21	Exuberance	.93	.78	.85
U.I. 23	Mobilization	.71	.71	1.00*
U.I. 24	Anxiety	.90	.85	.94
U.I. 25	Realism	.62	.62	1.00*
U.I. 28	Asthenia	.66	.58	.88
U.I. 32	Exvia-vs-Invia	.74	.67	.91
U.I. 33	Discouragement-vs-Sanguineness	.81	.80	.99

NOTE: Consistency as homogeneity has not been calculated, being irrelevant to most purposes, since reduced homogeneity, to some appropriate point, is a deliberately sought ideal in personality subtests (Cattell & Tsujioka, 1964). The remaining consistency coefficient—transferability—involves substantial cross-cultural and subcultural research on factor structure change which lies largely in the future. However, it should be noted that transferability coefficients for a comparable battery can be calculated from the factor pattern matrices for American, Japanese, and German-Austrian subjects in the research of Cattell, Schmidt, and Pawlik (1973).

*Due to sampling effects in these two cases the coefficient for the long term (stability) retest actually exceeded the immediate retest reliability, yielding a constancy coefficient over 1.0. In these cases we have averaged the two values as a best general estimate of level and reported the highest possible constancy estimate at 1.00. It would be of scientific interest, when these values are more accurately determined, to see if the higher nature-nurture ratios for these traits go with higher trait constancy coefficients.

Table 5.2

DEPENDABILITY COEFFICIENTS CORRECTED TO ONE HOUR LENGTH PER FACTOR BATTERY

Universal Index No.	Factor Label	Dependability Coefficient
U.I. 16	Ego Standards	.92
U.I. 19	Independence	.92
U.I. 20	Evasiveness	.92
U.I. 21	Exuberance	.98
U.I. 23	Mobilization-vs-Regression	.91
U.I. 24	Anxiety	.97
U.I. 25	Realism-vs-Tensidia	.85
U.I. 28	Asthenia	.86
U.I. 32	Exvia-vs-Invia	.92
U.I. 33	Discouragement-vs-Sanguineness	.95

$$\mathbf{V}_{fe} = \mathbf{R}_{v}^{-1}\,\mathbf{V}_{fs} \qquad (5.2)$$

From this formula, which will be discussed again later, we obtain the multiple correlations of the factor batteries with the pure factors as *squared values in the diagonal* of the matrix $\mathbf{R}_b$, where:

$$\mathbf{R}_b = \mathbf{V}_{fe}\,\mathbf{V}_{fs} \qquad (5.3)$$

Within the defined concept validity there can be direct and indirect validities. The above are what are called *direct validities*.[2] The calculation

---

[2]The contrast of supposed ''predictive'' and ''concurrent'' validity coefficients by the APA Committee of several decades ago has always been a misleading proposition. Whether a test which predicts well *concurrently*, i.e., without time lapse, will also predict well into *future* occasions has nothing to do with the test, but only with the ''natural history'' of the traits, i.e., any inaccuracy in prediction is reducible only by using what we know about the change of the source traits themselves with age, circumstance, etc., and does not refer at all to the properties of the test, per se. ''Predictive validity'' (in the sense of that obsolete definition) thus confounds test and trait properties.

Table 5.3

CONCEPT ("CONSTRUCT") VALIDITIES OF THE 10 MAIN BATTERY FACTORS

Universal Index No.	Factor Label	R
U.I. 16	Ego Standards	.92
U.I. 19	Independence	.79
U.I. 20	Evasiveness	.68
U.I. 21	Exuberance	.80
U.I. 23	Mobilization-vs-Regression	.76
U.I. 24	Anxiety	.92
U.I. 25	Realism-vs-Tensidia ("Psychosis")	.74
U.I. 28	Asthenia	.64
U.I. 32	Exvia-vs-Invia	.71
U.I. 33	Discouragement-vs-Sanguineness	.85

(Using only the subtests belonging to the separately administered factor, as one factor battery, with unweighted, i.e., unit weight, subtests)

NOTE: The values are from a sample of 394 14-16-year-olds (193 boys; 201 girls) in the research of Cattell and Klein (1975).

of *indirect validities* may be illustrated as follows. If pure Factor A correlates with pure Factors B, C, D, E, F, etc., according to a vector of correlations .3, —.2, .0, —.1, .3, etc., then the test *battery* for A should ideally show the *same* vector of correlations with these other factors. The indirect validity is calculated as the congruence coefficient, r_c, or pattern similarity coefficient, r_p, between these two vectors of correlations. The correlations among the pure factors and all of them with any one factor battery are insufficiently determined at present to dependably determine the indirect validities. In any case, the indirect validity values may be regarded as supports rather than substitutes for the direct validity values.

Table 5.4

CONCEPT VALIDITIEŞ USING COMPUTER SYNTHESIS ("VARIANCE ALLOCATION") SCORING

Universal Index No.	Factor Label	R
U.I. 16	Ego Standards	.96
U.I. 19	Independence	.91
U.I. 20	Evasiveness	.87
U.I. 21	Exuberance	.89
U.I. 23	Mobilization-vs-Regression	.85
U.I. 24	Anxiety	.94
U.I. 25	Realism-vs-Tensidia	.86
U.I. 28	Asthenia	.82
U.I. 32	Exvia-vs-Invia	.87
U.I. 33	Discouragement-vs-Sanguineness	.89

NOTE: These are from the Cattell and Klein (1975) sample of 394 14-16-year-olds (193 boys; 201 girls) and are thus strictly comparable to values in Table 5.3.

Table 5.3 gives the numerical values if one uses source-trait batteries one at a time, resting measurement of the factor only on the eight or so subtests in that battery. But, as explained above, if one can afford time for the whole Kit, then each factor can take some weight from *all* subtests, in what has been called computer synthesis scoring. This procedure raises the validities considerably, as shown in Table 5.4.

However, since most users will use only one or two factors from the Kit at any one time, it has seemed best to base the standardization on the subtests special to one factor and to which scoring is normally restricted. The use of the full Kit of source-trait batteries is probably more likely to be made in research, and there, with the aim of comparing experimental and control groups or obtaining the correlation of the 10 traits with some criterion, standardization is unnecessary, and computer synthesis scoring is clearly the desirable method. Its technicalities are discussed under Scoring in Chapter 7, where it is pointed out that if one is prepared to accept the weights for the general population a standardization table for computer synthesis scoring *can* be set up, just as for single factor scoring here.

What are designated *concrete* validities (or more properly, perhaps, concrete relevancies) are to be obtained, of course, only when a test aims at predicting some one concrete performance, e.g., performance on a lathe, or number of times disciplined in class. A personality test measuring, as here, a *concept* such as anxiety or superego strength has only *conceptual validity* and the other correlations are strictly, as stated, *concrete relevances*. Correlation with a concrete "criterion" such as amount of salivation, amount of upset of cancellation, or a psychiatrist's rating of anxiety (which correlates only 0.3 with another psychiatrist's; see Cattell & Scheier, 1961) cannot be taken as a validity coefficient because these measures are not supposed to represent pure anxiety. They are only single manifestations of anxiety, partly determined by other source traits such as ego strength and depression. So the correlation of such a concrete variable tells us only the relative relevance of anxiety in causing that symptom. Numerous concrete relevances are given in Chapter 11, and they help enrich the concept of the given source trait in our minds, but it would be absurd to take them as true measures of *validity*, for only the unique *central factor in each concept* is the real criterion against which the given battery is to be evaluated.

To meet the aim of allowing this "practical" Handbook to simultaneously illustrate and refer to matters of basic "theoretical" importance in personality study, it is desirable to add a further insight into concept validity. Concept validity is the correlation of a test with the pure factor, and it is, of course, obtainable by simple structure factor analysis. Even so, if the factoring is within only one modality or instrumentality, it can be biased. The real validating factor concept is that underlying several instrumentalities and defined as an instrument-transcending personality trait (Cattell, Pierson, & Finkbeiner, 1976). Such a trait will show itself as a source trait in observer ratings (L-data), questionnaire responses (Q-data), and objective tests (T-data) for factors that can be matched across media.

So far, the equivalents of T-data *primary* factors (as in the O-A; see Chapter 9) have appeared, where discovered, as *secondary* (second-order, second-stratum) factors in Q-data. The equivalent of T-data U.I. 24, anxiety, for example, is found in the second-stratum Q-data Factor QII, and to fully demonstrate the validity of the U.I. 24 battery as an instrument-transcending anxiety trait measure, we should also validate it against this questionnaire second-order QII. Such refinement, depending on the setting aside of instrument factors and the definition of the instrument-transcending factor, lies mainly in the future. Meanwhile, however, we should note in use of the O-A Battery that success has been achieved in three to six (depending on the rigor of statistical significance) cross-media validations. Possibilities can be pointed out to the research psychologist by reminding him that, so far, L- and Q-data alignments with T-data (U.I.) factors in various researches (Cattell, 1955a, 1973; Cattell & Scheier, 1961; Schmidt, 1975; Wardell & Yeudall, 1970) cover: U.I. 17 with Q VIII, control; U.I. 19 with Q IV, independence; U.I. 22 with Q III, cortertia; U.I. 24 with Q II, anxiety; U.I. 25 (reversed) with Q XIV, general psychoticism; and U.I. 32 with Q I, exvia-invia.

Table 5.5 shows for three factors in the O-A, whose match with second-order Q-data factors has been most checked, the agreement between the loadings of the questionnaire primaries on the objective test factors, defined largely by objective test variables, and in the questionnaire secondaries.

It will be seen that with minor exceptions (set in brackets) the parallelism gives clear evidence of these personality source traits transcending the particular instrumentality (medium) of observation.

Validity needs to be examined also with respect to use of the Supplementary Battery (Appendix B) and the 10 factors in the Extended Battery (Appendix A). As to the former, it should go without saying that the addition of three or four tests (Appendix B) to the eight or so already in the battery for each factor should appreciably raise the validities above those in Table 5.3. With these additions one is approaching half an hour of actual test performance and an hour of elapsed testing time, and it is encouraging that in the few instances where the Supplemented Battery has been given, notably U.I. 24, the concept validity has reached 0.9, putting objective personality batteries on the same level as intelligence test batteries. Consequently, for the most exact research, where one particular source trait is involved, we would advocate adding the Supplementary Batteries, though the experimenter will need to develop his own distribution to give norms.

The validities of source-trait batteries in the Extended Battery (Appendix A) are only roughly known. The reader can draw his own inferences regarding validities at various ages and in normal and clinical groups from the main published research sources. At present these are Cattell (1955b), Cattell and Damarin (1968), Cattell, Delhees, and Tatro (1971), Cattell, Dubin, and Saunders (1954), Cattell and Howarth (1964), Cattell and Killian (1967), Cattell and Klein (1975), Cattell and Scheier (1961), Cattell and Schiff, et al. (1953), Cattell, Schmidt, and Bjerstedt (1972), Cattell, Schmidt, and Pawlik (1973), Cattell, Schuerger, Klein, and Finkbeiner (1976), Dielman, Schuerger, and Cattell (1970), Hundleby (1973a), Hundleby and Cattell (1968), Hundleby, Pawlik, and Cattell (1965), Knapp (1962), Nesselroade (1966), Rickels and Cattell (1965), Reuterman, Howard, and Cartwright (in press), Scheier, Cattell, and Mayeske (1960), Wardell and Yeudall (1976), and others indicated in the bibliographies to the above. Incidentally, the keen researcher will find in these sources not

Table 5.5

VALIDATION OF O-A PRIMARIES FOR U.I. 17, 24, AND 32
AGAINST QUESTIONNAIRE SECONDARIES

	Superego U.I. 17		Anxiety U.I. 24		Exvia U.I. 32	
	O-A	16 PF	O-A	16 PF	O-A	16 PF
A					39	58
B						
C			—56	—66		
E	—13	—18			(46)	
F	—45	—27			46	51
G	47	67				
H			—33	—38	43	50
I						
L			54	54		
M			(46)			
N						
O			66	78		
Q_1	(31)					
Q_2					—25	—65
Q_3	39	47	—60	—43		
Q_4			74	80		

NOTE: The O-A Pattern for 17 is from Wardell and Yeudall's (1976) identification of their factor V with U.I. 17. All values over .30 have been included here from the correlations in these researches of the questionnaire primaries with the second-order factor. The O-A factor loadings of U.I. 24 and U.I. 32 on questionnaire primaries are taken from the Cattell (1955) study of 750 air force men, using combined Q- and T-data measures. The questionnaires loading patterns in the second column in each pair are the "target" criteria against which these objective factor correlations are compared. The values are the means of 14 studies with questionnaire primaries in their own second-order space as reported in Cattell (1973b, p. 116). Only significant loadings are given in this table.

only the correlation and loading evidence on the 10 factors in Appendix A, but also further, yet-unindexed, patterns beyond those of U.I. 16 through U.I. 36. These are patterns that have been replicated only sporadically or not at all, but, like the heap of cracked shards beside a potter's workbench, offer ideas of what is yet to be accomplished. Someday systematic and careful researchers will find perhaps 10 more patterns in this heap already sufficiently replicated to call for a full-scale factor-analytic experiment to put them in position among older factors, to sharpen their patterns, and to establish their true psychological nature.

Meanwhile, it should be pointed out that among the 10 Extended Battery source traits—U.I. 17, 18, 22, 26, 27, 29, 30, 31, 34, and 35—there are some, as the work of Nesselroade, Scheier, Schmidt, Schuerger, Wardell, and Yeudall, referenced above, particularly shows— that are as high in validity as those in the Main Battery. This is true of U.I. 17, 18, 22, and 29, which were not included in the Main Kit for other reasons (U.I. 22, because mainly individual tests; U.I. 18, the "manic factor," because of having only clinical relevance; and so on). On the other hand, though U.I. 30, 31, and 35 promise many criterion relevances, they, and the rest of the Extended traits beyond U.I. 26, show (as their rank-order numbering indicates), lesser variance contribution to personality—at least in all objective tests yet created—than the earlier U.I. numbers. They are therefore likely to have lower concept validity coefficients than those reached for the 10 in the Main Kit, and for U.I. 17, 18, 22, and 29 in the Extended Kit.

For the Main Kit it is evident that if the same time is given for objective batteries as intelligence tests, namely, about an hour, the reliabilities and validities are of the same order of magnitude. Since only one form of the Kit is presently available with half-an-hour per factor, the psychologist wishing the most exact possible evaluations is advised to retest after a month with the same battery (no "practice" effects have yet been shown significant over an interval of that length). Actually, this should be done with intelligence tests if a stable *trait* I.Q. is to be obtained, and complaints about I.Q. instability largely arise from ignoring test sophistication and state fluctuation effects. As stated, more trait change is to be expected on most personality source traits, though at least three appear to be temperament traits and substantially genetic in nature (Cattell, Stice, & Kristy, 1957), as is general fluid intelligence.

6
Test Administration: Detailed Instructions

To use the O-A Battery, one needs this Handbook, the audio cassette tapes of administration instructions, the Main Kit of test booklets, and the associated answer sheets. Once the psychologist is informed and practiced, he will need, for an actual test session, only the last three items mentioned above. However, it has seemed desirable, in order that the psychologist may be fully in control, that this Handbook should go to the expense of setting out a detailed replication of what is on the tapes.

Once familiar with the O-A Battery, the psychologist will commonly have no regular use for Chapter 6; but it is vital to have it on hand for reference in case of difficulties.

Of course, the administrator may, if he wishes, set the tapes aside and give the instructions orally from the Handbook. But it is almost certainly preferable to use the tapes, because the voice expression is standardized and because there are almost always some slips in individual use of stopwatches, whereas the tapes have the timing built in. However, if individual timing is used it is advantageous to employ an "alarm-clock" timer instead of a stopwatch. A timer can be set to time each test (at 2 minutes, or whatever), can be released with the instruction "Begin," and will then signal with the bell the moment to call out "Put down your pencils." Nowadays, audio aids are almost universally available, and machines have reached sufficient reliability in adjustment of running speed to permit the timing of the test to be left to the tapes. If, however, there is any doubt of machine reliability, the psychologist should check the times on the tapes against a good stopwatch and adjust the machine rate. These Standard Administration Tapes are normally purchased with the Main Battery test booklets, but extra copies may be obtained from IPAT, 1602 Coronado Drive, Champaign, Illinois 61820.

Despite the mechanicalness which can be thus invoked for the actual instruction, skill is still required in group administration to deal with questions and to switch the tape on or off at necessary moments. Moreover, if short of proctors one must watch for cheating or casualness in responding to instructions. Indeed, it is well to show one's alertness by correcting, early in the testing session, any definite cases of ignoring instructions.

The instructions, factor by factor, are given in Table 6.1. Factors need not be given in any particular order, and, of course, one will frequently be using only one or two factors from the Kit. To aid this practice, the instructions for each factor begin in this Handbook on a separate page. The Handbook is of a size convenient for opening on a desk to have the instructions before one for any given factor, and it will be helpful to have it open there even when the taped instructions are being used. The psychologist should make sure that each person (or the one individual in an individual test) has all the necessary test material before him and knows just what each piece is. That material can be of three kinds:

1) the reusable test booklets, to be used with answer sheets,
2) the answer sheets for the reusable booklets,
3) the expendable booklets, for which responses are entered directly in the test booklets.

After the testing, the reusable booklets—1)—will need to be collected for further use elsewhere. The actual test results for subjects are to be collected together in materials 2) and 3), since scoring will be done on them simultaneously.

It is probably unnecessary to remind the experienced psychologist of the need to prepare the subjects here, as in any testing, by a preliminary talk on the purpose of the testing and its role in the individual's field of interest. The subject can correctly be told that—quite apart from the scholastic, clinical, or other counseling help that will accrue to him from testing—he is going (a) to take part in a very varied and interesting set of situations—most of them like games—in which he is asked to cooperate as much as he can; (b) that he should respond as he thinks best, and not bother about what others are doing, adding that these are not ability tests; and (c) that as each test is explained he should at once raise his hand if anything is not clear. He should be instructed to contact a proctor at once if any adverse circumstance—a broken pencil, a missing answer sheet or booklet —occurs during a timed test.

The test administrator should note that there is a slight difference—a necessary adaptive one—between the Instructions as set out in Table 6.1 and those on the actual Standard Administration Tapes. It is that the examiner is left in the written instructions of Table 6.1 to (a) read aloud the instructions printed at the head of each test (These are incorporated in the Tapescript as part of the "voice."), and (b) time the tests, pauses, etc., to the required number of seconds, by use of a timer (a self-timer, as used in laboratories is recommended). These two tasks are indicated by notes in parentheses in the Text of Table 6.1.

Table 6.1

ADMINISTRATION OF THE O-A MAIN KIT
Detailed Instructions and Timing for Subtests on 10 Source Traits

The printed instructions correspond exactly to those on the *tape*, and it is assumed that they will normally be given by playing the tape on a standard, audio cassette taperecorder, checked to run at a constant speed of 1 7/8 inches per second (ips).

Both the instructions here, and those on the tapes, are broken down into 10 separate units, so that any source trait can be lifted from the Main Kit and given separately.

Before the tape is started, make sure that everyone has a pencil (with spares available to the examiner) and has the correct test booklets and answer sheets. Be sure that the name or I.D. number of each individual is written on all answer sheets and any *Expendable Booklets* (but not the Main Booklet which is to be used again by others).

Instructions for

Administering

U.I. 16

Ego Standards

Test Time 16:00 Mins

**Total Time with Instructions, as on Tape
Approx. 30:00 Mins**

Eight Subtests

No apparatus needed

Instructions [as on Tape] for U.I. 16 — Ego Standards

Time required: Actual testing time: 16 mins.
Approximate total time with instructions and other time expenditures: 30 mins.

(Before playing the tape, be sure everyone has the test booklet, answer sheet, and pencils; have them write name, etc., on the answer sheet.)

No. in Battery for U.I. 16	Identifying T No.	Time Required†	Directions
		0:25	Now look at your answer sheet and find the block where you answer the questions for Test 1 on side 1 of the answer sheet. The words "Test 1" are printed at the left of the block. There are 30 questions in the block for Test 1. If you have not found the place to answer the questions in Test 1, put up your hand (pause).
1	361	0:40	Now open your test booklet to page 1 and look at Test 1—Attitudes. Read the directions to yourselves while I read them aloud. (Here examiner reads aloud instructions at top of Test 1, T361.):* "Fill in the 'a' box on your answer sheet next to the item number if you strongly agree with a statement, 'b' if you agree, 'c' if you are uncertain, and so on. When you are told to begin, work quickly." If you finish the first page before time is called, go right on to the second. Any questions? (pause) Pencils ready. Begin Attitudes. (Switch on timer.)
		2:00	(After 1 min., say): "Don't forget, go right on to the second page." (After 2 mins., say): "Stop working. Pencils down while we get ready to work on Test 2."
2	49a	1:15	Now turn to page 3 in the booklet and look at Test 2, Coding. I will read the directions aloud. (Read T49a) "In this test you are to look for the vowels (A, E, I, O, U) in the rows of letters below and mark next to the item number on the answer sheet as follows. If you find

† Actual testing times are in **bold face.**
* Notes to examiner, not actually on tape to examinees, are put in parentheses.

A, fill in the 'A' box on the answer sheet; if you find E, mark the 'E' box; if you find I, mark 'I'; if you find O, mark 'O'; if you find U, mark 'U.' There is only one vowel in each row." Now look at the block of answer spaces for Test 2 on the answer sheet. Notice the letters A, E, I, O, U. (pause) Any questions? (pause) Do this whole page if you can before time is called, but do not go on to the next page until told to do so. Pencils ready. Begin Coding, Part I. (Switch on timer.)

1:00 (After 1 min. by timer, say): "Stop working."

0:30 On the next page is Part II of this test. Do not turn the page yet. The questions on the next page start with item 41. Find that now on the answer sheet. (pause) Now turn the page, to page 4, and get ready to do Part II of Coding. Pencils ready. Begin Coding, Part II.

1:00 Stop working. Pencils down while we get ready to do Test 3.

1:35

44a

3

Now turn to page 5 in the booklet and look at Test 3, Letter and Number Comparison. I will read the directions aloud. (Read T44a): "When sets of letters or numbers are the same and in the same order, mark 'S' next to the item number on the answer sheet. If one or more letters or numbers in a set are different, mark 'D' next to the item number on the answer sheet. Look at the letters next to number 1 below. 'ous' is not the same as 'oys,' so for number 1 fill in the 'D' box for 'different' next to 1 on the answer sheet. Next to number 2, 'haz' is the same as 'haz,' so mark the 'S' box for 'same.' When you are told to begin, work quickly." If you have not already done so, find the place to mark the answers for Test 3 on your answer sheet. Any questions? (pause) Do this whole page if you can before time is called, but do not go on to the next page until told to do so. Remember, mark S for same, D for different. Pencils ready. Begin Letter and Number Comparison, Part I.

1:00 Stop working. Pencils down.

0:25		Part II of this test is like Part I. The questions on Part II start with item 41 on the answer sheet. Find that now. (slight pause) Now turn to page 6. Pencils ready. Begin Letter and Number Comparison, Part II.
1:00		Stop working. Pencils down while we get ready for Test 4.
0:55	8a	Now turn to page 7 of the booklet and look at Test 4, Goodness of Work I. I will read the directions aloud. (Read T8a): "Fill in the 'a' box on the answer sheet next to the item number if you think the work done is very good, 'b' on the answer sheet if it is good, 'c' if it is average, and so on." Turn the sheet over now and find the place to answer Test 4 (slight pause). Any questions? (pause) If you finish this page before time is called, go right on to the next page. Pencils ready. Begin Goodness of Work I.
1:30		(After 1 min., say): "Don't forget, go right on to the next page." Stop working. Pencils down while we get ready for Test 5.
1:00	20a	Now turn to page 9 in the booklet and look at Test 5, Modernistic Drawings. I will read the directions aloud. (Read T20a): "Look at these phrases below marked a, b, and c. If you see something like 'a' in the picture above, mark the 'a' box next to the item number on the answer sheet. If you see something like 'b,' mark the 'b' box on the answer sheet for that item. If you do not see either, mark the 'c' box on the answer sheet. Mark only 'a,' 'b,' or 'c' for each item." Find the place to mark your answers for Test 5 on the answer sheet (slight pause). Any questions? (pause) Pencils ready. Begin Modernistic Drawings, Picture 1.
0:30	5	Stop working. Pencils down.
0:20		Picture 2, on the next page, starts with question 11. Find the place to mark question 11 on

65

the answer sheet (slight pause). Now turn to page 10 and get ready to do Picture 2. Pencils ready. Begin Picture 2.

0:30 Stop working. Pencils down.

0:25 Picture 3, on the next page, starts with question 21. Find the place to mark question 21 on the answer sheet (slight pause). Now turn to page 11 and get ready to do Picture 3. Pencils ready. Begin Picture 3.

0:30 Stop working. Pencils down while we get ready to work on Test 6.

2:05 / 11a / 6 Now turn to page 12 in the booklet and look at Test 6, Assumptions I. I will read the directions aloud. (Read T11a): "In this test there are six sentences like this one: Example A: Bossie is contented because she is a cow. For this to be true, it must be true that: 1) all contented animals are cows, 2) all cows are contented, 3) Bossie is not a horse, 4) Bossie gives more milk, 5) cows may or may not be contented depending on how well they are cared for. Under the example you see five statements. You are to decide which ones must be true for the sample sentence to be true. In the example above, number 2) must be true, and number 3) must be true. If Bossie is contented because she is a cow, then it must be true that all cows are contented, and that she is not a horse. In the rest of the test there will be six problems like this one. If the statement must be true for the sentence to be true, fill in the 'T' box on the answer sheet next to the item number; if it does not have to be true, mark the 'F' box. In each problem there can be one or two statements which must be true." Find the place to mark your answers to Test 6 on the answer sheet (slight pause). Any questions? (pause) Just mark T for true or F for false. If you finish one page before time is called, go right on to the next. Now turn to page 13. Pencils ready. Begin Assumptions I.

3:00

(After 1½ mins., say): "Remember, go right on to the next page." Stop working. Pencils down while we get ready for Test 7.

1:25   35a

Now turn to page 15 in the booklet and look at Test 7, Rapid Calculation, Part I. I will read the directions aloud. (Read T35a): "Work the problems *across* the page, one row at a time. Number 1) is addition, 2) is subtraction, 3) multiplication, 4) division, 5) addition again, and so on. If the answer given here is correct, mark the 'a' box next to the item number on the answer sheet. If the answer given is wrong, mark the 'b' box next to the item number on the answer sheet. When you are told to start, work as quickly as you can, but don't be surprised if you don't finish. Not many people will. Be sure to do both pages. Remember, 'a' for right, 'b' for wrong." Find the place to mark your answers for Test 7 on the answer sheet (slight pause). If you finish the first page before time is called, go right on to the second. Remember, a for right, b for wrong. Pencils ready. Begin Rapid Calculation, Part I.

1:00

(After 30 sec., say): "Don't forget, go right on to the second page." Stop working. Pencils down.

0:30

Part II is like the first, except with different problems. Part II starts with item 41 in Test 7. Find that now on the answer sheet (slight pause). Now turn to page 17 in the booklet, Rapid Calculation, Part II. Pencils ready. Begin Part II.

1:00

(After 30 sec., say): "Don't forget, go right on to the second page." Stop working. Pencils down while we get ready to work on Test 8.

1:05   43b   8

Turn to page 19 in the booklet and look at Test 8, My Interests. I will read the directions aloud. (Read T43b): "If you had an hour to spare, which of the following would you like to talk about with someone who knows about them? Mark the 'I' (interested) box next to the correct number on the answer sheet if you would like to talk about it, 'N' (not interested) if you're not interested in that thing. Example A: Building boats." Find the place to mark your answers for Test 8 on the answer sheet. (slight pause) Any questions? (pause) Remember, "I" for interested, "N" for not interested. Pencils ready. Begin My Interests.

2:00 Please sit quietly while materials are collected.

End of tape for U.I. 16

Total time: 30:00 mins.

Instructions for

Administering

U.I. 19

**Independence
vs
Subduedness**

Test Time 15:15 Mins

**Total Time with Instructions, as on Tape
Approx. 29:00 Mins**

Seven Subtests

No apparatus needed

Instructions [as on Tape] for U.I. 19 — Independence

Time required: Actual testing time: 15 mins. 15 sec.
Approximate total time with instructions and other time expenditures: 29 mins.

(Before playing the tape, be sure everyone has the test booklet, answer sheet, and pencils; have them write name, etc., on the answer sheet.)

No. in Battery for U.I. 19	Identifying T No.	Time Required†	Directions
		0:25	Now look at your answer sheet and find the block where you answer the questions for Test 1, on the side of the answer sheet that says U.I. 19.** The words "Test 1" are printed at the left of the block. There are 20 questions in the block for Test 1. If you have not found the place to answer the questions in Test 1, put up your hand. (pause)
1	35b	1:00	Now open your test booklet to page 1 and look at Test 1, Problems. Read the directions to yourselves while I read them aloud. (Read T35b): "Work the following problems as fast as you can. If you think 'a' is the correct answer, fill in the 'a' box on your answer sheet; if 'b' is correct, mark 'b,' and so on. Example A: If you multiply 2 x 2 and add 3, you have: a) 5, b) 6, c) 7, d) 8, e) 9." The answer is 7, so you would blacken the space under the little c for that item on the answer sheet. Do not make any mark in the test booklet, however. Any questions? (pause) Pencils ready. Begin Problems, Part I.
		1:00	Stop working. Pencils down.
		0:25	Part II of this test is like Part I. The questions in Part II start with item 11. Find item 11

† Actual testing times are in **bold face.**
** Some answer sheets may use HSOA instead of the more general U.I. notation.

for Test 1 on the answer sheet (slight pause). Now turn to page 2, Problems, Part II. Pencils ready. Begin Problems, Part II.

1:00 Stop working. Pencils down while we get ready for Test 2.

1:40 Now turn to page 3 and look at Test 2, Hidden Shapes. I will read the directions aloud. (Read T37): "Look at the row of boxes in the example. One box at the left is separate from the next five boxes marked a, b, c, d, and e. First look at the drawing in the single box on the left. Then find one of the five boxes on the right that has the same parts in it as the one on the left. If you look at the example you see it has a circle and a triangle in it. So has 'c' on the right, so box 'c' is the right answer. The parts will sometimes be moved up or down, and there may be extra lines. But the right answer will contain all parts shown in the box at the left. In the rest of the test, when you decide on your answer, fill in the 'a,' 'b,' 'c,' 'd,' or 'e' box next to the number on your answer sheet, depending on which box you think has the same parts in it as the one on the left." Find the place to mark the answers for Test 2 on the answer sheet (pause). Any questions? (pause) If you finish this page before time is called, DO NOT go on to the next page. Pencils ready. Begin Hidden Shapes, Part I.

1:00 Stop working. Pencils down.

0:25 Part II of this test is like Part I. The questions in Part II start with item 7. Find item 7 for Test 2 on the answer sheet (slight pause). Now turn to page 4, Hidden Shapes, Part II. Pencils ready. Begin Hidden Shapes, Part II.

1:00 Stop working. Pencils down while we get ready for Test 3.

1:05 Turn to page 5 and look at Test 3, Reading Comprehension. I will read the directions aloud. (Read T6a): "On the following pages are three stories which you will be asked to read and answer questions on later. DO NOT turn any pages until told to do so. When you are told to

2

37

3

6a

turn the page, start reading the first story. Read at your ordinary, natural rate, as if you were reading for pleasure. It is NOT a test to see how fast you can read. The stories are too long for anyone to reach the end. Wait for instructions before beginning." When you get the signal, turn to page 6 and begin reading What Makes the Wind Blow. Any questions? (pause) Turn the page and begin reading.

0:30 Stop reading.

0:45 Turn to page 7 and get ready to answer the memory questions when you get the signal. I will read the directions aloud. (Read Reading Memory 1): "Mark the 'Y' box next to the item number on your answer sheet if you remember the phrase or word, 'N' if you do not remember it." Find the place to mark your answers for Test 3 on the answer sheet. Any questions? (pause) Remember, mark the Y for Yes, remembered, the N for not remembered. Pencils ready. Begin Reading Memory 1.

0:15 Stop working.

0:15 When you get the signal, turn to page 8 and begin reading "A Natural Radar System." Now turn to page 8 and begin reading.

0:30 Stop reading.

0:15 Turn to page 9 and get ready to answer the memory questions as before. This part starts with question 11. Find that now on the answer sheet. Pencils ready. Begin Reading Memory 2.

0:15 Stop working.

0:15 When you get the signal, turn to page 10 and begin reading "Boy or Man." Now turn to page 10 and start reading.

0:30 Stop reading.

0:15 Turn to page 11 and get ready to answer the memory questions as before. This part starts with question 21. Find that now on the answer sheet. Pencils ready. Begin Reading Memory 3.

0:15 Stop working. Pencils down while we get ready for Test 4.

1:40   4   422

Now turn to page 12 and look at Test 4, What Is the Right Design? I will read the directions aloud. (Read T442): "Look at the two examples below. Notice that each example has two rows of designs with five boxes in it. The first row is marked 'A,' and the second marked 'B.' The row marked 'A' has a series or pattern in it, but with one square of the pattern missing. This square has a question mark in it. Your job on this test is to choose the design from the lower row, 'B,' which fits best in the square with the question mark. In example 1 below, you would mark the 'b' box on your answer sheet because the design in the square marked 'b' fits best in place of the question mark. In example 2, you would mark 'd' on your answer sheet. On the next page, there are 15 problems of the same sort. When you are told to do so, turn the page and begin." Find the place to mark Test 4 on your answer sheet. Any questions? (pause) Turn to page 13, turn the booklet sideways, and get ready to begin. Pencils ready. Begin What Is the Right Design?

2:00 Stop working. Pencils down while we get ready for Test 5.

1:05   5   328

Now turn to page 14 and look at Test 5, Searching. I will read the directions aloud. (Read T328): "On the following two pages, which are lettered 'A' and 'B' at the top, there are some pictures. The questions below ask you to search among these pictures to answer questions about them. Read each question, look at the pictures, and then fill in the 'a' box on your answer sheet if you think choice 'a' is the correct answer, 'b' if you think choice 'b'

73

is correct, and so on. When you are told to begin, work as fast as you can." Find the place to answer Test 5 on your answer sheet. Any questions? (pause) When you get the signal, get ready to look up the answers on the next two pages. Pencils ready. Begin Searching.

2:30 Stop working. Pencils down while we get ready to work Test 6.

242a

6

1:00 Now turn to page 17 and look at Test 6, Picture Memory. I will read the directions aloud. (Read T242a): "On the next two pages are 10 rows of pictures (5 rows on each page). When you are told to turn the page, start memorizing the LEFT column of pictures on the first page. Remember, concentrate on memorizing the pictures on the left, but DO NOT cover the ones on the right. You will be given a few minutes for this. You will then be told to turn to the second page and there again you should begin memorizing the pictures on the LEFT on that page." Any questions? (pause) Now turn the page, to page 18, and memorize the pictures on the left. Begin.

0:30 Stop working.

0:10 Now turn to page 19 and memorize the pictures on the left. Begin.

0:30 Stop working.

0:45 Turn to page 20, Picture Memory 1. You will have to turn this page sideways. I will read the directions aloud (Read T242a): "Below are 10 rows of pictures. One of the pictures in each row is one that you've just memorized. Find the picture you memorized, then mark the 'a,' 'b,' 'c,' 'd,' or 'e' box next to the item number on your answer sheet." Find the place to mark the answers for Test 6 on the answer sheet. Any questions? (pause) Pencils ready. Begin Picture Memory 1.

1:00 Stop working. Pencils down while we get ready to work on Test 7.

7   114

2:00 Now turn to page 21 in the booklet and look at Test 7, Observation. I will read the directions aloud. (Read T114): "This is a test of your powers of observation. On the next pages are some figures (circles, squares, etc.) which have dots or lines in them. Look at these examples: This figure is DOTTED and ROUNDED. This figure is DOTTED and SQUARED. This figure is LINED and ROUNDED. This figure is LINED and SQUARED. This figure is CROSS-LINED. This figure is EMPTY. You will be given six seconds to look at each figure and mark your answer sheet. Here are the instructions for how to mark. 1. On your answer sheet, fill in the 'a' box if the figure is DOTTED and ROUNDED. 2. On your answer sheet, fill in the 'b' box if the figure is DOTTED and SQUARED. 3. On your answer sheet, fill in the 'c' box if the figure is LINED and ROUNDED. 4. On your answer sheet, fill in the 'd' box if the figure is LINED and SQUARED. 5. On your answer sheet, fill in the 'e' box if the figure is CROSS-LINED or EMPTY." Find the place to answer Test 7 on the answer sheet. Take a last look at the instructions: a if it is dotted and rounded, b if it is dotted and squared, c if it is lined and rounded, d if it is lined and squared, e if it is cross-lined OR empty. (pause) Pencils ready. Turn the page and do number 1.

2:30 (Have clock running before you; allow six seconds per item including time for the words "number 1.")

Number 2 number 3 4 5 6 7 8 9 10 11 12 13 14 15 16 17 18 19 20 21 22 23 24 25

Stop working. Pencils down. Please sit quietly while we collect materials.

End of tape for U.I. 19

Total time: 29:00

Instructions for

Administering

U.I. 20

Evasiveness

Test Time 15:00 Mins

Total Time with Instructions, as on Tape
Approx. 24:00 Mins

Seven Subtests

No apparatus needed

Instructions [as on Tape] for U.I. 20 — Evasiveness

Time required: Actual testing time: 15 mins.
Approximate total time with instructions and other time expenditures: 24 mins.

(Before playing the tape, be sure everyone has the test booklet, answer sheet, and pencils; have them write name, etc., on the answer sheet.)

No. in Battery for U.I. 20	Identifying T No.	Time Required†	Directions
		0:25	Now look at your answer sheet and find the block where you answer the questions for Test 1, on the side of the answer sheet that says U.I. 20.** The words "Test 1" are printed at the left of the block. There are 10 questions in the block for Test 1. If you have not found the place to answer the questions in Test 1, put up your hand. (pause)
1	10b(1)	1:20	Now open your test booklet to page 1 and look at Test 1, Opinions I. Read the directions to yourselves while I read them aloud. (Read T10b): "For each item in this test there are two sentences, the first in capital letters and the second in small letters. You are asked to show how much you agree or disagree with the sentence in capital letters. The second sentence, in small letters and brackets, is there to give you some information that may help you make up your mind about the first sentence. Fill in the 'a' box if you strongly agree, 'b' if you agree, 'c' if you are uncertain, 'd' if you disagree, and 'e' if you strongly disagree. Example A: IN ORDER TO GET AHEAD IN LIFE, YOU HAVE TO WORK HARD. [Definitely agree, because stories about the lives of important men show most of them worked hard.] a) strongly agree, b) agree, c) uncertain, d) disagree, e) strongly disagree." Any questions? (pause) If you finish the first page before time is called, go right on to the next page. (pause) Pencils ready. Begin Opinions I.

† Actual testing times are in **bold face.**
** Some answer sheets may use HSOA instead of the more general U.I. notation.

1:30 (After 1 min., say): "Don't forget, go right on to the next page." Stop working. Pencils down while we get ready for Test 2.

9g(1) **0:55** Now turn to page 3 in the booklet and look at Test 2, Opinions II. I will read the directions aloud. (Read T9g(1)): "Fill in the 'a' box next to the item number on the answer sheet if you strongly agree with the sentence, 'b' if you agree, 'c' if you are uncertain, and so on. Use the following key in marking your answers: a) strongly agree, b) agree, c) uncertain, d) disagree, e) strongly disagree." Find the place to mark your answers for Test 2 on the answer sheet. Any questions? (pause) If you finish the first page before time is called, go right on to the next. Pencils ready. Begin Opinions II.

3:30 (After 2 mins., say): "Don't forget to go right on to the next page." Stop working. Pencils down while we get ready for Test 3.

9bj(1) **0:40** Now turn to page 5 in the booklet and look at Test 3, Opinions III. I will read the directions aloud. (Read T9bj(1)): "Fill in the 'a' box next to the item number on the answer sheet if you strongly agree with the sentence, 'b' if you agree, 'c' if you are uncertain, and so on. Use the following key in marking your answers: a) strongly agree, b) agree, c) uncertain, d) disagree, e) strongly disagree." Find the place to mark your answers for Test 3 on the answer sheet. Any questions? (pause) Pencils ready. Begin Opinions III.

2:30 Stop working. Pencils down while we get ready for Test 4.

9bj(2) **1:30** Now turn to page 6 and look at Test 4, Memory. I will read the directions aloud. (Read T9bj(2)): "This is a memory test. Fourteen of the 28 phrases below are from the last test. You are to fill in the 'Y' box for yes on your answer sheet next to the item number if you remember the phrase from the last test. Fill in the 'N' box for no if you don't remember it. Don't look at the last test. There should be only 14 marked 'Y' for yes, remembered. When you are told to begin, work quickly." Find the place to mark your answers for Test 4 on the answer sheet. Any questions? (pause) Mark Y for remembered, N for not remembered.

2:00 Pencils ready. Begin Memory.

1:00 Stop working. Pencils down while we get ready for Test 5.

5   10b(2)

Now turn to page 7 and look at Test 5, Opinions IV. I will read the directions aloud. (Read T10b(2)): "For each item in this test there are two sentences, the first in capital letters and the second in small letters. You are asked to show how much you agree or disagree with the sentence in capital letters. The second sentence, in small letters and brackets, is there to give you some information that may help you make up your mind about the first sentence. Fill in the 'a' box if you strongly agree, 'b' if you agree, 'c' if you are uncertain, 'd' if you disagree, and 'e' if you strongly disagree." Find the place to answer Test 5 on the answer sheet. Any questions? (pause) If you finish the page before time is called, go right on to the next page. Pencils ready. Begin Opinions IV.

1:30 (After 1 min., say): "Don't forget to go right on to the next page." Stop working. Pencils down while we get ready for Test 6.

7   38a

1:05 Now turn to page 9 and look at Test 6, Common Annoyances. I will read the directions aloud. (Read T38a): "Fill in the 'a' box on your answer sheet next to the item number if you get very annoyed and angry about the thing mentioned in that item. Mark 'b' if you get a little annoyed by it, and mark 'c' if you don't get at all annoyed by it. Use the following answers: a) very annoyed, b) a little annoyed, c) not at all annoyed. Example A. Windows that stick when you try to close them. a) very annoyed, b) a little annoyed, c) not at all annoyed." Find the place to answer Test 6 on the answer sheet. Any questions? (pause) If you finish this page before time is called, go right on to the next page. Pencils ready. Begin Common Annoyances.

2:00 (After 1 min., 30 sec., say): "Don't forget, go right on to the next page." Stop working. Pencils down while we get ready for Test 7.

0:55 Now turn to page 11 and look at Test 7, Human Nature I. I will read the directions aloud. (Read T16b): "Fill in the 'a' box next to the item number on your answer sheet if you strongly agree with a statement, 'b' next to the item number if you agree, 'c' if you are uncertain, and so on. When you are told to begin, work as quickly as you can. Use the following key in marking your answers: a) strongly agree, b) agree, c) uncertain, d) disagree, e) strongly disagree. Example A: Most teachers are really interested in helping their students learn. a) strongly agree, b) agree, c) uncertain, d) disagree, e) strongly disagree." Find the place to answer Test 7 on the answer sheet. Any questions? (pause) If you finish this page before time is called, go right on to the next page. Pencils ready. Begin Human Nature I.

2:00 (After 1 min., 30 sec., say): "Don't forget, go right on to the next page." Stop working. Please sit quietly while materials are collected.

End of tape for U.I. 20

Approximate total time: 24:00

16b

8

80

Instructions for

Administering

U.I. 21

_____

Exuberance

_____

Test Time 17:50 Mins

Total Time with Instructions, as on Tape
Approx. 29:00 Mins

_____

Eight Subtests

_____

Sound Tape and recorder needed for Test 4 "Can you hear the word?"

Instructions [as on Tape] for U.I. 21 — Exuberance

Time required: Actual testing time: 17 mins. 50 sec.
Approximate total time with instructions and other time expenditures: 29 mins.

(Before playing the tape, be sure everyone has the test booklet and pencils; have them write name, etc., on the booklet.)

No. in Battery for U.I. 21	Identifying T No.	Time Required†	Directions
1	411d	1:25	Take up the U.I. 21 expendable booklet. Make sure your name is on the front, where it says "Name," because for these tests all answers go right in the book. Now open the booklet to page 1 and look at Test 1, Following Directions Quickly. I will read the directions aloud. (Read T411d): "You are to fill in the boxes below as you would on a regular answer sheet. Be neat, but work fast and follow directions carefully. Count the boxes either from the left or the right, according to the directions, filling in the boxes listed. If you start at the LEFT, count boxes from the left. If you start at the RIGHT, count boxes from the right. STOP. Wait for the signal to begin then read the following directions." After the signal to start, you may look back at the directions as often as you wish. When you get the signal, work as fast as you can through the whole test. Any questions? (pause) Pencils ready. Begin.
		1:00	(After 20 sec., say): "Don't forget, work right on through the whole test." Stop. Pencils down while we get ready for the next test.
2	43a	0:40	Turn to page 2, and look at Test 2, Ideas. I will read the directions aloud. (Read T43a): "When told to begin, write in the left-hand column as many words as you can think of that

† Actual testing times are in **bold face**.

begin with the letter 'M.' When time is up, you will be told to write in the right-hand column as many words as you can that begin with the letter 'T.' Don't start until you are told." Any questions? (pause) When told to begin, write M words. Pencils ready. Begin M words.

0:45 Stop working.

0:10 Get ready to write T words next to the M words. Pencils ready. Begin T words.

0:45 Stop working.

0:35 Turn the page, to page 3. I will read the directions aloud. (Read p. 3): "When told to begin, write as many things as you can think of that would go where the 'X' is, under the tree. Next you will be told to write things that could go where the other 'X' is, on the rug. Wait for directions to start." Any questions? (pause) Get ready for what might be under the tree. Pencils ready. Begin.

0:45 Stop working.

0:05 Get ready for what might be on the rug. Pencils ready. Begin.

0:45 Stop working. Pencils down while we get ready for the next test.

1:00 Turn to page 4 and look at Test 3, Drawings I. I will read the directions aloud. (Read T88a): "This is a simple drawing test. The lines in each box are parts of designs. Change each one so that it is either a pleasing design or so it looks like something. Add as few lines as possible in making the changes. Work quickly. For example, this could be changed to this or this. Don't start until you are told." The example shows that the two lines could be

88a

3

changed into a flag, or they could be changed into just a design, not any real object. You will have 1 minute to do the drawings on this page. Any questions? (pause) Pencils ready. Begin Drawings, Part I.

1:00 Stop working.

0:10 Pencils down. Turn to page 5 and get ready to do Part II. Ready. Begin Part II.

1:00 Stop working.

0:25 Now go back over all the drawings you have made, on this page and on the last one. If any of these drawings were meant to be real things in any way at all, write in the name of the thing inside the picture. Write the name of the thing only if it was meant to be a real thing when you drew it. Start now, writing the names of the drawings. You will have to work quickly.

1:30 Stop working. Pencils down while we get ready for the next test.

1:20 Now turn to page 6, Can You Hear the Word? I will read the directions aloud. (Read T164a): "In this test you will listen to a series of sounds played on the tape recorder. These will often seem a little muffled to you. However, most of the sounds contain a real word, that is, a word you would find in the dictionary. You are to listen to each sound. A number will be called before each sound. Put your answer next to that number on the Answer Sheet below. If you are pretty sure you heard a word in the sound, write it in the correct blank space below. The word you put down doesn't have to be absolutely correct—you get some credit for it if you write a word that sounds almost like it. If you aren't sure whether or not there was a real word, underline 'could not tell' on that line." You will hear the example first, then the test words. Any questions? (pause) Be ready to write the example and the test words.

4   164a   CUT HERE—PLAY 164a TAPE. (Note: Included in taped instructions.)

4:20 Stop working. *Do not* turn the page yet.

5

2d

0:40 On the next page you will see some pictures that are not complete, even though they are pictures of real things. It will be hard to tell what they are, but your job will be to give each picture a name. You must write the name on the line right under the picture. (pause) Now turn to page 7 and get ready to do the test Incomplete Pictures. Be ready to write a name for each picture on the line below the picture. DO NOT go on to Part II if you finish before time is called. Pencils ready. Begin Part I.

0:30 Stop working.

0:10 Turn to page 8 for Part II, Incomplete Pictures. Begin Part II.

0:30 Stop working. Pencils down while we get ready for the next test.

6

3

1:00 Now turn to page 9 in the booklet, In and Out. I will read the directions aloud. Do not begin until I give the signal (Read T3): "Look at the picture below. Notice that it looks like a vase if you let the white part of the picture stand out, or as two faces if you let the black part of the picture stand out. When told to start, stare at the picture and make a mark like this / on the line below where it says 'MARK HERE' each time it changes from vase to faces or from faces to vase." Do not begin yet. Some of you will find that the picture changes rapidly, while others may find that it does not change at all. What you are to do is simply put a mark on the line below, where it says "mark here" each time the figure changes during the time allowed. Any questions? (pause) Pencils ready. Begin In and Out.

1:00 Stop working.

0:45 Pencils down while we get ready for the next page. Turn to page 10 and read silently while I read the directions aloud. (Read T3, p. 10): "On this test you are to do the same as you did with the 'vase and faces' picture. Look at the dot in the middle of the box below. It is possible to see the box in two different ways. In one way, the dot appears to be on the front of the box, toward you. In another way, the dot appears to be on the back, away from you. Make a mark like this **/** on the line below each time the box changes for you. Don't start until you are told." Any questions? (pause) Pencils ready. Begin.

21

1:00 Stop working. Pencils down while we get ready for the next test.

0:30 Now turn to page 11 in the booklet, Listening and Writing. I will explain the test. When I give the signal, I will start reading words that you are to copy down on the lines provided. Just copy them as well as you can while I read. Any questions? (pause) Pencils ready. Here are the words for Part I.

7

1:00 (Set timer for 1 min. As timer starts): "I start reading the next words every 3 seconds."

3   6   9   12
I was / sheltered by / a couple / of coconut /

15   18   21   24
leaves. No / one but / Jim could / have dragged /

27   30   33   36   39
me far / from the / water and / put up / a couple /

42   45   48   51
of leaves / for shade. / He was / lying quietly /

54   57   60
beside me. / I went / off again. /

(Buzzer)

86

0:15 Now turn to page 12 and get ready to copy the words for Part II. Here are the words for Part II.

1:00 (Set timer for 1 min. As timer starts): "I start reading words, 3 words per 2 seconds."

2   4   6
The next time / I came round / it was evening, /

8   10   12
and Jim was / pressing a cooling / coconut drink to /

14   16   18
my lips. We / were the only / people alive after /

20   22   24
the wreck and / even we would / have starved if /

26   28   30
it had not / been for the / natives who found /

32   34   36
us next day. / They performed with / us the rite /

38   40   42
of changing names, / which surprised us. / But this rite /

44   46   48
binds two men / closer together than / a blood brothership /

50   52   54

and the natives / treated us most / kindly . Two weeks /

56   58   60

later we were / taken home by / an American cruiser . /

Stop working. (Read 2 seconds after the word "cruiser.")

0:15 Pencils down while we get ready for the next test.

0:45 136a 8 Now turn to page 13 and look at Test 9, Tapping. This one is sideways on the page. I will read the directions aloud. (Read 136a): "In this test you are to tap four little dots with your pencil inside each of the blocks you see on this sheet. There must be four dots in each block. Don't expect to finish, but put four dots in as many blocks as you can, following the blocks right around the curves. Start when the signal is given." Just tap with your pencil, putting four dots in each block. Any questions? (pause) Time is short, so work quickly. Please start and stop exactly on the signal. Pencils ready. Begin Tapping.

0:30 Stop working.

0:10 Turn the page, to page 14, and be ready to work on the second part of Tapping. Pencils ready. Begin Tapping, Part II.

0:30 Stop working.

0:05 Pencils down while test materials are collected.

End of tape for U.I. 21

Total time: 29:00 min.

Instructions for

Administering

U.I. 23

**Mobilization
vs
Regression**

Test Time 16:00 Mins

**Total Time with Instructions, as on Tape
Approx. 27:00 Mins**

Eight Subtests

No apparatus needed

Instructions [as on Tape] for U.I. 23 — Mobilization vs. Regression

Time required: Actual testing time: 16 mins.

Approximate total time with instructions and other time expenditures: 27 mins.

(Before playing the tape, be sure everyone has test booklets, answer sheet, and pencils; have them write name, etc., on the answer sheet.)

No. in Battery for U.I. 23	Identifying T No.	Time Required†	Directions
		0:30	Now look at your answer sheet and find the block where you answer the questions for Test 1, on the side of the answer sheet that says U.I. 23.** The words "Test 1" are printed at the left of the block. There are 20 questions in the block for Test 1. If you have not found the place to answer the questions in Test 1, put up your hand. (pause)
1	38b	0:40	Now open your test booklet to page 1 and look at Test 1, Annoyances. Read the directions to yourselves while I read them aloud. (Read T38b): "Mark 'a' on the answer sheet next to the item number if you are *very* annoyed and angry about one of the things mentioned, 'b' if you are a *little bit* annoyed, and 'c' if you are *not* annoyed. Don't start until you are told. Example A: Toys that break easily. a) very much, b) a little, c) not." Any questions? (pause) If you finish the first page before time is called, go right on to the second. Pencils ready. Begin Annoyances.
		2:00	(After 1 min. 30 sec., say): "Don't forget, go right on to the second page." Stop working. Pencils down while we get ready for Test 2.
2	44c	0:50	Now turn to page 3 in the booklet and look at Test 2, Comparing Letters. I will read the directions aloud. (Read T44c): "There are two sets of letters after each number. If both

† Actual testing times are in **bold face.**

** Some answer sheets may use HSOA instead of the more general U.I. notation.

sets are exactly the *same* and in the same order, fill in the 'S' box next to the item number on the answer sheet. If one or more letters in a set are *different*, mark 'D' next to the item number on the answer sheet. Work quickly, when you are told to begin. Remember, 'S' for the same, 'D' for different." Find the place to mark your answers for Test 2 on the answer sheet. Any questions? (pause) Pencils ready. Begin Comparing Letters, Part I.

0:30 Stop working.

0:20 On the next page is another part of this test. It starts with item 41; find that now on your answer sheet. Now turn to page 4 and get ready to do Part II of Comparing Letters. Pencils ready. Begin Part II.

0:30 Stop working. Pencils down while we get ready for Test 3.

2:05

112

3

Now turn to page 5 and look at Test 3, Where Do the Lines Cross? I will read the directions aloud. (Read T112): "Your job in this test is to decide just where two lines would cross. The lines are *not* drawn in for you. You will be given the end points of the imaginary lines. For example, AB-CD means that the first imaginary line is from A to B, and the second line is from C to D. The problem is to find the place marked by a small letter where those lines cross. In the example below, the problem is to find the letter where the two lines, 1B and DC cross. We have dots near the letters and numbers so you will know exactly where the lines start. In this example we have drawn the imaginary lines. You see that they cross near the small 'a,' so for that item on the answer sheet you would mark 'a.' Don't actually draw any lines in the test booklet. Just imagine where they will be. Just look for the small letter where the two imaginary lines cross, and fill in that box next to the item number on your answer sheet." Find the place to mark your answers for Test 3 on the answer sheet. Any questions? (pause) Now turn to page 6 and get ready to do Part 1. If you finish before time is called, do *not* go on to Part 2. Remember, do NOT draw any lines in the booklet. Any questions? (pause) Pencils ready. Begin Part 1.

1:15 Stop working. Part 2 is like Part 1. It starts with item 9. Find that now on the answer sheet. Pencils ready. Begin Part 2.

1:15 Stop working. Pencils down while we get ready for Test 4.

0:40   **4**   Now turn to page 7 and look at Test 4, Which Would You Rather Do? I will read the directions aloud. (Read T197): "Mark 'a' on the answer sheet next to the item number if you would rather do 'a.' Mark 'b' if you would rather do 'b.'" Find the place to mark your answers for Test 4 on the answer sheet. Any questions? (pause) If you finish the first page before time is called, go right on to the second page. Pencils ready. Begin Which Would You Rather Do?

197

(After 1:30, say): "Don't forget, go right on to the second page."

2:30 Stop working. Pencils down while we get ready for Test 5.

1:50   **5**   Now turn to page 9 and look at Test 5, Assumptions II. I will read the directions aloud. (Read T11b): "In this test there are four sentences like this one: Example A: *Bossie is contented because she is a cow*. For this to be true, it must be true that: 1) all contented animals are cows, 2) all cows are contented, 3) Bossie is not a horse, 4) Bossie gives more milk, 5) cows may or may not be contented depending on how well they are cared for. Under the example you see five statements. You are to decide which ones must be true for the sample sentence to be true. In the example above, number 2) must be true, and number 3) must be true. If Bossie is contented because she is a cow, then it must be true that all cows are contented, and that she is not a horse. In the rest of the test there will be four problems like this one. If the statement must be true for the sentence to be true, fill in the 'T' box on the answer sheet next to the item number; if it does not have to be true, mark the 'F' box. In each problem there can be one or two statements which must be true." Find the place to answer Test 5 on the answer sheet. Any questions? (pause) Turn to page 10. Pencils ready. Begin Assumptions II.

11b

(After 1:30, say): "Don't forget, go right on to the second page."

3:00 Stop working. Pencils down while we get ready for Test 6.

6   **20b**

0:45 Now turn to page 12 and look at Test 6, What Do You See? I will read the directions aloud. (Read T20b): "On this and the next page you will see a drawing with some words under it. For each word, fill in the 'Y' box on your answer sheet if you see it in the picture, and 'N' if you don't see it." Find the place to answer Test 6 on your answer sheet. Any questions? (pause) Pencils ready. Begin What Do You See, Part I.

0:45 Stop working.

0:15 Turn to page 13 for Part II of What Do You See? This part starts with question 21. Find that on your answer sheet. Pencils ready. Begin Part II.

0:45 Stop working. Pencils down while we get ready for Test 7.

7   **224b**

1:00 Now turn to page 14 and look at Test 7, Matching Words. I will read the directions aloud. (Read T224b): "In this test, pick one of the three words—a, b, or c, that goes best with the word in capital letters. If you think the word next to 'a' would go best with the key word in capital letters, fill in the 'a' box. If you think the word next to 'b' would go best, mark 'b.' If you think the word next to 'c' would go best, mark 'c.' By *go best*, we mean pick the word you would most naturally think of. Don't begin until you are told." Find the place to answer Test 7 on the answer sheet. Any questions? (pause) Time will be short, so work quickly. Pencils ready. Begin Matching Words.

1:30 Stop working. Pencils down while we get ready for the next test.

8   **1a**

1:20 Now put aside booklet 23 and the answer sheet. We are finished with them. Take up the U.I. 23 expendable booklet and be sure your name is on the front. Your answers for this test will go right in the booklet. Now open the booklet to page 1 and look at Test 8, How

93

Fast Can You Write? I will read the directions aloud. (Read T1a): "On this test we want to see how fast you can write. When you are told to start Part I, write 'ready' as many times are you can below the word 'ready.' Use both columns if you need them. When you are told to start Part II, write 'ten big dogs' as many times as you can in the space below the words 'ten big dogs.' Work as fast as you can. Do not start until you get the signal." If you finish Part I before time is called, do NOT go on to Part II. I will tell you when to start and stop each part. Any questions? (pause) Pencils ready. Begin Part I.

0:30 Stop writing.

0:10 Get ready to write "ten big dogs" in Part II. Pencils ready. Begin Part II.

0:30 Stop writing. Pencils down.

0:35 Turn the page and look at Parts III and IV. You are to write the same words, "ready" on Part III and "ten big dogs" in Part IV, but you are to write them backwards just like the example at the top, beginning with the "y" in "ready." Start with Part III when I give the signal, but do NOT go on to Part IV until I tell you to do so. Any questions? (pause) Begin Part III.

0:30 Stop working. Get ready to write "ten big dogs" backwards in Part IV. You should begin with the "s" in "dogs." Pencils ready. Begin Part IV.

0:30 Stop working. Pencils down. Please sit quietly while materials are collected.

End of Tape for U.I. 23

Total time: 27:00 mins.

Instructions for

Administering

U.I. 24

Anxiety

Test Time 16:30 Mins

**Total Time with Instructions, as on Tape
Approx. 25:25 Mins**

Eight Subtests

No apparatus needed

Instructions [as on Tape] for U.I. 24 — Anxiety

Time required: Actual testing time: 16 mins. 30 sec.
Approximate total time with instructions and other time expenditures: 25 mins. 25 sec.

(Before playing the tape, be sure everyone has the test booklet, answer sheet, and pencils; have them write name, etc., on the answer sheet.)

No. in Battery for U.I. 24	Identifying T No.	Time Required†	Directions
		0:30	Now look at your answer sheet and find the block where you answer the questions for Test 1, on the side of the answer sheet that says U.I. 24.** The words "Test 1" are printed at the left of the block. There are 14 items in the block for Test 1. If you have not found the place to answer the questions in Test 1, put up your hand. (pause)
1	430	0:45	Now open your test booklet to the first page and look at Test 1, Humor Test. I will read the directions aloud. (Read T430): "Below are some jokes. Show how funny you think each joke is by filling the 'a' box next to that item number on your answer sheet if you think it is *very funny,* 'b' if you think it is *funny,* 'c' if you think it is *a little funny,* and 'd' if you think it is *not funny at all.* Don't start until you are told." Any questions? (pause) If you finish the first page before time is called, go right on to the second page. Pencils ready. Begin Humor Test.
		2:00	(After 1:30, say): "Don't forget, go right on to the second page."
			Stop working. Pencils down while we get ready for Test 2.

† Actual testing times are in **bold face.**
** Some answer sheets may use HSOA instead of the more general U.I. notation.

2

27b

1:00 Now turn to page 3 and look at Test 2, How Do You Like. . .? I will read the directions aloud. (Read T27b): "Fill in the 'a' box next to the item number on the answer sheet if you would like or do like the thing *very much*, 'b' if you *like it*, 'c' if you are *uncertain*, and so on. Work very quickly. Don't bother to think much about each item, but just give your first impression. Use the following key: a) like very much, b) like, c) uncertain, d) dislike, e) dislike very much. Example A: Amusement parks. a) like very much, b) like, c) uncertain, d) dislike, e) dislike very much." Find the place to mark your answers for Test 2 on the answer sheet. Any questions? (pause) If you finish the first page before time is called, go right on to the second page. Pencils ready. Begin How Do You Like. . .?

(After 1:30, say): "Don't forget to go right on to the second page."

2:00 Stop working. Pencils down while we get ready for Test 3.

3

41a

1:10 Now turn to page 5 and look at Test 3, Do You Sometimes. . .? I will read the directions aloud. (Read T41a): "All of us have sometimes done something we shouldn't, or something we're ashamed of later. Nobody is perfect, but sometimes it's hard to admit things we've done wrong. If there is one of these things you have done *very often*, mark 'a' on your answer sheet next to that number. If you have done or thought it *often*, mark 'b'; if *sometimes*, mark 'c'; and so on. Use the following key: a) very often or almost always, b) often, c) sometimes, d) seldom, e) very seldom." Find the place to mark your answers for Test 3 on the answer sheet. Any questions? (pause) If you finish the first page before time is called, go right on to the second page. Pencils ready. Begin Do You Sometimes. . .?

(After 1:30, say): "Don't forget, go right on to the second page."

2:00 Stop working. Pencils down while we get ready for Test 4.

4   36   1:10   Now turn to page 7 and look at Test 4, What's Your Comment? I will read the directions aloud. (Read T36): "Below are 12 statements about some things which have happened or could possibly happen in the future. Underneath each statement there are comments somebody might make when hearing it for the first time. Select the *one* comment that comes nearest to what you would probably say. Mark either the a, b, or c on the answer sheet by filling in that box. Example A: *Mr. Jones was fired from his job yesterday.* a) He didn't do a good job, anyway. b) His boss was probably in a bad mood. c) It will be hard for him to find a new one." Find the place to mark your answers for Test 4 on the answer sheet. Any questions? (pause) If you finish the first page before time is called, go right on to the second page. Pencils ready. Begin What's Your Comment?

(After 1 min., say): "Don't forget to go right on to the second page."

2:00   Stop working. Pencils down while we get ready for Test 5.

5   187a   0:45   Now turn to page 9 and look at Test 5, Jokes and Tricks. I will read the directions aloud. (Read T187a): "In front of you is a list of practical jokes that when you were a teen-ager you might have thought it would be fun to play on someone. Mark 'Y' for 'Yes' on your answer sheet if you think you would probably have considered it a good trick to play. Mark 'N' for 'No' if you would not think it suitable." Find the place to answer Test 5 on the answer sheet. Any questions? (pause) Pencils ready. Begin Jokes and Tricks.

2:00   Stop working. Pencils down while we get ready for Test 6.

6   163a   0:45   Now turn to page 10 and look at Test 6, Putting Up With Things (A). I will read the directions aloud. (Read 163aA): "Mark 'Y' on your answer sheet next to the item number if you like or don't mind doing the thing listed. Mark 'N' if you don't like to do it." Find the place to answer Test 6 on the answer sheet. Any questions? (pause) Remember, Y for yes, I would like it, N for no, I wouldn't like it. Pencils ready. Begin Putting Up With Things (A).

1:00 Stop working. Pencils down while we get ready for the next page.

0:55 Turn to page 11, Putting Up With Things (B). I will read the directions aloud. (Read T163aB): "You just marked some things you like or don't like doing. Now tell us whether you *would* do them, regardless of whether you like doing them, if your family and friends asked you to. Mark 'a' if you would *always* do it, 'b' if you would do it *most of the time*, 'c' if you would do it *sometimes*, and so on. Use the following key: a) always, b) most of the time, c) sometimes, d) rarely, e) never." This part of Test 6 starts with question 13. Find that now on your answer sheet. Any questions? (pause) Pencils ready. Begin Putting Up With Things (B).

1:30 Stop working. Pencils down while we get ready for Test 7.

7 38c

1:00 Now turn to page 12 and look at Test 7, What Bothers Me. I will read the directions aloud. (Read T38c): "Mark 'a' on your answer sheet if you are *very much bothered* or angry or angry about the thing mentioned in each item; mark 'b' if you are *a little bothered*, and 'c' if you are *not at all bothered*. Use the following key: a) very much bothered, b) a little bothered, c) not bothered. Example A: A television breaking down during your favorite show. a) very much bothered, b) a little bothered, c) not bothered." Find the place to mark your answers for Test 7 on the answer sheet. Any questions? (pause) If you finish the first page before time is called, go right on to the second page. Pencils ready. Begin What Bothers Me.

(After 1:30, say): "Don't forget to go right on to the next page."

2:00 Stop working. Pencils down while we get ready for Test 8.

8 25

0:55 Now turn to page 14 and look at Test 8, Favorite Titles. I will read the directions aloud. (Read T25): "Here are 12 pairs of book titles, with a brief description telling what the book is about. You are to decide which book of the two you would rather read. Fill in the 'a' box on your answer sheet next to the item number if you prefer the first book, and 'b' if you prefer the second book. When you are told to begin, work as quickly as you can." Find the place to answer Test 8 on the answer sheet. Any questions? (pause) If you finish the first page before time is called, go right on to the second. Pencils ready. Begin Favorite Titles.

(After 1:30, say): "Don't forget to go right on to the second page."

2:00 Stop working. Please sit quietly while materials are collected.

End of Tape for U.I. 24

Total tape time: 25:25 mins.

Instructions for

Administering

U.I. 25

———————

Realism
vs
Tensidia

———————

Test Time 16:50 Mins

Total Time with Instructions, as on Tape
Approx. 27:00 Mins

———————

Seven Subtests

———————

No apparatus needed

Instructions [as on Tape] for U.I. 25 — Realism vs. Tensidia

Time required: Actual testing time: 16 mins. 50 sec.
Approximate total time with instructions and other time expenditures: 27 mins.

(Before playing the tape, be sure everyone has the test booklet, answer sheet, and pencils; have them write name, etc., on the answer sheet.)

No. in Battery for U.I. 25	Identifying T No.	Time Required†	Directions
		0:40	Now look at your answer sheets. For this booklet we will need both sides, side 1 and side 2. The answers for the first test are on the side that says U.I. 25, ** side 1. Find the block for the answers to Test 1 now on side 1. There are 13 items in the block for Test 1. If you have not found the place to answer the questions in Test 1, raise your hand (pause).
1	16b	0:35	Now open the booklet to page 1 and look at Test 1, Human Nature II. Read the directions to yourselves while I read them aloud. (Read T16b): "Mark 'a' next to the item number on your answer sheet if you *strongly agree* with a statement, 'b' next to the item number if you *agree*, 'c' if you are *uncertain*, and so on. Work as quickly as you can. Use the following key: a) strongly agree, b) agree, c) uncertain, d) disagree, e) strongly disagree." Any questions? (pause) Pencils ready. Begin Human Nature II.
		2:00	Stop working. Pencils down while we get ready for Test 2.

† Actual testing times are in **bold face.**
** Some answer books may use USOA instead of the more general U.I. notation

2   9bk   0:55   Now turn to page 2 and look at Test 2, Memory. I will read the directions aloud. (Read T9bk): "This is a memory test. Of the 26 phrases below, 13 are from the last test. If you remember the phrase from the last test, mark the 'Y' box on your answer sheet next to the item number. Mark 'N' if you do not remember it. Do not look back at the last test. There should be only 13 marked 'Y' for remembered. Work quickly." Find the place to answer Test 2 on the answer sheet. Any questions? (pause) Pencils ready. Begin Memory.

2:00   Stop working. Pencils down while we get ready for Test 3.

3   431   1:25   Now turn to page 3 and look at Test 3, Memory for Numbers. I will read the directions aloud. (Read T431): "In this test you will hear some numbers read to you aloud. There will be six or more numbers in each set. Try to remember the numbers as you would a telephone number. After the number is read, the examiner will tell you to turn this page, look at the first example, and decide which of the two rows of numbers is the one that was read. For example, you might hear numbers like 5—1—2—3, and you have to choose between 5—1—2—3 and 5—1—3—2. In this case you would mark the 'a' box on your answer sheet because 'a' is the same as the numbers that were read. Now wait for the instruction to turn the page." Each time after I read the numbers I will tell you which page to turn to for the answer. Please do not turn pages until told to do so. Any questions? (pause) Find where to answer Test 3 on the answer sheet. Pencils ready. Here is the first set of numbers.

6:00 (Start timer, visible to reader, without buzzer, for 6 minutes.)

Questions:

#	Numbers	Instruction
1	5 8 7 9 2 6	Turn to page 4: Choose the right numbers and mark A or B on your answer sheet (pause for 7 seconds)
2	2 9 4 5 8 1	Turn to page 5
3	5 9 4 3 2 8 1	Turn to page 4
4	7 6 9 2 1 4 8	Turn to page 5
5	9 5 4 6 1 3 7	Turn to page 4
6	4 7 6 8 2 9 3	Turn to page 5
7	3 9 7 6 2 8 1 4	Turn to page 4
8	9 4 2 5 3 6 8 1	Turn to page 5
9	7 3 4 1 9 5 2 6	Turn to page 4
10	1 7 6 2 4 5 8 3	Turn to page 5
11	6 4 3 7 5 4 2 9	Turn to page 4
12	8 5 7 3 6 4 2 1	Turn to page 5
13	3 5 2 8 7 9 6 4 1	Turn to page 4
14	7 1 4 6 2 5 3 9 8	Turn to page 5

Stop working. Pencils down while we get ready for Test 4.

4 — **31**

0:55 Now turn to page 6 and look at Test 4, Wise Statements. I will read the directions aloud. (Read T31): " Fill in the 'a' box next to the item number on your answer sheet if you think the statement makes sense, and is wise and helpful in our lives. Mark 'b' next to the item number if the statement is weak, a little silly, doubtful, or not really worth following. Example A: There's never enough time to do all the things you want to do." Find the place to answer Test 4 on the answer sheet. Any questions? (pause) Remember, a if it is wise, b if it is not. Pencils ready. Begin Wise Statements.

2:00 Stop working. Pencils down while we get ready for Test 5.

5 — **224a**

1:05 Now turn to page 7 and look at Test 5, Best Word to Fit. I will read the directions aloud. (Read T224a): "In this test, pick one of the three words—a, b, or c, that goes best with the word in capital letters. If you think the word next to 'a' would go best with the key word in capital letters, fill in the 'a' box. If you think the word next to 'b' would go best, mark 'b'. If you think the word next to 'c' would go best, mark 'c'. By *go best*, we mean pick the word you would most naturally think of. Don't begin until you are told. Example A: GOOD a) luck, b) bad, c) time." Find the place to answer Test 5 on the answer sheet. Any questions? (pause) Work quickly. Pencils ready. Begin Best Word to Fit.

(After 1 min., say): "Work quickly, time is almost up."

1:30 Stop working. Pencils down while we get ready for Test 6.

6 — **118a**

0:55 Now turn to page 8 and look at Test 6, Memory. I will read the directions aloud. (Read T118a): "This is a test of your memory. On the next page is a list of words for you to memorize. When told to 'turn the page,' read the list to yourself from beginning to end and over again until 'Time' is called. Don't try to memorize one word at a time. Learn as many of the words as you can. After a short time, you will be told to turn to another page and pick out the words that you have memorized. Don't start until you are told." Time to memorize is very short. Any questions? (pause) Turn to page 9 and memorize the words for Memory, Part I. Begin.

0:15 Stop.

0:45 Turn to page 10, Recognizing Words. Pencils should still be down. I will read the directions aloud. (Read Recognizing Words): "Some of the words that you just memorized are in the following list. If a word *is* one that you remember from the list you just memorized, fill in the 'Y' (yes) box next to the item number on the answer sheet. If the word is *not* one that you remember from the list you just memorized, mark 'N' (no) next to the item number on the answer sheet." Find the place to answer Test 6 on the answer sheet. Any questions? (pause) Pencils ready. Begin Recognizing Words, Part I.

0:45 Stop working. Pencils down.

0:10 Turn back to page 9 and quickly memorize the words in Part II. Begin.

0:15 Stop.

0:20 Turn to page 11 and get ready to mark the words you remember. Answers start with item 25. Find that now on the answer sheet. Pencils ready. Begin Recognizing Words, Part II.

0:45 Stop working. Pencils down while we get ready to work on Test 7.

1:05 For this test, turn the answer sheet over and find the place for the answers to Test 7. Now turn to page 12 in the booklet and look at Test 7, Counting Letters and Numbers. I will read the directions aloud. (Read T49c): "In this test you are to count letters in one column

49c

7

(Part I) and numbers in the other (Part II). In the left-hand column, Part I, count the A's in each row of letters. If you find one A, mark '1' on the answer sheet next to the item number. If you find two A's, mark '2'; if you find three A's, mark '3'; and so on. Do the same in Part II, counting 3's." Any questions? (pause) If you finish Part I before time is called, do NOT go on to Part II. Pencils ready. Begin Part I.

0:20 Stop working.

0:15 Part II starts with item 21 on the answer sheet. Find that now. Get ready to count "3's" in Part II. Begin.

0:20 Stop working.

0:20 Part III starts with item 41 on the answer sheet. Find that now. Turn to page 13 and get ready to count "G's" in Part III. Begin Part III.

0:20 Stop working.

0:15 Part IV starts with item 61 on the answer sheet. Find that now. Get ready to count "6's" in Part IV. Begin Part IV.

0:20 Stop working. Pencils down while we collect materials.

End of tape for U.I. 25

Total time: 27:00 mins.

Instructions for

Administering

U.I. 28

Asthenia
vs
Self-Assurance

Test Time 18:40 Mins

Total Time with Instructions, as on Tape
Approx. 27:30 Mins

Seven Subtests

Apparatus needed: Stop watch or clock with bell for signaling time intervals in Test 7, "Longer or Shorter."

Instructions [as on Tape] for U.I. 28 — Asthenia

Time required: Actual testing time: 18 mins. 40 sec.
Approximate total time with instructions and other time expenditures: 27 mins. 30 sec.

(Before playing the tape, be sure everyone has the test booklet, answer sheet, and pencils; have them write name, etc., on the answer sheet.)

No. in Booklet for U.I. 28	Identifying T No.	Time Required†	Directions
		0:30	Now look at your answer sheet and find the block where you answer the questions for Test 1, on the side of the answer sheet that says U.I. 28.** The words Test 1 are printed at the left of the block. There are 33 items in the block for Test 1. If you have not found the place to answer the questions in Test 1, put up your hand. (pause)
1	9c(a) 9ek, 9d	0:45	Now open your booklet to page 1 and look at Test 1, Opinions V. Read the directions to yourselves while I read them aloud. (Read Opinions V): "In this test you will find a number of opinions with which you might agree or disagree. Fill in the 'a' box next to the item number on the answer sheet if you strongly agree with the opinion, 'b' if you agree, 'c' if you are uncertain, and so on. Use the following key in marking your answers: a) strongly agree, b) agree, c) uncertain, d) disagree, e) strongly disagree. Example A: Time is valuable and shouldn't be wasted." Find the place to answer Test 1 on the answer sheet. Any questions? (pause) If you finish the first page before time is called, go right on to the second and third pages. Pencils ready. Begin Opinions V.
		5:00	(After 2 min., say): "Don't forget, go right on to pages 2 and 3."
			Stop working. Pencils down while we get ready for Test 2.

† Actual testing times are in **bold face.**
** Some answer sheets may use HSOA instead of the more general U.I. notation.

2   16a   0:35   Now turn to page 4 and look at Test 2, Human Nature III. I will read the directions aloud. (Read T16a): "In this test you are asked to show your judgment about human nature. Use the following key in marking your answers: a) strongly agree, b) agree, c) uncertain, d) disagree, e) strongly disagree." Find the place to answer Test 2 on the answer sheet. Any questions? (pause) Pencils ready. Begin Human Nature III.

    2:00   Stop working. Pencils down while we get ready for Test 3.

3   19   0:55   Now turn to page 5 and look at Test 3, How Long Would It Take You? I will read the directions. (Read T19): "Look at the following list of jobs and pastimes. Below each are two guesses of how long it would take you personally, going at normal speed, to do each. Check the one that seems right for *you*. If neither number seems right for you choose the nearer one. This is a test to see how well you know how long it takes you to do things." Find the place to answer Test 3 on the answer sheet. Any questions? (pause) If you are not sure, make the best guess you can. Work quickly. Pencils ready. Begin How Long Would It Take You?

    (After 1:45, say): "Don't forget, go right on to page 6."

    3:00   Stop working. Pencils down while we get ready for Test 4.

4   149   0:50   Now turn to page 8 in the booklet and look at Test 4, What Will Happen? I will read the directions aloud. (Read T149): "In this test you are to imagine that you're the main character in each of the following situations. The story can end in one of two ways. You are to choose which way you think the story will end. Fill in the 'a' box next to the item number on your answer sheet if you think the first ending is better, or mark 'b' if you think the second ending is better." Find the place to answer Test 4 on the answer sheet. Any questions? (pause) If you finish the first page before time is called, go right on to the second page. Pencils ready. Begin What Will Happen?

(After 1 min., say): "Don't forget to go right on to the second page."

2:00 Stop working. Pencils down while we get ready for Test 5.

1:15 Now turn to page 10 and look at Test 5, What Does It Take? I will read the directions aloud. (Read T96): "People get on in the world partly through ability and hard work and partly through luck or the influence of friends, and sometimes even by breaking the rules, or what we might call 'cutting corners.' But this happens differently in different jobs, such as are shown in the list below. In this part of the test you are asked to decide how important *ability* and *hard work* are relative to other things in succeeding in each of these kinds of jobs. Mark each item on your answer sheet using the following key: Hard work and ability are: a) very important, b) important, c) less important, d) unimportant, e) very unimportant." Find the place to answer Test 5 on the answer sheet. Any questions? (pause) Pencils ready. Begin What Does It Take?

1:00 Stop working.

0:30 Turn to page 11 and get ready to mark the same activities on the importance of having the right friends or of cheating. Answers start with item 19. Find that now on the answer sheet. (pause) Now get ready to mark How important are the *right friends* or *cheating*. Pencils ready. Begin.

1:00 Stop working.

0:25 Turn to page 12 and get ready to mark the same activities on the importance of good luck. Answers start with item 37. Find that now on the answer sheet. (pause) Now get ready to mark How important is *good luck*. Pencils ready. Begin.

1:00 Stop working. Pencils down while we get ready for Test 6.

96

5

111

6	9c(2)	0:40	Now turn to page 13 and look at Test 6, Opinions VI. I will read the directions aloud. (Read T9c): "Fill in the 'a' box next to the item number on the answer sheet if you strongly agree with the opinion, 'b' if you agree, 'c' if you are uncertain, and so on. Use the following key in marking your answers: a) strongly agree, b) agree, c) uncertain, d) disagree, e) strongly disagree. Example A: Writing letters is a waste of time." Find the place to answer Test 6 on the answer sheet. Any questions? (pause) Pencils ready. Begin Opinions VI.
		1:30	Stop working. Pencils down while we get ready for Test 7.
7	76	1:00	Now turn to page 14 and look at Test 7, Longer or Shorter? I will read the directions aloud. (Read T76): "Now you will be given a series of short rest periods. You will be asked to judge whether one period is longer or shorter than another. Please do not look at clocks or watches. If a period is 6 seconds longer than the other period, fill in the 'a' box for that item number on the answer sheet. If it is 3 seconds longer, mark 'b'; if it is 3 seconds shorter, mark 'c'; if it is 6 seconds shorter, mark 'd'. Wait for the first rest period." Find the place to answer Test 7 on the answer sheet. Any questions? (pause) Here is the first rest period. Begin.
		0:10‡	Here is the second rest period. Begin.
		0:12‡	Now answer question 1, "Was the second rest period longer or shorter than the first rest period?" (pause)
		0:14‡	Here is the third rest period. Begin.
			Now answer question 2. (pause) Remember, mark your answers on the answer sheet.
		0:14‡	Here is the fourth rest period.
			Now answer question 3. (pause)
		0:10‡	Here is the fifth rest period. Begin.
			Now answer question 4. (pause)

‡ Times marked ‡ are for the rest periods in Test 7 (T76).

112

Here is the sixth rest period. Begin.

0:12‡ Now answer question 5. (pause)

Here is the seventh rest period. Begin.

0:08‡ Now answer question 6. (pause)

Here is the eighth rest period. Begin.

0:12‡ Now answer question 7. (pause)

Here is the ninth rest period. Begin.

0:16‡ Now answer question 8. (pause)

Here is the tenth rest period. Begin.

0:14‡ Now answer question 9. (pause)

Here is the eleventh rest period. Begin.

0:10‡ Now answer question 10. (pause)

Pencils down. Please sit quietly while materials are collected.

End of tape for U.I. 28

Total time: 27:30 mins.

Instructions for

Administering

U.I. 32

Exvia-vs-Invia
(Popularly "Extraversion")

Test Time 15:30 Mins

Total Time with Instructions, as on Tape
Approx. 28:00 Mins

Eight Subtests

Apparatus needed: Sound Tape and recorder needed for Test 6, "Can you hear the word? II"

Instructions [as on Tape] for U.I. 32 — Exvia vs. Invia

Time required: Actual testing time: 15 mins. 30 sec.
Approximate total time with instructions and other time expenditures: 28 mins.

(Before playing the tape, be sure everyone has the test booklets, answer sheet, and pencils; have them write name, etc., on U.I. 32 expendable booklet and the answer sheet.)

No. in Battery for U.I. 32	Identifying T No.	Time Required†	Directions
		0:30	Now look at your answer sheet and find the block where you answer the questions for Test 1, on the side of the answer sheet that says U.I. 32.** The words "Test 1" are printed at the left of the block. There are 80 items in the block for Test 1. If you have not found the place to answer the questions in Test 1, put up your hand. (pause)
1	45	1:05	Now open your booklet to page 1 and look at Test 1, Judging Lines. Read the directions to yourselves while I read them aloud. (Read T45): "In this test you are asked to decide whether two lines are the same length or whether one is longer than the other. Use the following key in marking your answers: (L) right-hand line is longer, (S) right-hand line is shorter, (E) both lines equal. Mark 'L' on your answer sheet next to the item number if you think the right-hand line of a pair is LONGER; check 'S' if you think the right-hand line is SHORTER; and check 'E' if you think both lines are the same length." If you finish Part I before time is called, do NOT go on to Part II. Any questions? (pause) Pencils ready. Begin Part I.
		0:30	Stop working. Pencils down.

† Actual testing times are in **bold face.**
** Some answer sheets may use HSOA instead of the more general U.I. notation.

0:15   Part II starts with item 21 on the answer sheet. Find that now. Get ready for Part II. Pencils ready. Begin Part II.

0:30   Stop working. Pencils down.

0:20   Part III starts with item 41. Find that now on the answer sheet. Now turn to page 2 and get ready for Part III. Pencils ready. Begin Part III.

0:30   Stop working. Pencils down.

0:15   Part IV starts with item 61. Find that now on the answer sheet. Get ready for Part IV. Pencils ready. Begin Part IV.

0:30   Stop working. Pencils down while we get ready for Test 2.

1:15   Now turn to page 3 and look at Test 2, Which Is More? I will read the directions aloud. (Read T62b): "Below, and on the next page, are pairs of circles. Each one has a set of numbers in it. Try to tell at a glance whether the numbers in the left circle, marked 'A', or the numbers in the right circle, marked 'B', add up to a bigger number. Don't actually add the numbers, because you won't have time. On your answer sheet, mark 'A' next to the item number if you think the total in the *left* circle is bigger, or 'B' next to the item number if you think the total in the *right* circle is bigger." Find the place to answer Test 2 on the answer sheet. Any questions? (pause) Work quickly. You will have a very short time to do both pages. If you finish the first page before time is called, go right on to the second page. Pencils ready. Begin Which Is More?

(After 20 sec., say): "Don't forget to go right on to the second page."

0:40   Stop working. Pencils down while we get ready for Test 3.

62b

2

3   142a   1:20   Turn to page 5 in the booklet and look at Test 3, Qualities I. I will read the directions aloud. (Read T142a): "In this test you are to compare each of the figures in the boxes with the solid black figure at the top of that column and decide whether it is a) taller, b) shorter, c) wider, d) narrower, or e) equal. Look at example A, the triangle. It is taller than the solid black triangle at the top, so on your answer sheet you would mark the 'a' box for 'taller' for that item. In example B, the rectangle is wider than the solid black one at the top, so you would mark the 'c' box for 'wider.' Mark only one answer for each item. You will have just a short time to do all the problems on this page. Use the following key: a) taller, b) shorter, c) wider, d) narrower, e) equal." Now find the place to mark your answers for Test 3 on the answer sheet. (slight pause) Any questions? (pause) Pencils ready. Begin Qualities I.

0:20   Stop working. Pencils down while we get ready for the next page.

1:05   Turn to page 6, Qualities II. I will read the directions aloud. (Read Qualities II): "This test is just like the last, except that here you must choose the opposite each time. Look at example A, the triangle. It is taller than the one at the top, so you must mark the 'b' box, shorter, on that item on your answer sheet. In the same way, example B is wider than the square at the top, so you would mark the 'd' box, narrower, on the answer sheet. If it is the same size, mark 'e', equal, as before. Mark only one answer for each item. Use the following key: a) taller, b) shorter, c) wider, d) narrower, e) equal." Qualities II starts with item 21. Find item 21 on the answer sheet now. (slight pause) Any questions? (pause) Pencils ready. Begin Qualities II.

0:30   Stop working. Pencils down while we get ready for the next page.

0:55   Turn to page 7, Qualities III. I will read the directions aloud. (Read Qualities III): "In this test you must look at each block and decide whether the picture shows something that is: a) cold, b) light, c) noisy, d) sharp, or e) wet. Look at example A. It's a picture of the sun, so

117

for that questions you would mark 'b', light, next to the item number on your answer sheet. Mark only one answer for each picture. Use the following key: a) cold, b) light, c) noisy, d) sharp, e) wet." Qualities III starts with item 41. Find item 41 on the answer sheet now. (slight pause) Any questions? (pause) Pencils ready. Begin Qualities III.

0:20 Stop working. Pencils down while we get ready for the next page.

1:00 Turn to page 8, Qualities IV. I will read the directions aloud. (Read Qualities IV): "This test is like the last one except that you must choose the opposite of what is shown in the picture. If it is cold, mark hot; if it is sharp, mark dull, and so on. Look at example B. It is a picture of the sun, which is light, so on your answer sheet you would mark 'b' for shadow. Use the following key: a) hot, b) shadow, c) quiet, d) dull, e) dry." Qualities IV starts with item 61. Find item 61 on the answer sheet now. (slight pause) Any questions? (pause) Pencils ready. Begin Qualities IV.

0:30 Stop working. Pencils down while we get ready for Test 4.

1:05 Turn to page 9 and look at Test 4, Crime and Punishment. I will read the directions aloud. (Read T97): "If the crime described below seems to you to be very serious, and punishment 'a' seems the best one for that crime, fill in the box marked 'a' next to the item number on your answer sheet. Fill in the 'b' box next to the item number on your answer sheet if you think the crime described is *rather serious*, and punishment 'b' is the best. Use choices 'c', 'd', and 'e' in the same way. Try to decide quickly. Example: Two young boys broke into a school building and caused $300 worth of damage. a) 1 year in reform school (very serious) b) fine parents $300 (rather serious) c) 1 year probation (serious) d) suspension from school (slight) e) warning from judge (trivial)" Find the place to answer Test 4 on the answer sheet. Any questions? (pause) If you finish the first page before time is called, go right on to the second page. Pencils ready. Begin Crime and Punishment.

97

4

118

(After 1:30, say): "Don't forget to go right on to the next page."

2:30 Stop working. Pencils down while we get ready for the next test.

5   13a   1:15   Now put aside booklet 32 and the answer sheet. We are finished with them. Take up the U.I. 32 expendable booklet and be sure your name is on the front. Your answers for this test will go right in the booklet. Now open the booklet to page 1 and look at the first test, What People Are Like. I will read the directions aloud. (Read T13a): "You are to write below some good or bad things about the way you and other people you know act. For example, if the question asks in what way most people fell down at some time or another, you might write 'selfish' on one line, 'bad-tempered' on the next, and so on. Put just one word or phrase on each line. Don't start until you are told." Any questions? (pause) I will tell you when to go on to the next sections. Pencils ready. Begin to list some things that get people into trouble.

(After 30 sec., say): "Go on to list things you like in children you know."

(After 1 min.): "Go on to list some habits that children often have."

(After 1:30): "Go on to list some things you have done to help others."

2:00 Stop working. Pencils down while we get ready for the next test.

6   164b   1:25   Now turn to page 2 and look at Test 6, Can You Hear the Word? II. I will read the directions aloud. (Read T164b): "In this test you will listen to a series of sounds played on the tape recorder. These will often seem a little muffled to you. However, most of the sounds contain a real word, that is, a word you would find in the dictionary. Listen to each sound. If you think there was a word in the sound, then write on your answer sheet what the word

119

is. If you don't think there was a word, write 'no'. Each sound will be preceded by a number, and you have to put down your answer next to that number in the place for answers below. You will only have a few seconds for each item. Never leave an item blank. If you don't know it, guess." You will hear the example first, then the test words. Any questions? (pause) Be ready to write the example and the test words.

CUT HERE—PLAY T164b TAPE (Note: Tape T164b is included in instruction tapes.)

2:40 Stop working. Do not turn the page yet.

2:30 Now turn to page 3 and look at Test 7, Obstacles. I will read the directions aloud. (Read T121): "This test is a game in which you try to get as many points as you can in running four obstacle courses. Here are the rules of the game. 1. You get one point for each UPRIGHT line you cross. 2. You LOSE one point for each SLANTED line you cross. 3. If you come to a number of upright lines in a bunch, you may circle the bunch and get as many points as you would be crossing each one separately. 4. You may use only SIX circles on each obstacle course. 5. You LOSE one point for each slanting line in a bunch which you circle. 6. In crossing the upright lines each one must be crossed separately like this rather than a number of them at once like this. Look at the example below to see how it's done. (pause) Remember, the purpose of the game is to get as many points as you possibly can. Time will be very short, so work as fast as you can. When you are told to begin, turn the page and start on the obstacle course at the top of the page, marked '1'. Listen for more instructions which will be given while you work." When you are told to turn the page, you will start on the first line, numbered 1; if you finish with the part of game 1 on the first page, turn the page and go on with game 1 on the next page. Do not start game 2 until you are given the signal. Any questions? (pause) Now turn to page 4 and turn the booklet sideways. You see game 1 running across the top of the page. It is continued at the top of the next page. Do not start until you get the signal. Any questions? (pause) Pencils ready. Begin game 1.

121

7

120

0:30 Stop working.

0:10 Get ready to begin game 2 on page 4. Begin game 2.

0:30 Stop working.

0:10 Get ready to begin game 3 on page 4. Begin game 3.

0:30 Stop working.

0:10 Get ready to begin game 4 on page 4. Begin game 4.

0:30 Stop working. Pencils down while we get ready for the next test.

8   1d   1:00 Now turn to page 6, Writing Signatures. I will read the directions aloud. (Read T1d): "This is a test to see how rapidly you can write your signature under various conditions. When you are told to begin at Part I, write your last name and your initials before it. Thus, if you were called John Richard Adams, you would write J. R. Adams, and if Jane Smith, then J. Smith. At the word 'go,' start at line 1 and write one signature on each line as fast as you can, on lines 1, 2, 3, etc., until 'stop' is called. (½ min.)" If you finish Part Ia before time is called, do NOT go on to Part Ib. I will tell you when to start and stop each part. Any questions? (pause) Pencils ready. Begin Part Ia.

0:30 Stop. Now I will read you the instructions to Part Ib. (Read aloud): "Now I want you to write your signature in an unusual way. Begin at the last letter and work backwards, letting your pencil go just the opposite direction to the usual. Thus, if your name were J. Adams, your pencil would move as shown by these arrows. When I say 'go,' see how many backward written signatures of your name you can write here." Is that understood? Ready. Start writing.

121

0:30 Stop working. Turn to page 7. Read instructions while I read them aloud: "Now we are going to do two more runs in Part II in just the same way. First, write your signature as fast as you can in the ordinary way, when I say 'go.'" Go!

0:30 Stop working. Read instructions as I read them aloud: "Now do your best at backward writing again (as in J. Adams) using your own signature when I say 'go.'" Now are you ready? Go!

0:30 Stop working. Pencils down while we collect materials.

End of tape for U.I. 32

Total time: 28:00 mins.

Instructions for

Administering

U.I. 33

———————

Discouragement
vs
Sanguineness

———————

Test Time 14:00 Mins

Total Time with Instructions, as on Tape
Approx. 21:00 Mins

———————

Seven Subtests

———————

No apparatus needed

Instructions [as on Tape] for U.I. 33 — Discouragement vs. Sanguineness

Time required: Actual testing time: 14 mins.
Approximate total time with instructions and other time expenditures: 21 mins.

(Before playing the tape, be sure everyone has the test booklet, answer sheet, and pencils; have them write name, etc., on the answer sheet.)

No. in Battery for U.I. 33	Identifying T No.	Time Required†	Directions
		0:30	Now look at the answer sheet and find the block where you answer the questions for Test 1, on the side of the answer sheet that says U.I. 33.** The words "Test 1" are printed at the left of the block. There are 14 items in the block for Test 1. If you have not found the place to answer the questions in Test 1, put up your hand. (pause)
1	22b	0:40	Now open your booklet to page 1 and look at Test 1, Performance Estimates. I will read the directions aloud. (Read T22b): "Below is a list of things which not many people have tried. Mark on the answer sheet how well you think you could do each of them *without much experience or practice.* Use the following key for marking your answers: a) very well, b) well, c) fairly well, d) poorly, e) very poorly. Example A: Never having trained an elephant, I think I would be able to do it: a) very well, b) well, c) fairly well, d) poorly, e) very poorly." If you finish page 1 before time is called, go right on to the second page. Any questions? (pause) Pencils ready. Begin Performance Estimates.
			(After 1:00, say): "Don't forget to go right on to the second page."
		1:30	Stop working. Pencils down while we get ready for Test 2.

† Actual testing times are in **bold face**.
** Some answer sheets may use HSOA instead of the more general U.I. notation.

2   64b   1:10   Now turn to page 3 and look at Test 2, How Many Friends? I will read the directions aloud. (Read T64b): "Good friends are people you want to continue to know for a long time. You trust them and they trust you. If you ever need them you know they will stand by you, and you would do the same for them. According to the above definition of a friend, mark your answer sheet, next to the number corresponding to each item below. Use the following key: a) if you have *no friends* whom you could call on the situation described, b) if you have only *one friend* you could call on, and c) if you have *two or more friends* you could call on in this situation." Find the place to answer Test 2 on the answer sheet. Any questions? (pause) If you finish the first page before time is called, go right on to the second page. Pencils ready. Begin How Many Friends?

(After 1 min., say): "Don't forget, go right on to the second page."

2:00   Stop working. Pencils down while we get ready for Test 3.

3   40c   0:50   Now turn to page 5 and look at Test 3, What Is Fun? I will read the directions aloud. (Read T40c): "Mark the 'Y' box (for 'yes') on your answer sheet next to the item number if you would like to do what is said in the item. Mark the 'N' box next to the item number if you would *not* like to do it. Don't start until you are told." Find the place to answer Test 3 on the answer sheet. Any questions? (pause) Pencils ready. Begin What Is Fun?

2:00   Stop working. Pencils down while we get ready for Test 4.

4   156b   0:55   Turn to page 6 and look at Test 4, My Feelings. I will read the directions aloud. (Read T156b): "The following items ask you to tell how you have felt at certain times. Read each item and try to remember how you felt at that time. Use the following key in marking your answers: a) if you felt *very happy*, b) if you felt *fine*, c) if you felt *O.K.*, d) if you felt

not really good, and e) if you felt *unhappy.*" Find the place to answer Test 4 on the answer sheet. Any questions? (pause) If you finish the first page before time is called, go right on to the second page. Pencils ready. Begin My Feelings.

(After 1:30, say): "Don't forget to go right on to the second page."

2:00 Stop working. Pencils down while we get ready for Test 5.

5 39 0:50 Now turn to page 8 and look at Test 5, Chances of Success. I will read the directions aloud. (Read T39): "Below is a list of things which many people would like to be able to do. Show whether you think your chances are low, average, or good of doing these things. *We are not asking you what your chances of doing these things are now, but what your chances are for reaching these goals in the future.* Use the following key in marking your answers: a) *good* chance, b) *average* chance, c) *low* chance." Find the place to answer Test 5 on the answer sheet. Any questions? (pause) Pencils ready. Begin Chances of Success.

2:30 Stop working. Pencils down while we get ready for Test 6.

6 9e1 0:45 Now turn to page 9 and look at Test 6, Opinions VII. I will read the directions aloud. (Read T9e1): "Fill in the 'a' box next to the item number on your answer sheet if you strongly agree with the statement, 'b' if you agree, 'c' if you are uncertain, and so on. Use the following key in marking your answers: a) strongly agree, b) agree, c) uncertain, d) disagree, e) strongly disagree." Find the place to answer Test 6 on the answer sheet. Any questions? (pause) If you finish the first page before time is called, go right on to the second page. Pencils ready. Begin Opinions VII.

(After 1:30, say): "Don't forget, go right on to the second page."

2:00 Stop working. Pencils down while we get ready for Test 7.

7

24

1:00 Now turn to page 11 and look at Test 7, How Would Events Affect You? I will read the directions aloud. (Read T24): "Things happen fairly far away in the world that can nevertheless affect you personally. A list of such things is given below. Try to decide whether in the end its effects on your life are likely to be good or bad. You have five possible choices from 'very bad' through 'rather bad,' 'neither good nor bad,' and 'rather good' to 'very good' effects. Mark one only for each event." Find the place to answer Test 7 on the answer sheet. Any questions? (pause) If you finish the first page before time is called, go right on to the second page. Pencils ready. Begin How Would Events Affect You?

(After 1:30, say): "Don't forget, go right on to the second page."

2:00 Stop working. Pencils down while materials are collected.

End of tape for U.I. 33

Total time: 21:00 mins.

7

Scoring: I. Principles for Scoring the O-A

In actual daily practice the psychologist using this book strictly as a Handbook will be able to put his fingers in Chapter 6 on Administration and Chapter 8 on Practical Scoring Procedures, and not be concerned with the rest—at least until he needs to study final criterion relations for the scores. However, in order to satisfy his curiosity about the psychometric rationale of the seemingly arbitrary mechanical rules given in Chapter 8, as well as to tie into the general theoretical position of objective personality assessment, this chapter discusses the basic principles for deriving scores. Some users, pressed for time, may prefer simply to score the tests as Chapter 8 indicates and omit this chapter on the underlying rationale.

The general psychometric principles are by now clear. The score for each personality factor is based on a set of seven or eight subtests which 30 years of programmatic research have shown to have the steadiest significant correlations with the factor. It would have given *apparently* good psychometric properties, i.e., coefficients of validity and reliability, to pick the two tests, or even one, with the highest validity correlation and call it a factor measure. But we know, psychologically and psycho-metrically, (a) that wider spread of measures over many areas and types of expression is desirable in order to soundly measure a broad personality factor, and (b) that it is in the nature of changing human subpopulations that loadings on particular tests can change rather markedly with age, sex, social class, etc., so that it would be foolish to "put all our eggs in one basket" (as was done, formerly, in various objective approaches such as the Rorschach, hinging on a special perceptual performance, or the TAT, depending on one particular defense mechanism—projection).

Not only do we sample here across (typically) eight different subtests for any one factor, but we also have the option of considering behavior across all 76 subtests in the Main Kit, if we wish to put the examinee through the whole Kit. The best of the 76 for any one factor, it is true, are in the eight we can measure when giving only a single factor battery from the whole Kit, but though the rest are primarily chosen for other factors, the complexity of personality behavior is such that certain tests have appreciable contributions to make to the first factor chosen. This gives a still broader base of general behavior upon which to estimate the trait, and, psychometrically, we can see that it gives a significant and sometimes quite appreciable boost to the concept validity of the score.

The first method we shall call the *single factor* method, and the second, the *computer synthesis* method (Cattell, Eber, & Tatsuoka, 1970), and it will be noted that the latter requires use of the whole Kit (10 factors,

76 subtests, roughly 3½ to 4 hours) and gives scores on all 10 source traits, of course, whereas the former can alone be used with a single battery (typically 30 minutes).

The psychometric principles in the two are, however, the same, namely, that one weights every performance score by its appropriate weight to give the best possible estimate of the trait score. The only difference is that these weights are worked out for just eight subtests in the single battery method and for 76 in the computer synthesis method. In many batteries with component subtests which psychologists have been accustomed to, it has been traditional—and easiest—to add their scores without a weighting system, as in the WAIS or WISC. As any sophisticated psychometrist knows, this nominal equal weight falls short of real equal weight because of the varying raw score deviations and correlations among the subtests. Even if real equal weighting were reached, it would be inferior to the particular weights for each subtest required to give maximum regression on the criterion. Psychometrists (Horn, 1964) have sometimes noted that the gain from going from true equal weights to optimum weights is negligibly small when the weights from the first are applied to a second sample. Recognizing this, we nevertheless would argue that if the first is on a sufficiently large sample, as with the O-A, its carryover to new groups is good enough to bring gains. Indeed, if one is going beyond the crude addition of subtest raw scores at all it is very little more trouble to go the whole way. (Parenthetically, the raw score sigma differences in personality subtests are so great that it would be indefensible to use the rough method sometimes used with intelligence tests.) However, since there is always *some* loss of validity when weights from one sample are applied to another, large-scale users of the Kit may wish to redetermine the values on their own samples.

Let us consider briefly the obtaining of a factor score from an optimal weighting table for subtests. This is, in fact, just the same formally as obtaining regression weights for a nonfactor, ordinary variable *criterion.* In the latter case, if we know the intercorrelations of the n predictors, the matrix for which we will call $\mathbf{R}_n$, and their correlations with the criterion, a column vector we will call $\mathbf{C}$, then the column vector of weights, which we will call $\mathbf{B}$, is obtained by:

$$\mathbf{B} = \mathbf{R}_n^{-1} \cdot \mathbf{C} \tag{7.1}$$

$$n \begin{bmatrix} \\ \end{bmatrix}^{1} \;=\; n \begin{bmatrix} \end{bmatrix}^{n} \;\times\; n \begin{bmatrix} \\ \end{bmatrix}^{1}$$

In the case of factor score estimation, we have correlations among the variables, which give a square matrix, $\mathbf{R}_{v \cdot x}$, x being the given factor, and a column vector from the given factor structure matrix (correlations with the factor) which we will call, as usual, $\mathbf{V}_{fs \cdot x}$, the x indicating a particular factor x column in $\mathbf{V}_{fs}$. Then the weight column vector, which we will call $\mathbf{V}_{fe \cdot x}$ (because the entries are e's—estimation weight values), will be obtained by:

$$\mathbf{V}_{fe \cdot x} = \mathbf{R}_{v \cdot x}{}^{-1} \, \mathbf{V}_{fs \cdot x} \qquad (7.2)$$

$$n_x \begin{bmatrix} 1 \\ \\ \end{bmatrix} = n_x \begin{bmatrix} n_x \\ \\ \end{bmatrix} \quad \text{x} \quad n_x \begin{bmatrix} 1 \\ \\ \end{bmatrix}$$

Here n_x is the number of variables (7 or 8) used in the particular factor, x, battery, and $\mathbf{R}_{v \cdot x}$ is the correlations among that particular x factor set of variables.

This is for the single battery method. If we use computer synthesis with the whole battery, we have:

$$\mathbf{V}_{fe} = \mathbf{R}_v{}^{-1} \, \mathbf{V}_{fs} \qquad (7.3)$$

$$n_t \begin{bmatrix} k \\ \\ \end{bmatrix} = n_t \begin{bmatrix} n_t \\ \\ \end{bmatrix} \quad \text{x} \quad n_t \begin{bmatrix} k \\ \\ \end{bmatrix}$$

Here n_t (total) is all the variables (76 in the present battery) and k is the number of factors (10 in the O-A) since it is usual to estimate all factors at once when using this method.

The calculations just indicated give e weights that apply to standard scores on the variables, not raw scores. In matrix terms, we go from standard scores on the variables on N people, arranged in a matrix, $\mathbf{S}_v$, to the estimated scores on the factors, $\widehat{\mathbf{S}}_f$, by the computer calculation:

$$\widehat{\mathbf{S}}_f = \mathbf{S}_v \, \mathbf{V}_{fe} \qquad (7.4)$$

$$N \begin{bmatrix} k \\ \\ \end{bmatrix} = N \begin{bmatrix} n \\ \\ \end{bmatrix} \quad \text{x} \quad n \begin{bmatrix} k \\ \\ \end{bmatrix}$$

In principle, this is basically what is done in getting factor scores on the O-A, both for the single battery and the total (computer synthesis) method, but there are some refinements to consider. Any reader who drove an automobile in the 1940s will recollect that it was far harder to drive but far easier to understand than its 1970 equivalent. Similarly, in psychometrics it is possible for a good designer to make the scoring calculations simpler, but at the cost of more complex statistical devices back of the offered procedures. For example, when the raw score deviations of the subtests are different, and the weights to be assigned to the standard scores for estimating the factor are different, as shown in the V_{fe} (factor estimation matrix), it simplifies the actual working procedure to combine the two multipliers in one as instructed in the next chapter. Some readers will simply carry out that procedure as instructed, but here, as stated, we propose to make the rationale for the step explicit. Although single battery weighting and total computer synthesis are the same in principle, there are some differences which call for setting out their translation into procedures separately.

Approximate or Exact Standard Scores for a Single Factor Battery from the Main Kit

Obviously, the first step, since the $V_{fe \cdot x}$ is for standard scores, is to convert each test's raw score, by our norms, to standard scores. To get the standard scores from raw scores we subtract m, the raw score mean, computed from the raw scores in the standardization sample, from the individual's raw score, thus getting his score as a positive or negative deviation in raw score terms. We then divide this raw score deviation by s, the standard deviation of the raw scores for that test as found by our norms. If the reader will turn to the practical steps, at this point, set out, say, for U.I. 16, in Chapter 8, he will see that the first column, headed "Derived Raw Score" simply calls for the original raw score to be put in it. (The word "derived" merely means that it is derived sometimes as a ratio or difference from values obtained directly by the test key.) The scorer subtracts the mean value in the second column (given by our norms) from this raw score and sets the result down as a raw score deviation in the third column. (See Table 8.1.)

At this point weighting begins. To give equal nominal weight to all subtests it would suffice simply to add such standard scores, but we wish to weight instead by the optimal weight of the subtest, as given in $V_{fe \cdot x}$ described above, for getting the best factor score estimate. For we have decided that even the eight or so salients chosen to measure each factor can differ appreciably in their loadings and their correlations with the factor, i.e., their validites.

Here the user might perhaps think to get the weights from the $V_{fe \cdot x}$'s (which are set out in Table 7.1 and could be arranged in the fourth column of the summary sheet for U.I. 16: see page 174). He would multiply the values just inserted in the third column of the summary sheet, after bringing them to standard score deviations, to get the final contribution of the test to the individuals' factor scores. The deviations in standard scores he would, of course, obtain by dividing the raw score deviation by the "s"

Table 7.1

**TRANSITIONS FROM RAW SCORES: Weights To Be Applied
To Subtests To Obtain Factor Scores When Using Single Trait
Batteries of the O-A Main Kit**

U.I. 16   Ego Standards

Test Performance Factor No. in Factor	T and MI number		"e" from V$_{fe}$ for U.I. 16	m mean of raw score	s s.d. of raw score	w weight
	T	MI				
1	361	244	.07	10.71	3.92	.02
2	49a	6d	.21	29.24	7.38	.03
3	44a	307	.28	38.00	7.77	.04
4	8a	288	.17	9.81	2.67	.07
5	20a	282	.09	13.29	5.07	.02
6	11a	2409	.06	19.59	9.40	.01
7	35a	199	.27	26.70	8.31	.04
8	43b	2410	.09	34.37	3.24	.03

given in the fifth column of Table 7.1. Table 7.1 is in fact presented here in case he wants to do that, and also to show the basis for the further calculation.

However, we intend a further calculation and, for the good reason that if the standard scores multiplied by the e weights were used, they would not add up directly to a standard score on the factor. The factor scores would have a mean of zero, but a sigma that falls short of unity by the amount that the obtained multiple correlation from all subtests falls short of 1.0. To correct this, and come as close as possible to factor standard scores, all the e weights from the V$_{fe·x}$ must be multiplied down the column by the reciprocal of R (multiple correlation) of the eight subtests with the factor criterion. This has been done to convert the e values to

133

Table 7.1 (Continued)

U.I. 19   Independence

Test Performance Factor No. in Factor	T and MI number		"e" from V$_{fe}$ for U.I. 19	m mean of raw score	s s.d. of raw score	w weight
	T	MI				
1	35b	120f	.23	.71	.170	1.53
2	37	206	.18	.73	.138	1.47
3	6a	167c	.12	.84	.115	1.17
4	422	2367	.14	.60	.204	.78
5	328	1387	.20	7.60	1.960	.12
6	242a	689	.33	.84	.180	2.07
7	114	51	.16	.77	.206	.88

p values. Probability (p) values are the corrections for e weights in terms of finally giving standard scores for estimated factors, obtained by summing the column of test contributions (see column 5, p. 174).

For the convenience of the user, however, it would be best to have a type of p value that can be applied directly to the *raw* score deviations he has written in column 3 of the Score Summary Sheet. Consequently, p, the value to apply to a standard score deviation, is divided by s, the standard deviation of the given test, to yield a value w that can be applied directly to the raw score deviation. This is set ouf in the last column of Table 7.1 and has then been transferred for use to the fourth column of the Score Summary Sheets in Chapter 8. [1]

---

[1]The values in Tables 7.1 and 7.2 are all exact, based on the actual data used in the final norm group, for the O-A Battery. A few w's in Table 7.1 are negative and, hence, contradictory to overall previous findings. The test user is advised that the w's reported in the Score Summary Sheets (Chapter 8) have been modified slightly to reflect all research findings presently available.

Table 7.1 (Continued)

U.I. 20   Evasiveness

Test Performance Factor No. in Factor	T and MI number		"e" from V_{fe} for U.I. 20	m mean of raw score	s s.d. of raw score	w weight
	T	MI				
1	10b	34	.08	1.14	.756	.13
2	9g	65	.17	2.67	.972	.23
3	9bj	38	—.004	.74	1.320	—.01
4	38a	211a	—.03	2.04	.555	—.07
5	16a	100b	.22	.49	.331	.85
6		152b	.10	3.58	.308	.42
7		67a	.52	2.20	.222	3.02

Let us set the above transformations down more concisely in algebraic form. We have said that:

$$p = \frac{e}{R} \quad \text{(correction to bring to factor standard scores)} \tag{7.5}$$

$$w = \frac{p}{s} \quad \text{(correction if } w \text{ is to apply to raw score deviation)} \tag{7.6}$$

so that the total calculation made in getting w from e is:

$$w = \frac{e}{Rs} \tag{7.7}$$

The way in which the e's are typically obtained is shown in Equation (7.3) above. But this uses V_{fs}, the factor structure matrix, and we have not paused yet to explain how that is obtained. The usual culmination of a factor analysis, as in the two studies (Cattell & Klein, 1975; Cattell,

135

Table 7.1 (Continued

U.I. 21   Exuberance

Test Performance Factor No. in Factor	T and MI number		"e" from V_{fe} for U.I. 21	m mean of raw score	s s.d. of raw score	w weight
	T	MI				
1	411d	335b	.12	15.11	3.00	.05
2	43a	271	.36	44.40	7.11	.07
3	88a	853	.16	5.90	5.24	.04
4	164a	699	.23	11.30	4.86	.07
5	2d	7	.12	12.00	2.82	.06
6	3	8	.04	45.70	38.91	.01
7	51	286	.17	57.10	10.54	.02
8	136a	264	.17	62.20	20.11	.01

Schuerger, Klein, & Finkbeiner, 1976) on which present results are based, is a factor pattern matrix, $\mathbf{V}_{fp}$ (see articles concerned). The $\mathbf{V}_{fs}$, used to obtain the $\mathbf{V}_{fe}$ for the Table 7.1 values, is calculated by:

$$\mathbf{V}_{fs} = \mathbf{V}_{fp}\,\mathbf{R}_f \qquad (7.8)$$

where $\mathbf{R}_f$ is the correlation matrix among the factors.

Possibly the only step in the above that is novel to the reader is the correction of e weights to p weights. In explanation, we would remind the reader that the e-weighted sum of standard scores of subtests falls short of unity because any battery can only estimate the factor imperfectly,

Table 7.1 (Continued)

U.I. 23   Mobilization-vs-Regression

Test Performance Factor No. in Factor	T and MI number T	MI	"e" from V_{fe} for U.I. 23	m mean of raw score	s s.d. of raw score	w weight
1	38b	242	—.02	1.05	.093	—.32
2	44c	120b	.07	.880	.104	.96
3	112	609	.37	.697	.294	1.80
4	197.	401	.15	.712	.136	1.54
5	11b	36	.39	.695	.139	4.03
6	20b	105	—.03	.654	.205	—.20
7	224b	714	—.003	.870	.180	—.02
8	1a	2a	—.006	.204	.058	—.16

so the variance will be short of 1.0. (The multiple R, which is the validity of the whole battery, might be, say, 0.8, in which case these estimated factor scores, when e is used, will have a variance of only $[0.8]^2 = 0.64$, instead of 1.0.) Accordingly, the last step is to change the obtained e to a p value by multiplying all values in the e column by the inverse of the multiple correlation, R, for that factor.

Any psychometrist will recognize that the values of m (subtest means) and w (subtest weights) in the Score Summary Sheets for Chapter 8 are not universal. That is to say, they are bound to the particular samples (Cattell & Klein, 1975; Cattell, Schuerger, Klein, & Finkbeiner, 1976) and to time. Although most parameter values from samples of this size vary

Table 7.1 (Continued)

U.I. 24   Anxiety

Test Performance Factor No. in Factor	T and MI number		"e" from V_{fe} for U.I. 24	m mean of raw score	s s.d. of raw score	w weight
	T	MI				
1	430	2404	—.01	3.04	.244	—.04
2	27b	117b	.20	3.40	.543	.44
3	41a	219	.39	2.89	.637	.72
4	36	205	.09	.29	.163	.67
5	187a	218	.31	.62	.256	1.45
6	163a	1370	.04	2.28	.844	.06
7	38c	211b	.21	4.15	.357	.70
8	25	321	.11	.70	.192	.68

little, it must be recognized that beta weights are among the least stable of parameters. Consequently, the user must not expect that when he applies these m and w values to the raw scores of his particular sample, e.g., students, clinical cases, delinquents, etc., he will get for a given factor battery, on his given sample, *exact* standard scores. The standard scores are likely to have a mean different from zero and a standard deviation slightly different from 1.0. However, if our late high school samples were reasonably representative of the general population (at that age), as we believe them to be, then the above kinds of deviations from standard score means and standard deviations in further groups will be largely real, due to the psychologist having a sample, e.g., neurotics, university students,

Table 7.1 (Continued)

U.I. 25   Realism-vs-Tensidia

Test Performance Factor No. in Factor	T and MI number		"e" from V_{fe} for U.I. 25	m mean of raw score	s s.d. of raw score	w weight
	T	MI				
1	16b	100b	.11	.51	.331	.51
2	9bk	2411	.24	.87	.129	2.95
3	431	2408	.25	.89	.163	2.45
4	31	144	—.03	.63	.198	—.25
5	224a	714	—.02	.80	.175	—.17
6	118a	249	.21	.31	.050	6.60
7	49c	120h	.25	.93	.090	4.44

delinquents, really differing from the general population. But these differences will also be due, in some degree, to the changing correlations of and among subtests, and therefore the resulting ideal w weights will be different for his sample. If the user wants scores in exact standard scores for his sample, he can, of course, always treat the scores obtained via Table 8.1 as "raw" scores and transform them, knowing his present sigma, to precise standard scores, but they will be standard then only for his sample.

Only some years of experience and experiment can show whether the refinement we have used of giving unequal, truly adjusted weights to the different subtests in the single batteries justifies the work involved therein, relative to the more casual practice of adding subtests

Table 7.1 (Continued)

U.I. 28   Asthenia

Test Performance Factor No. in Factor	T and MI number		"e" from V_{fe} for U.I. 28	m mean of raw score	s s.d. of raw score	w weight
	T	MI				
1	9c	152b	.15	6.30	.598	.35
2	9ek	116	.27	2.80	.363	1.02
3	9d	125	.37	2.60	.625	.82
4	16a	100	.02	3.00	.386	.08
5	19	192	.22	1.59	.480	.63
6	149	364	.21	.40	.189	1.53
7	96	1160	.16	1.69	.390	.56
8	76	97	—.08	2.49	.247	—.44

with equal nominal weights. But meanwhile we offer column 8 in Table 7.1 as a best rounded estimate at present of the weights to be assigned to raw score deviations on the subtests to get the best standard score estimate of each. There will be circumstances, of course, where the psychologist will already have put the subtest scores in standard form, and he can then use the e or the p column directly, according to his choice.

The Computer Synthesis Method for Use When the Full Kit Is Used

We described three scoring possibilities above: (1) crude addition of raw subtest scores; (2) weighting for optimal estimation when

Table 7.1 (Continued)

U.I. 32   Exvia-vs-Invia

Test Performance Factor No. in Factor	T and MI number		"e" from V_{fe} for U.I. 32	m mean of raw score	s s.d. of raw score	w weight
	T	MI				
1	45	309	.34	47.80	12.32	.05
2	62b	737	.21	12.91	4.05	.09
3	142a	356a	.13	19.91	7.29	.03
4	97	1169	.21	.79	.224	1.56
5	13a	763a	.11	14.00	4.30	.04
6	164b	2412	.14	.40	.627	.37
7	121	15	—.03	25.30	7.02	—.01
8	1d	2a	.23	.40	.110	3.45

only a single battery has been used; and (3) computer synthesis, which is possible only when the entire Kit is used.

This third method gives greater validity, but will also give slightly different correlations among the factor scores from those reached by Method 2. (Both, of course, will be only an approximation to correlations among the true factors.) Let us repeat that it can be used only when the whole Kit is given, and it requires a standardization table totally different from that for single factor use. For all the single factor values, calculated above, are from "isolated" 8 x 8 matrices for each factor. Computer synthesis scoring uses the same multiple regression principle as Method 2, but now brings in all subtests in the Main Kit and requires regard for the correlations among all 76 of them. It is unnecessary, also, to repeat the derivations, since it uses just the same matrix equations as in Equations 7.3 and

Table 7.1 (Continued)

U.I. 33   Discouragement-vs-Sanguineness

Test Performance Factor No. in Factor	T and MI number		"e" from V_{fe} for U.I. 33	m mean of raw score	s s.d. of raw score	w weight
	T	MI				
1	22b	108	.39	3.22	1.290	.40
2	64b	473	.09	3.39	1.210	.10
3	40c	2413	.04	.34	.209	.24
4	156b	1245	.01	2.35	.881	.01
5	39	212	.47	2.00	.761	.81
6	9e1	116a	.08	2.83	.993	.11
7	24	112	.35	3.14	.280	1.64

7.4 above. The $\mathbf{R}_v$ matrix to be inverted is now 76 x 76 and $\mathbf{V}_{fe}$ and $\mathbf{V}_{fs}$ are no longer vectors (single columns) but comprise 10 columns, i.e., are matrices 76 x 10.

Table 7.2 will provide the w's to apply to the obtained raw score deviations from the mean. They are obtained from the $\mathbf{V}_{fe}$ *for the whole Kit* by just the same transformation as are used in Table 7.1 for single factor batteries, i.e., by responding to differences in the raw score deviation size and the multiple R sizes in the formula $w = e/R_s$. The w values are thus reached by multiplying each variable row in the $\mathbf{V}_{fe}$ by $1/s$, the raw score sigma, and then each column by $1/R$, where R is the multiple R for the given factor.

In the full matrix of 76 variables and 10 factors, this is best done by matrix algebra methods as shown in Table 7.2, which involves a simple computer program and is quite rapid.

In the use of single batteries, the final step of applying the w values to raw score deviations has been set out in the Score Summary Sheets of Chapter 8 in a way to permit it to be done by hand without recourse to the computer. But in the computer synthesis method, where the psychologist would be dealing generally with many examinees, and where the weighting and adding of 76 subtests even for one examinee would be time consuming, the last step of obtaining factor scores is also best transferred to a computer.

The essential form of the matrix calculation has already been set out in Equation 7.4 above, and it hardly needs to be said that it—and the fuller details of procedure below—can also be used with single batteries if desired.

In what follows, the designations of the matrices are:

1) S_t = The raw scores on the subtest. This will be an N x 76 score list (N being the number of examinees).

2) M_t = The raw score means for each test (from column 5 of our Table 7.1 or the user's own sample), arranged with the same value repeated down the whole of each test column, in an N x 76 matrix. Make sure these are in the right order by MI numbers, matching those in Table 7.2.

3) S_f = The resultant matrix of people's estimated factor scores in (approx.) standard score form. A matrix of N people x 10 factor scores.

The procedure for computer synthesis scoring uses the following elementary matrix formula:

$$S_f = (S_t - M_t)\, V_w \qquad\qquad (7.9)$$

which states that the matrix of factor scores, S_f, for the group of interest (one score per factor per individual) is equal to the deviation of the individual's subtest scores from the respective subtest means ($S_t - M_t$), multiplied by the appropriate weights (V_w) of the individual factors. The V_w values are adjusted for the fact that ($S_t - M_t$) is in raw score units.

As stated earlier, this can be used also for the single factor procedures too, in which case S_f will be an N x 1 column matrix and S_t and N x 8 matrix, while V_w will be an 8 x 1 set of weights, and M_t, an 8 x 1 column of transformed means. It is pointed out, here and later, however, that the actual factor score estimates will not be quite the same from the two sources, because, although the high marker variables for a given factor will have big w's on both, the computer synthesis method will also bring in other variables. This is the same as saying that the norms, if one dealt in raw score transformations to standard scores, would not be precisely

Table 7.2

WEIGHT MATRIX (V$_W$) VALUES FOR COMPUTER SYNTHESIS SCORING OF THE O-A MAIN BATTERY

V$_W$

	MI Number	U.I. 16	U.I. 19	U.I. 20	U.I. 21	U.I. 23
1	244	0.02	0.00	0.00	-0.02	0.01
2	6d	0.02	0.00	0.00	0.01	0.00
3	307	0.03	0.00	0.00	0.01	-0.01
4	288	0.06	0.01	0.00	0.00	0.00
5	282	0.02	0.00	0.00	0.00	0.00
6	2409	0.00	0.00	0.00	0.00	0.01
7	199	0.03	0.00	0.00	0.01	0.00
8	2410	0.02	0.01	0.0	0.00	0.00
9	120f	0.02	0.99	-0.10	0.07	0.32
10	206	-0.05	1.11	-0.41	0.00	0.30
11	167c	-0.50	0.98	0.03	-1.01	-0.26
12	2367	-0.04	0.60	-0.12	-0.02	-0.01
13	1387	0.01	0.08	-0.01	-0.01	-0.02
14	689	0.11	1.38	-0.09	-0.01	0.35
15	51	0.07	0.59	-0.25	-0.14	0.31
16	34	-0.02	0.00	0.10	0.02	-0.02
17	65	0.00	0.00	0.21	0.00	0.01
18	38	0.02	0.02	0.01	-0.01	0.01
19	211a	0.01	-0.13	0.01	0.00	-0.34
20	100b	-0.04	-0.05	0.73	0.03	-0.08
21	152b	0.08	0.08	0.35	-0.06	0.22
22	67a	-0.08	0.01	2.55	-0.14	-0.47
23	335b	0.01	0.00	-0.01	0.04	0.01
24	271	0.00	0.00	0.00	0.04	0.00
25	853	0.00	0.00	0.00	0.03	0.01
26	699	0.00	0.00	0.00	0.05	0.00
27	7	0.00	0.01	0.00	0.04	0.00
28	8	0.00	0.00	0.00	0.00	0.00
29	286	0.00	0.00	0.00	0.01	0.00
30	264	0.00	0.00	0.00	0.00	0.00
31	242	0.0	0.21	0.29	-0.50	-0.22
32	120b	0.08	0.80	-0.15	0.16	0.62
33	609	-0.04	0.18	-0.23	0.15	1.20
34	401	-0.15	0.20	-0.03	-0.03	0.82
35	36	-0.19	-0.22	-0.13	0.20	2.49
36	105	-0.03	0.25	-0.11	0.45	0.05
37	714	0.20	-0.40	-0.02	0.38	0.07
38	2a(1)	-0.33	-0.28	-0.22	0.51	0.10

NOTE: V$_W$ was calculated using the following formula:

$$V_W = D_S{}^{-1} V_{fe} D_R{}^{-1}$$

where D_S is a diagonal matrix of sigmas for the 76 subtests, D_R is a diagonal matrix of multiple R's for the 10 factors, and V_{fe} is the factor estimation matrix for the entire battery of 76 subtests.

Table 7.2 (Continued)

	MI Number	U.I. 24	U.I. 25	U.I. 28	U.I. 32	U.I. 33
1	244	0.01	0.00	−0.01	−0.02	0.02
2	6d	0.00	0.00	0.00	0.00	0.00
3	307	0.00	0.00	0.01	0.00	−0.01
4	288	−0.01	0.03	−0.01	0.04	0.00
5	282	0.00	0.00	0.00	−0.02	0.00
6	2409	0.00	0.00	0.00	0.00	0.00
7	199	0.00	0.00	0.00	0.02	0.00
8	2410	0.00	0.01	0.00	0.02	0.00
9	120f	−0.08	0.11	−0.20	0.09	−0.32
10	206	−0.42	−0.19	−0.03	0.54	−0.06
11	167c	0.0	−0.19	0.35	−1.33	0.50
12	2367	0.01	−0.05	−0.06	0.19	−0.01
13	1387	−0.01	0.08	0.00	0.00	0.05
14	689	−0.59	0.30	0.16	−0.90	0.50
15	51	−0.01	−0.01	0.12	0.15	−0.24
16	34	−0.03	−0.02	0.04	0.00	0.04
17	65	0.00	0.09	−0.01	0.00	0.02
18	38	−0.04	0.03	−0.03	−0.01	−0.01
19	211a	0.25	−0.14	0.20	0.07	−0.17
20	100b	0.26	−0.37	0.16	0.01	−0.14
21	152b	−0.31	0.12	−0.15	−0.10	0.12
22	67a	−0.15	−0.09	−0.35	0.01	−0.23
23	335b	0.00	0.01	0.00	0.00	0.00
24	271	0.00	0.01	0.00	0.02	0.00
25	853	0.00	0.02	−0.02	0.00	0.00
26	699	−0.01	0.01	0.00	−0.01	0.00
27	7	0.00	0.00	0.00	0.00	0.00
28	8	0.00	0.00	0.00	0.00	0.00
29	286	0.00	0.00	0.00	0.00	0.00
30	264	0.00	0.00	0.00	0.00	0.00
31	242	0.17	0.55	−0.10	−0.76	0.45
32	120b	−0.37	1.39	−0.30	−0.13	0.01
33	609	0.08	0.25	−0.03	0.16	0.19
34	401	−0.31	−0.03	0.06	0.09	0.60
35	36	−0.06	−0.48	0.04	0.40	−0.21
36	105	−0.39	0.59	−0.54	0.06	0.01
37	714	0.24	−1.32	0.19	0.09	0.08
38	2a(1)	0.63	−0.77	0.19	0.17	−0.31

Table 7.2 (Continued)

	MI Number	U.I. 16	U.I. 19	U.I. 20	U.I. 21	U.I. 23
39	2404	-0.08	-0.10	0.25	-0.01	-0.33
40	117b	0.03	0.00	-0.04	-0.05	0.02
41	219	-0.14	-0.09	0.02	-0.01	-0.06
42	205	-0.12	0.02	-0.05	0.0	0.42
43	218	0.16	0.01	0.22	-0.09	0.10
44	1370	0.06	0.01	-0.01	0.06	0.04
45	211b	0.06	-0.07	-0.43	0.10	0.11
46	321	0.06	-0.27	0.03	-0.31	-0.10
47	100b	0.04	0.04	-0.73	-0.02	0.08
48	2411	0.40	0.55	0.46	-0.07	0.47
49	2408	0.30	-0.05	-0.23	0.34	-0.29
50	144	0.19	0.24	0.05	0.06	0.16
51	714	0.04	0.73	0.14	-0.62	0.26
52	249	0.23	-1.18	-0.47	0.17	0.21
53	120h	0.09	0.85	-0.37	0.61	0.46
54	152b	-0.01	-0.07	0.04	0.09	0.07
55	116	-0.04	-0.27	-0.15	-0.05	0.00
56	125	0.06	0.02	-0.09	0.11	0.01
57	100	0.06	0.06	-0.11	-0.06	-0.07
58	192	0.09	0.09	-0.08	-0.01	0.07
59	364	-0.31	-0.51	0.37	0.09	-0.88
60	1160(2)	-0.09	-0.08	0.00	-0.07	-0.09
61	97	0.29	0.47	-0.21	0.09	0.15
62	309	0.00	0.00	0.00	0.00	0.00
63	737	0.00	-0.01	0.00	0.00	0.00
64	356a	0.00	0.00	0.00	0.00	0.00
65	1169	0.00	-0.13	-0.09	-0.08	0.04
66	763a	-0.02	-0.01	0.00	0.04	0.00
67	2412	0.08	-0.02	0.03	0.21	-0.04
68	15	0.00	0.00	0.00	0.00	0.00
69	2a(2)	0.32	0.42	-0.28	0.31	1.57
70	108	0.00	0.00	0.00	0.04	-0.12
71	473	-0.02	0.02	-0.01	-0.03	-0.02
72	2413	-0.04	0.08	0.13	-0.40	0.04
73	1245	0.00	0.06	-0.07	0.02	0.03
74	212	-0.01	0.07	0.00	-0.10	0.17
75	116a	0.00	-0.01	0.00	-0.03	0.01
76	112	0.34	0.10	-0.07	0.08	-0.22

Table 7.2 (Continued)

	MI Number	U.I. 24	U.I. 25	U.I. 28	U.I. 32	U.I. 33
39	2404	-0.07	0.00	0.15	0.06	-0.16
40	117b	0.41	0.20	-0.10	-0.04	0.13
41	219	0.60	-0.04	0.19	0.20	-0.18
42	205	0.60	0.42	-0.02	-0.12	0.29
43	218	-1.20	0.11	-0.03	-0.42	0.30
44	1370	-0.03	-0.14	-0.05	-0.05	-0.03
45	211b	0.42	-0.03	0.16	0.19	0.06
46	321	0.61	0.52	0.58	-0.26	0.03
47	100b	-0.26	0.37	-0.15	-0.01	0.14
48	2411	0.15	1.14	-1.00	-2.06	0.52
49	2408	-0.25	1.31	-0.10	0.41	-0.20
50	144	0.18	-0.01	-0.21	0.01	0.03
51	714	-0.27	-0.10	-0.60	0.00	0.35
52	249	0.95	3.45	-0.60	0.65	-0.48
53	120h	-0.04	2.34	-0.19	-0.88	0.35
54	152b	-0.06	0.02	-0.20	0.05	-0.03
55	116	0.11	-0.11	0.79	0.51	-0.16
56	125	0.04	0.00	0.61	-0.01	0.02
57	100	-0.04	0.00	0.09	-0.11	0.08
58	192	0.12	0.02	0.41	0.12	-0.04
59	364	0.25	-0.03	1.09	0.93	-0.48
60	1160(2)	0.05	0.05	0.44	0.11	0.06
61	97	-0.16	0.31	-0.34	-0.09	0.15
62	309	0.00	0.00	0.00	0.02	0.00
63	737	0.00	0.01	-0.03	0.04	0.00
64	356a	0.00	0.02	-0.01	0.02	0.00
65	1169	0.05	-0.25	-0.16	0.67	0.17
66	763a	0.00	0.00	0.0	0.02	0.00
67	2412	-0.14	-0.02	0.00	0.16	-0.02
68	15	0.00	0.00	0.00	0.00	0.01
69	2a(2)	-0.18	0.59	0.01	2.07	0.18
70	108	0.02	0.02	-0.08	0.01	0.39
71	473	-0.02	0.04	0.03	-0.02	0.10
72	2413	-0.19	0.03	0.20	-0.27	0.25
73	1245	0.00	0.01	-0.02	-0.04	0.05
74	212	-0.05	-0.08	0.00	-0.20	0.67
75	116a	0.02	-0.01	0.00	0.00	0.10
76	112	-0.30	-0.28	-0.02	0.18	0.65

comparable. However, the standard scores from the whole Kit and the single battery would both have zero mean and sigma 1.0, and the correlation over people on the scores is likely to be around 0.9.

The $\mathbf{V}_w$ and $\mathbf{M}_t$ values obtained from the present sample are set out in Table 7.2 and column 5 of Table 7.1, respectively, and should be sufficient basis for use of the computer synthesis method with whatever score matrix (raw scores) the psychologist derives from the full Kit applied to his given sample. The raw score matrix will, of course, be that of the derived scores as given by the key scoring procedures in the next chapter, in the first column of the Score Summary Sheets.

The Use of Corrections for Age, Sex, and Other Population Differences

The question of what reference population should be used to give meaning to a standard score is one of the persistent dilemmas of the practicing psychologist. Is the raw score to be interpreted against the distribution for *all* people of all ages, classes, and both sexes, or for one sex, or separately for students, or for certain minority groups? If people are to be treated equally, in, for example, job selection, regardless of origin and sex, there is much to be said for *general* norms from and for all people. The only exception to this is likely to be age, where (a) discrimination is sometimes appropriate on the ground that the individual is developing, and action is being considered that will concern his adjustment in years to come, and (b) clinical work often asks for diagnosis relative to the age group, e.g., a rather high raw score on anxiety in mid-adolescence would be less abnormal than at, say, 40. As regards age, if it is important where a person is going rather than whence he came, then it is not the absolute mental age of a child that counts, but rather his age-corrected score. We recognize this in the I.Q., and the same principle may be called for in regard to personality. In some further areas, e.g., such as studies in genetics or social status comparisons, it is again desirable to bring the people to be compared to the same age.

Recent research (Cattell, 1973b, 1977a) shows that on both Q- and T-data personality source trait measures there is substantial evidence of each trait having a characteristic age development curve, just as there is for primary abilities (Horn & Cattell, 1966, 1967). It is not yet known with any certainty, of course, how much of the age trend is genetic maturation and how much is the typical environmental learning effect in our culture. But some idea of the variety of trend over the years so far reliably tested can be gathered from Figure 7.1.

In Figure 7.1, as the article (Cattell, in press) reporting the basis (N = 1763) explains, the vertical scale units are standard deviation units for the variance within an age group—averaged over all ages taken. It will be seen that for some traits, such as ego standards (U.I. 16), independence (U.I. 19), and anxiety (U.I. 24), the mean change with age is quite

Figure 7.1a

U.I. 16, EGO STANDARDS

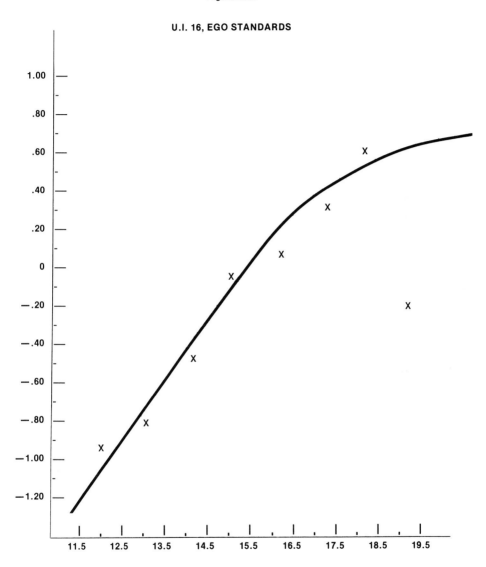

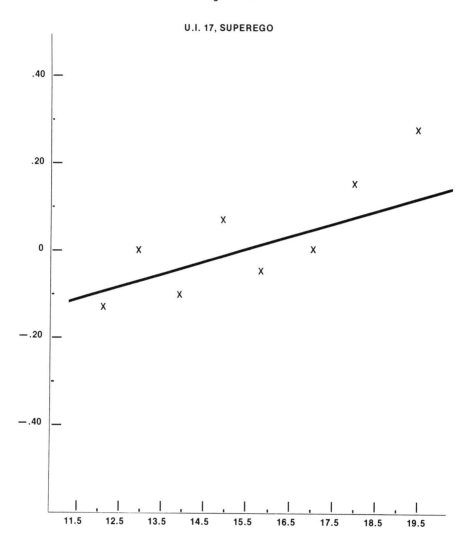

Figure 7.1b

U.I. 17, SUPEREGO

150

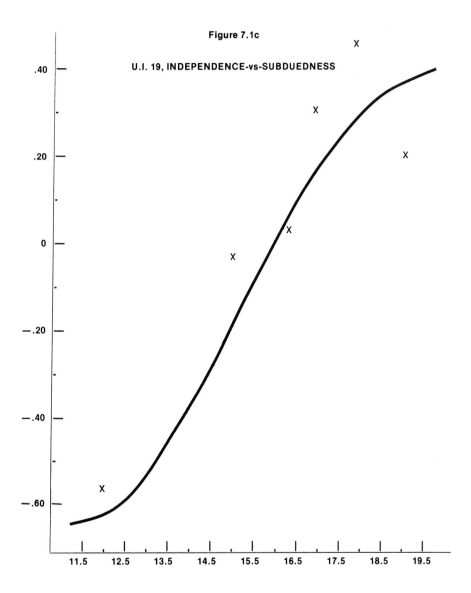

Figure 7.1c

U.I. 19, INDEPENDENCE-vs-SUBDUEDNESS

151

Figure 7.1d

U.I. 20, EVASIVENESS

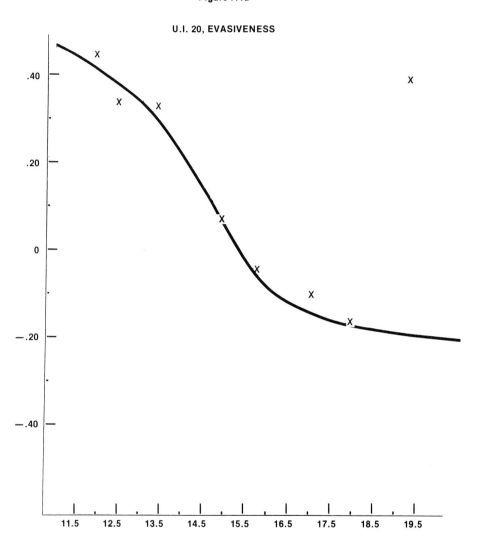

The 19.5 score is on an unduly small sample.

Figure 7.1e

U.I. 21, EXUBERANCE

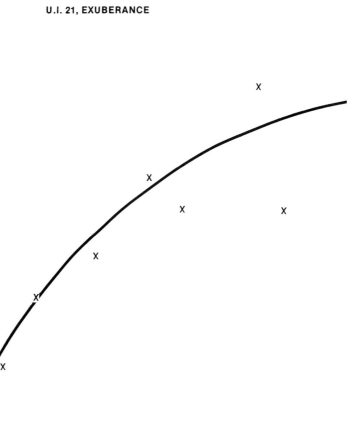

Figure 7.1f

U.I. 23, CAPACITY TO MOBILIZE-vs-REGRESSION

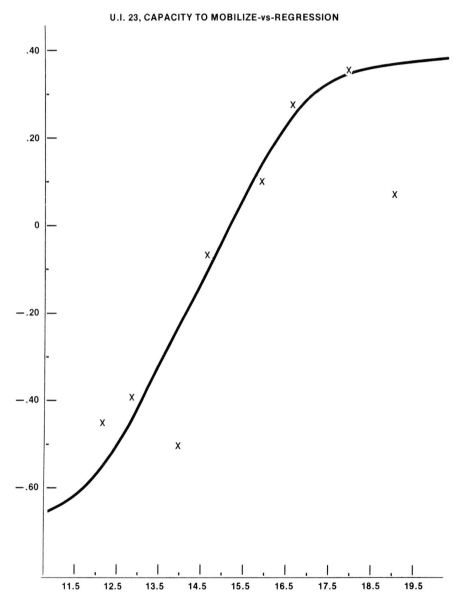

154

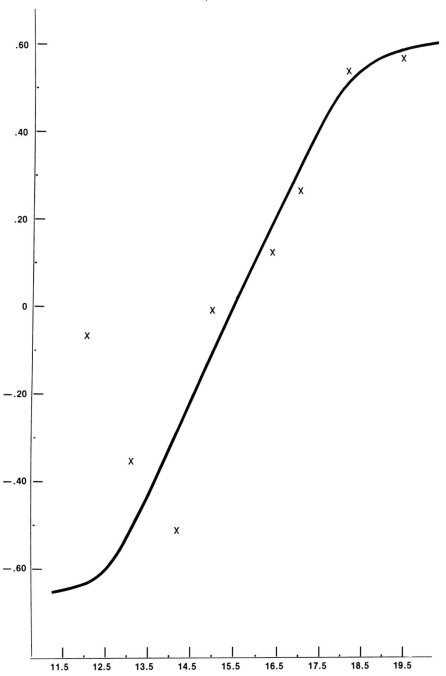

Figure 7.1g

U.I. 24, ANXIETY

Cattell and Scheier (1961) show this curve dropping steadily from 20 years into the 60s and then rising somewhat.

155

Figure 7.1h

U.I. 25, REALISM-vs-TENSIDIA

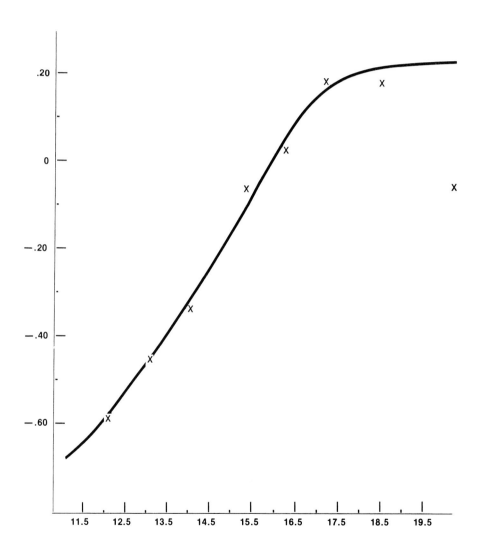

156

Figure 7.1i

U.I. 26, NARCISTIC EGO

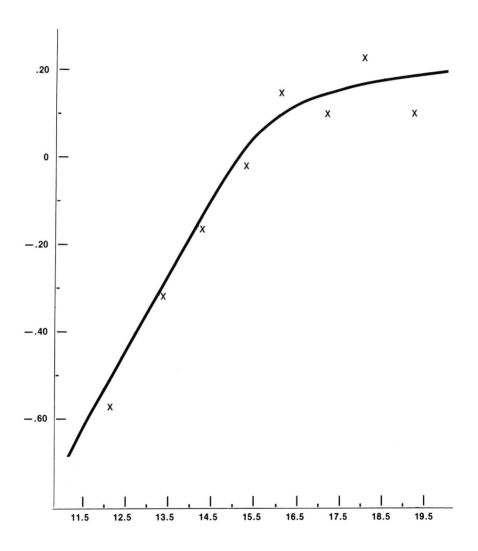

157

Figure 7.1j

U.I. 28, ASTHENIA-vs-SELF-ASSURANCE

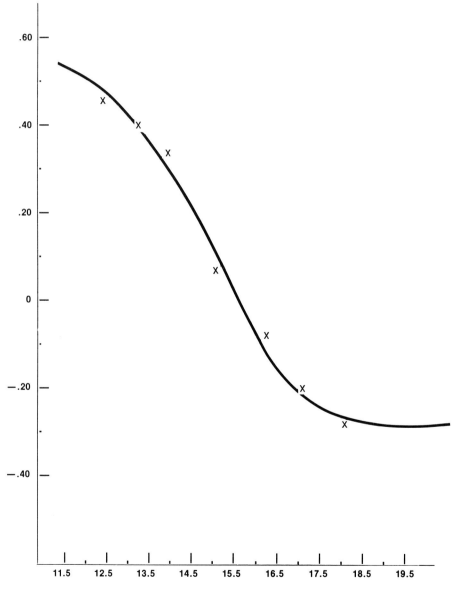

158

Figure 7.1k

U.I. 32, EXVIA-vs-INVIA

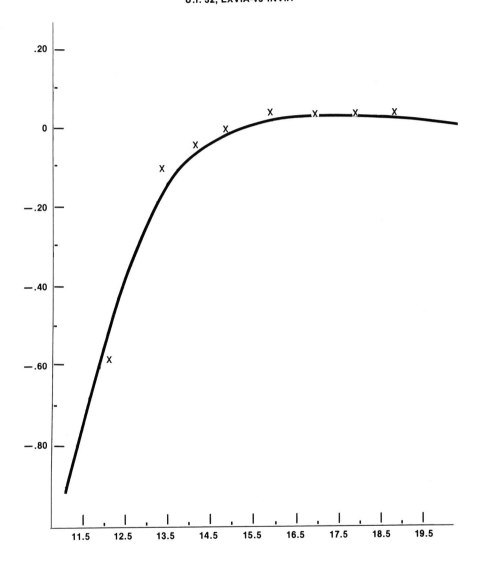

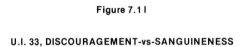

Figure 7.1 I

U.I. 33, DISCOURAGEMENT-vs-SANGUINENESS

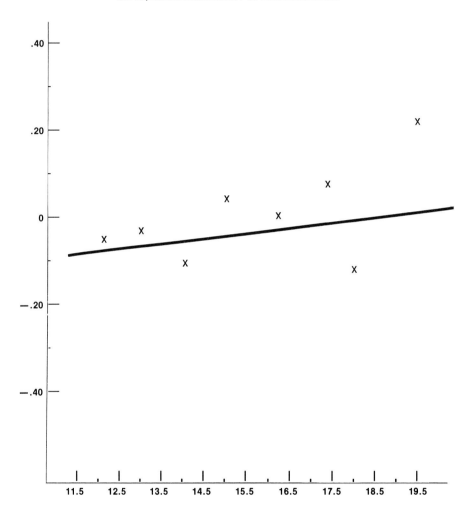

160

considerable relative to the within-age standard deviation; so in the situations where age corrections are appropriate they should and can be made for such traits.

It is convenient for practice to have age corrections in tabular form, and they are so arranged in Table 7.3. It does not much matter to what particular year the measures are brought for comparison, since an age-free score is an age-free score regardless of the reference year, hence we have chosen 15½ here as the reference point for comparison since this represented the largest number of subjects from the standardization group. Fortunately, the differences over the age range for which the O-A is intended are not massive in nature. Consequently, the scores obtained by either the single factor procedure or the computer synthesis process should suffice so far as regular use with individuals is concerned.

However, in research, where group means and standard deviations calculated to one or two decimal places are needed, age corrections may contribute significantly to the results of the study.

When other methods of controlling for age effects (e.g., the analysis of variance or covariance) are impractical or seem inappropriate, the values given in Table 7.3 may be used to make age corrections in O-A scores.

To use this table, simply enter with the standard score for the given subject, for the given trait, at the nearest year row, and *add* algebraically the value seen in that row. For example, if a child of 13 years and 1 month has an initial standard score of −.75 on U.I. 16, we should enter the row of 13½ (13.5), the nearest age, and find a correction of + .55, leading by addition to a final score of −.20. Or if a young man of 19 years and 3 months had an initial anxiety (U.I. 24) score of −.70, then adding −.60 as indicated would bring him to the low anxiety score of −1.30 for an age-standardized population.

Two qualifications should be mentioned on the age-corrected score: (1) The principal contributions so far to the standardization have been on males, and when eventually the age curves can be examined separately for boys and girls, men and women, some significant difference may be found. On the present limited samples we have found none. (2) The result of applying age corrections to an age-spread population sample with an initial sigma of unity will be to reduce the final sigma below unity. The variance over a mixed-age population sample is the sum of the variance within years and between years, and removal of the latter will require the restandardization of the sample to a sigma of unity, if that is what the experimenter wants to use. One assumes that most users in most situations will not need to bother with the age correction.

In the end, after procedures to get either the simple or the age-corrected standard scores have been performed, the psychologist will either use them as such, transform them further into centile ranks—if ranking is his interest—or condense from standard scores to stens if he

Table 7.3

CORRECTIONS OF STANDARD SCORES FOR AGE DIFFERENCES

(All Scores Brought to 15½-Year-Age-Group Distribution)

	Main Kit — Personality Source Traits										Extended Battery	
Age In Years	U.I. 16	U.I. 19	U.I. 20	U.I. 21	U.I. 23	U.I. 24	U.I. 25	U.I. 28	U.I. 32	U.I. 33	U.I. 17	U.I. 26
11.5	+1.19	+.66	−.47	+.60	+.60	+.62	+.63	−.51	+.76	+.05	+.12	+.58
12.5	+.86	+.62	−.42	+.38	+.54	+.58	+.51	−.45	+.33	+.04	+.08	+.40
13.5	+.55	+.49	−.33	+.24	+.42	+.41	+.38	−.34	+.10	+.03	+.05	+.25
14.5	+.26	+.24	−.17	+.11	+.22	+.22	+.18	−.17	+.03	+.02	+.03	+.11
15.5	0	0	0	0	0	0	0	0	0	0	0	0
16.5	−.27	−.22	+.08	−.10	−.19	−.19	−.12	+.17	−.01	−.01	−.03	−.08
17.5	−.44	−.39	+.12	−.17	−.31	−.38	−.18	+.25	−.01	−.02	−.05	−.10
18.5	−.56	−.48	+.15	−.22	−.37	−.56	−.21	+.28	−.01	−.03	−.08	−.11
19.5	−.64	−.52	+.17	−.27	−.38	−.60	−.22	+.23	0	−.04	−.11	−.11

Basis of Age Standardization: Numbers in Each Age Cohort

	11	12	13	14	15	16	17	18	19	20	
No. of S's:	2	39	233	275	426	325	260	175	23	5	Total N = 1763

Any year X.5 includes cases of age X plus 0 month through X plus 11 months. X.5 is mid-year, .5 being a decimal, not number of months.

162

Figure 7.2

TRANSLATION FROM STANDARD SCORES TO STENS AND TO CENTILE RANKS

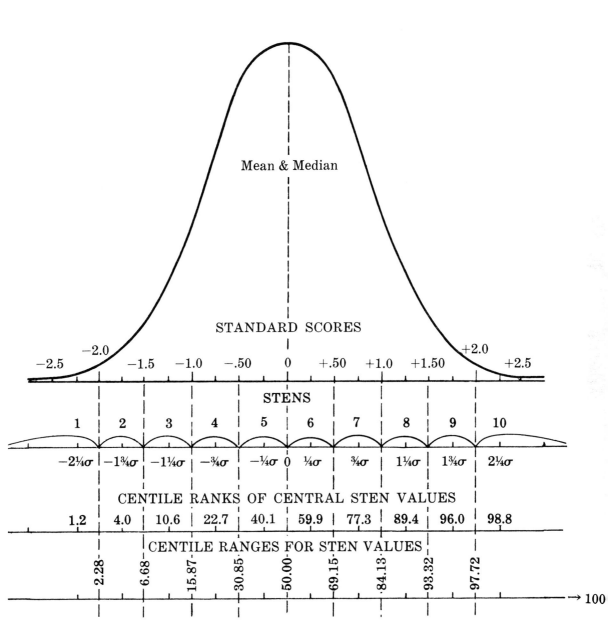

Mean & Median

STANDARD SCORES

| −2.5 | −2.0 | −1.5 | −1.0 | −.50 | 0 | +.50 | +1.0 | +1.50 | +2.0 | +2.5 |

STENS

| 1 | 2 | 3 | 4 | 5 | 6 | 7 | 8 | 9 | 10 |

| −2¼σ | −1¾σ | −1¼σ | −¾σ | −¼σ 0 ¼σ | ¾σ | 1¼σ | 1¾σ | 2¼σ |

CENTILE RANKS OF CENTRAL STEN VALUES

| 1.2 | 4.0 | 10.6 | 22.7 | 40.1 | 59.9 | 77.3 | 89.4 | 96.0 | 98.8 |

CENTILE RANGES FOR STEN VALUES

2.28 6.68 15.87 30.85 50.00 69.15 84.13 93.32 97.72

→ 100

wants a convenient point scale, realistically rounded and freed of the negative signs present in standard scores. Most statistics books have tables in the appendix for these transformations, but Figure 7.2 summarizes the relations and is itself adequate for each translation from standard scores to stens, and for centile ranks for the central value for each sten.

In Chapters 10, 11, and 12, the various criterion relations in which these standard scores on the 10 source traits can be put are described, while Chapter 8 turns to the mechanics of deriving the raw scores, either for individual calculation in the Score Summary Sheet or as a basis for computerized scoring procedures. Chapter 9 discusses scoring the broader and more general second- and third-stratum personality factors of major importance.

8

Scoring: II. Mechanics for Obtaining
Subtest Raw Scores

Scoring has two phases: (1) the obtaining of raw scores for each test, and (2) the conversion to suitable standard scores. Chapter 7 has dealt with the statistical rationale for the procedures for moving from raw scores to final standard scores. The present chapter goes on to describe those procedures in practical instructions and sets out the scoring keys for deriving the raw scores from answer sheets and booklets. But first a brief digression is called for to give perspective on the development, historically, of the present scoring practices.

Many leading psychometrists and psychologists—among them Anastasi (1975), writers in Buros (1972), Horn and Cattell (1966), Hundleby (1973a), Nesselroade and Delhees (1966), Scheier (1958), Schmidt (1975), and Wardell and Royce (1975)—have sometimes wondered, as we have above, what is preventing practicing psychologists from more vigorously advancing in the use of objective tests. The already published evidence shows there is every reason to believe such tests will bring new breadth of coverage and added precision into personality measurement. After noting the greater demands on time and skill in administration that we discussed above, such commentators generally mention finally the obstacle presented by the greater complication of scoring in behavioral tests, and, indeed, there are realities here with which progress has to cope.

One obstacle—the large demand on time—has been partly overcome by considerable reductions effected in testing time itself, as described in Chapter 6. At least we can now claim that a personality factor and an ability factor—both in objective form—are comparable in time demand. The transformation of all tests presented here from individual- to group-administrable form, and the simplification of administration by using sound tape, has removed other major obstacles. But there remain some complexities of scoring that perhaps may still intimidate some prospective users. These also, however, can be largely overcome. It is true that personality tests deal with more complex scoring than "right or wrong" answers, and involve ratios, speeds, changes under pressure, interference effects, and so on, necessary to encompass complex personal behavior. But by many successive adaptations of the tests toward convenience, proceeding from their first discovery as valid, but awkward, measures (often in individual test and apparatus-requiring form), they have now been brought even to the ultimate convenience of machine scoring of the responses, as will be explained in this chapter.

Until the gradual developments in the validation of new designs in the objective test area over the last 30 years, many of the early tests, like the Rorschach, were often "open-ended" in a way that required subjective, arbitrary personal decisions, differently made by different psychologists. Virtually all tests demanded hand scoring, and often according to some quite complex ritual. Some psychologists—deep in the crystal ball atmosphere of early testing—have not objected to the inventive (open-ended) answer, but those more keenly aware of the psychometric unreliability of open-ended designs, and those preferring to bring in their judgmental skills at the more complex and suitable level of interpreting the trait scores in predictive combinations rather than at the item level, have rightly demanded more mechanical dependability at the sheer test-scoring level.

Professional opinion increasingly favors *conspective test* designs, i.e., those where two psychologists, seeing the same behavior record, will proceed to the same score. Such a test *need* not be closed-ended (multiple choice) since there *are* means of conspectively scoring open-ended tests, but *generally* it is an advance to bring tests, wherever possible, to the former design, so that they become directly machine scorable. Many years of experiment concerning the effects of shifting to machine-scorable responses upon the factor validity of what had originally to be presented in the development of objective personality tests as open-ended designs, have preceded the design of the present answer sheets.

At present, the stage has been reached where the user is able to score *answer sheets* for over 80% of the O-A tests, and has to turn to the *expendable booklets*, i.e., tests where performances are wide open and recorded on the test form itself, only for a minority of tests. Seven of the source-trait batteries are completely free of the need to use expendable booklets.

Answer Sheet and Expendable Booklet Scoring Details

When dealing with just a few cases, or in some other special circumstances, such as the need for an immediate decision on a given case, the psychologist may decide to take the score patterns and score everything by hand himself. Generally, however, he is likely to want to call in mechanical aids. In that case, he may (a) clerically transfer the responses to computer cards and have the counting, addition, division, etc., done by programmed computer, or (b) invoke more specialized mechanical aids by using a special answer sheet sensitive to an optical scanner that "reads" the marks and transfers them directly into a computer which scores the tests and does all further manipulations with the scores desired.[1]

Regardless of which procedure is followed, the psychologist still needs to know his way about among the answer sheets and to recognize the

---

[1] The Institute for Personality and Ability Testing (address in this Handbook) is in the process of developing such a service for mailed-in O-A OpScan sheets, akin to its machine-scoring and interpretation service already available for the 16 PF, HSPQ, and other instruments.

various keys, as set out on the keyed answer sheets, for the 10 factors in this chapter. It has been thought best to have actual facsimiles of the answer sheets as seen by the examinee set out factor by factor here, just as was done above in Chapter 6 with the administration instructions from the audio tapes. These scoring instructions are set out below, beginning with trait U.I. 16, and giving a *Score Summary Sheet* for each, showing how the subtest scores are compounded for the whole factor.

The answer sheet is reproduced here just as it appears to the subject, though slightly reduced in size. However, in the quite common instances where only one particular response position has significance for the factor (corresponding to what would be a "right" answer if we dealt with ability tests), such "correct" responses are marked on the actual answer sheet here (these answers, of course, would not appear on the subject's answer sheet). Thus, the keyed answer sheets are presented both as showing the psychologist what the subject meets and as offering here the actual keys for immediate derivation from any examinee's answer of what we shall call the *derived raw score*. This is written in the first column of the Score Summary Sheet.

Directly following each keyed answer sheet—of which there is *one* for each factor, except for U.I. 16 and 25 (each of which has two)—there appears here what is to become a score record in the form of a *Score Summary Sheet*. There are 10 such Score Summary Sheets, each enabling one to proceed to the final standard score for a given factor battery. This sheet lists the subtests (by battery numbers, universal index numbers [T and MI], the Psychologist's Title, and, in parentheses, the Examinee's Title). It explains on the right, for each test title, how the derived raw score for each subtest is actually derived from the item responses on the answer sheet. This statement of derivation, e.g., number done, number right, the ratio of number right to number done, to the right of a given test title summarizes what is necessary and duplicates, for safety, what is written by the marks on the keyed answer sheet. The result of this scoring—be it a simple number, a ratio, a difference, or whatever— is entered in the first of the five numerical columns on the right of the Score Summary Sheet. Its treatment in regard to the four columns to its right will be explained in a moment, but meanwhile we call this *initial* result a *derived raw score*. For a scoring example, see Appendix C.

The Score Summary Sheet information takes care of the majority of the subtests, but in certain cases a special scoring instruction sheet is added. This happens either when an expendable booklet occurs in the battery or where the answer sheet scoring is somewhat complex and requires more than the phrase given on the Score Summary Sheet or on the keyed answer sheet.

In scores for more elementary types of psychological tests in psychometric practice, e.g., a standard score taken on an opinionnaire or an I.Q. score, one has only two numbers to deal with: a raw score and some final standard score derived from it. But here the transformation is carried out over five numerical columns on the right-hand side of the Score Summary Sheet.

As indicated earlier, what would sometimes be called the "raw score" is here called the *derived raw score;* for it is not always just the number right, but some difference, or quotient, etc., as just described. Some general points regarding these derived scores need to be set out here, as follows.

1) When a score is entitled "Sum" (more fully, "Sum of Scores on Items according to Key"), the usual order for five alternate choices is a $= 5$, b $= 4$, c $= 3$, d $= 2$, e $= 1$. Occasionally, one is instructed to reverse this order, but the above holds unless.

2) For three choices, the item scores (unless told otherwise) are based on a $= 3$, b $= 2$, c $= 1$. For two alternative answers, one is "right" (and equal to 1.0) and one is wrong (and equal to 0).

3) The expression "No. done" (number done) is the actual number of items the examinee marks, whether they are right or wrong.

4) A number of subtest scores are ratios, and with these some problems of distribution can arise. If the numerator is zero and the quotient zero, the score would be zero, which sometimes causes computer processing problems. In these cases, write .01. If the denominator is zero, the quotient is infinity. Skewed distributions of this source should be avoided by changing the denominator to 1.0. This is extremely rare, and still more rare is 0/0, in which case one assumes the examinee is not cooperating and one registers "no test."

5) In ratios and similar scores, go only to one decimal place in the answer written down. The psychologist must use his experience in deciding when a misunderstanding or "sabotage" has occurred to produce an egregious, unusable score. If it is an accident in one subtest, the factor contribution can be calculated on the remainder of the subtests, with the mean for the 'spurious' test being used instead of an invalid score. The net effect of this procedure will be a slight error toward the mean on this factor for the errant individual.

Using the Score Summary Sheet

From 1) the step of entering the derived raw scores from the answer sheet for each of the eight subtests in the first of the numerical columns, the procedures follow as now listed.

2) Subtract from the derived raw score for each test (column 1) the m (mean) value given in the second column and write the remainder in the third column. These values will be about as frequently negative as positive and *should be written with their signs.*

3) Now multiply each of these values in the third column by the weight in the fourth. Enter this product, with positive or negative sign, in the last column labeled "Special Subtest Standard Score."

4) Add the values down this fifth and last column. This is best done using a hand calculator. The result is the required standard factor score, positive or negative. The user may wish to convert this to a sten score (all stens being positive) by referring to Figure 7.2.

The pages which now follow set out for each of the 10 traits the answer sheet key, with the Score Summary Sheet immediately behind it. Before each answer sheet key is a page giving the factor and a statement of the number of subtests involved. This is intended to enable the busy practitioner, or his assistant, quickly to find the place in the Handbook where scoring instructions are found for a particular source trait.

At the moment, no stencil keys have been published for these answer sheets, and the user not employing an optical scanner is advised to take ordinary clerical folders or some transparent sheet and cut or mark the answer positions as given here. There is no other way of obtaining the first derived raw scores, though all other computations may be done with a computer, as described earlier, both for the single factor batteries and, with computer synthesis, for the whole Kit. However, even if scoring is to be done by hand as on the Score Summary Sheets, the process is very simple and quick—far simpler, say, than the citizen's task of completing a sheet from the Internal Revenue Service! With a little practice it should be reliably executed by clerical help in a few minutes.

It will often be helpful to have a specimen set of the actual O-A subtests on hand when scoring, as some anomalous uses of the answer sheet can then be more readily caught and perhaps "translated" into their proper meaning.

Table 8.1

**SCORING INSTRUCTIONS: Score Summary Sheets,
Specimen Answer Sheets, and Numerical Calculations
for Each Factor of the Main Kit**

Note

The means and weights for these single-factor score sheets have in general been derived from subtest means and sigmas in a late-high-school population, and from the factor estimation matrix in the study by Cattell, Schuerger, Klein, and Finkbeiner (1976). A few values have been modified to preserve consistency with earlier programmatic researches, and a policy of simplifying values has been followed here to facilitate computation. Greater precision may be obtained, as noted in Chapter 7, by using the computer synthesis method with the entire battery.

Scoring

for

U.I. 16

Ego Standards

Eight Subtests

Scoring Material

      1. Keyed Answer Sheets, Sides 1 and 2

      2. Score Summary Sheet

_____

No Expendable Booklets or Special Scoring Instruction Sheets involved.

PRINT YOUR NAME IN THE BOXES PROVIDED, THEN BLACKEN THE LETTER BOX BELOW WHICH MATCHES EACH LETTER OF YOUR NAME.

YOUR LAST NAME

YOUR FIRST NAME

MI

Use pencil only.

Be sure each mark is black and completely fills the space.

Erase completely any answer you wish to change.

IDENTIFICATION NUMBER

AGE To Nearest Year

SEX GRADE

TODAY'S DATE

HSOA 16 - Side 1

ATTITUDES   Score - Number Done

	a b c d e		a b c d e		a b c d e		a b c d e		a b c d e		a b c d e
	1	2		3		4		5		6	
a b c d e 7	a b c d e 8	a b c d e 9	a b c d e 10	a b c d e 11	a b c d e 12	a b c d e 13	a b c d e 14
a b c d e 15	a b c d e 16	a b c d e 17	a b c d e 18	a b c d e 19	a b c d e 20	a b c d e 21	a b c d e 22
a b c d e 23	a b c d e 24	a b c d e 25	a b c d e 26	a b c d e 27	a b c d e 28	a b c d e 29	a b c d e 30

CODING   Score - Number Done

a e i o u

1	2	3	4	5	6	7	8
9	10	11	12	13	14	15	16
17	18	19	20	21	22	23	24
25	26	27	28	29	30	31	32
33	34	35	36	37	38	39	40
41	42	43	44	45	46	47	48
49	50	51	52	53	54	55	56
57	58	59	60	61	62	63	64
65	66	67	68	69	70	71	72
73	74	75	76	77	78	79	80

LETTER AND NUMBER COMPARISON   Score - Number Done

D S

1	2	3	4	5	6	7	8
9	10	11	12	13	14	15	16	17	18	19	20	21	22	23	24
25	26	27	28	29	30	31	32	33	34	35	36	37	38	39	40
								41	42	43	44	45	46	47	48
49	50	51	52	53	54	55	56	57	58	59	60	61	62	63	64
65	66	67	68	69	70	71	72	73	74	75	76	77	78	79	80

IPAT

NAME

© 1971, IPAT

172

Use pencil only.

Be sure each mark is black and completely fills the space.

Erase completely any answer you wish to change.

IDENTIFICATION NUMBER

GOODNESS OF WORK I Score - Number Done

	a b c d e
1 2 3 4 5 6 7 8	
9 10 11 12 13 14 15 16	

MODERNISTIC DRAWINGS Score - Number Done

a b c
1 2 3 4 5 6 7 8 9 10
11 12 13 14 15 16 17 18 19 20
21 22 23 24 25 26 27 28 29 30

ASSUMPTIONS Score - Number Done T F

T F
1 2 3 4 5 6 7 8 9 10 11 12 13 14 15
16 17 18 19 20 21 22 23 24 25 26 27 28 29 30

RAPID CALCULATION Score - Number Right

a b
1 2 3 4 5 6 7 8 9 10 11 12 13 14 15 16
17 18 19 20 21 22 23 24 25 26 27 28 29 30 31 32
33 34 35 36 37 38 39 40 41 42 43 44 45 46 47 48
49 50 51 52 53 54 55 56 57 58 59 60 61 62 63 64
65 66 67 68 69 70 71 72 73 74 75 76 77 78 79 80

Sample

MY INTERESTS Score - Number Done

I N
1 2 3 4
5 6 7 8 9 10 11 12 13 14 15 16 17 18 19 20
21 22 23 24 25 26 27 28 29 30 31 32 33 34 35 36

TODAY'S DATE

HSOA 16 - Side 2

NAME

© 1971, IPAT

173

U.I. 16   SCORE SUMMARY SHEET

Test No. on Ans. Sht	T Number MI Number	Psychologist's Title (Examinee's Title)	Derived Raw-Score Formula	(1) Derived Raw Score	(2) Mean of Derived Raw Scores m	(3) (1) minus (2)	(4) Weight w	(5) Special Subtest Standard Score (3) multiplied by (4) = z'
1	361 244	Quicker Social Judgment (Attitudes)	Number done		10.71		.02	
2	49a 6d	Higher Coding Speed (Coding)	Number done (2 parts)		29.24		.03	
3	44a 307	Quicker Letter-Number Comparison (Letter and Number Comparison)	Number done (2 parts)		38.00		.04	
4	8a 288	Quicker Judgment (Goodness of Work I)	Number done		9.81		.07	
5	20a 282	More Seen in Unstructured Drawings (Modernistic Drawings)	Number done (3 pictures)		13.29		.02	
6	11a 2409	More Logical Assumptions Done (Assumptions I)	Number done		19.59		.01	
7	35a 199	Greater Simple Numerical Performance (Rapid Calculation)	Number right (2 parts)		26.70		.04	
8	43b 2410	Greater Fluency on Objects (selective) (My Interests)	Number done		34.27		.03	
							Sum =	Factor Score

Key: The pattern of answers, given in blocks of four for convenience in keeping track of the number of the item, is as follows:

babb abab bbaa aabb babb bbab aaaa aabb bbaa
abab babb abaa abba baab aabb abaa bbab aabb bbaa

For example, the answer to number 1 is "b", to number 2, "a", to number 3, "b", . . . , to number 80, "a".

To get the factor score in z-score form for each subject, obtain the "derived score" (Col. 1) according to formula for each subtest, subtract the appropriate "m" value (Col. 2) from Col. 1 score, multiply the difference (Col. 3) by the appropriate "w" value (Col. 4). This procedure gives the special subtest standard score, z' (Col. 5). Add Col. 5 to get the factor score in "z-score" form for the subject. Note the prime on the z is to remind one that these are not ordinary but "special" standard score components. See page 169.

174

Scoring

for

U.I. 19

Independence

Seven Subtests

Scoring Materials

    1. **Keyed Answer Sheet**

    2. **Score Summary Sheet**

No Expendable Booklets or Special Scoring Instruction Sheets involved.

PRINT YOUR NAME IN THE BOXES PROVIDED, THEN BLACKEN THE
LETTER BOX BELOW WHICH MATCHES EACH LETTER OF YOUR NAME

YOUR FIRST NAME

YOUR LAST NAME

MI

Use pencil only.

Be sure each mark is black and completely fills the space.

Erase completely any answer you wish to change.

IDENTIFICATION NUMBER

AGE   TEET   Nearest Year

SEX   G R A D E

HSOA 19

TODAY'S DATE

NAME

PROBLEMS No. right ÷ No. done

	a b c d e		a b c d e		a b c d e		a b c d e
1		2		3		4	

| 5 | 6 | 7 | 8 | 9 | 10 |

| 11 | 12 | 13 | 14 |

| 15 | 16 | 17 | 18 | 19 | 20 |

HIDDEN SHAPES No. right ÷ No. done

| 1 | 2 | 3 | 4 | 5 | 6 |

READING COMPREHENSION
No. right ÷ No. done

| 7 | 8 | 9 | 10 | 11 | 12 |

| 1 | 2 | 3 | 4 | 5 | 6 | 7 | 8 | 9 | 10 | 11 | 12 | 13 | 14 | 15 |

| 16 | 17 | 18 | 19 | 20 | 21 | 22 | 23 | 24 | 25 | 26 | 27 | 28 | 29 | 30 |

WHAT IS THE RIGHT DESIGN? No. right ÷ No. done

| 1 | 2 | 3 | 4 | 5 | 6 | 7 |

| 8 | 9 | 10 | 11 | 12 | 13 | 14 | 15 |

SEARCHING No. right

| 1 | 2 | 3 | 4 |

| 5 | 6 | 7 | 8 | 9 | 10 | 11 | 12 |

PICTURE MEMORY
No. right ÷ No. done

| 1 | 2 | 3 | 4 | 5 |

| 6 | 7 | 8 | 9 | 10 |

OBSERVATION No. right ÷ No. done

| 1 | 2 | 3 | 4 |

| 5 | 6 | 7 | 8 | 9 | 10 | 11 |

| 12 | 13 | 14 | 15 | 16 | 17 | 18 |

| 19 | 20 | 21 | 22 | 23 | 24 | 25 |

176

U.I. 19   SCORE SUMMARY SHEET

				(1)	(2)	(3)	(4)	(5)
Test No. on Ans. Sht	T Number MI Number	Psychologist's Title (Examinee's Title)	Derived Raw-Score Formula	Derived Raw Score	Mean of Derived Raw Scores m	(1) minus (2)	Weight w	Special Subtest Standard Score (3) multiplied by (4) = z'
1	35b 120f	High Accuracy/Speed — Numerical (Problems) Key: The pattern of answers, starting with number 1, is as follows: debda ecada cabeb acbda	$\dfrac{\text{Number right}}{\text{Number done}} =$		.71		1.5	
2	37 206	Gottschaldt Figures % Correct (Hidden Shapes) Key: The pattern of answers, starting with number 1, is as follows: ceabba eceace	$\dfrac{\text{Number right}}{\text{Number done}} =$		.73		1.5	
3	6a 167c	Immediate Memory (Reading Comprehension) Key: The pattern of answers, starting with number 1, is as follows: YNYYN YNNYN NYNNY YNNNY YNNYY	$\dfrac{\text{Number right}}{\text{Number done}} =$		.84		1.2	
4	422 2367	More Orderliness in Perceptual Series (What Is the Right Design?) Key: The pattern of answers, starting with number 1, is as follows: caaed addac eacca	$\dfrac{\text{Number right}}{\text{Number done}} =$		.60		.8	
5	328 1387	More Correct in Searching Task (Searching) Key: The pattern of answers, starting with number 1, is as follows: cebdca acdeab	Number right		7.60		.1	
6	242a 689	Greater Accuracy of Picture Memory (Picture Memory) Key: The pattern of answers, starting with number 1, is as follows: dbeac cbdae	$\dfrac{\text{Number right}}{\text{Number done}} =$		.84		2.1	
7	114 51	Higher Index of Carefulness (Observation) Key: The pattern of answers, starting with number 1, is as follows: aebee cedee deaab eeded cadac	$\dfrac{\text{Number right}}{\text{Number done}} =$		.77		.9	

Numerical Columns

Sum = Factor Score

To get the factor score in z-score form for each subject, obtain the "derived score" (Col. 1) according to formula for each subtest, subtract the appropriate "m" value (Col. 2) from Col. 1 score, multiply the difference (Col. 3) by the appropriate "w" value (Col. 4). This procedure gives the special subtest standard score, z' (Col. 5). Add Col. 5 to get the factor score in "z-score" form for the subject.

177

Scoring

for

U.I. 20

Evasiveness

Seven Subtests

Seven Performance Scores

Scoring Materials

1. Keyed Answer Sheet

2. Score Summary Sheet

3. Four Special Scoring Instruction Sheets

No Expendable Booklets involved.

U.I. 20 KEYED ANSWER SHEET

Use pencil only.

Be sure each mark is black and completely fills the space.

Erase completely any answer you wish to change.

IDENTIFICATION NUMBER

TEST / NEAREST Year — AGE

SEX — G B

GRADE

TODAY'S DATE

HSOA 20

TEST 1

Example: A. IN ORDER TO GET AHEAD IN LIFE, YOU HAVE TO WORK HARD.
[Definitely agree, because stories about the lives of important men show most of them worked hard.]
a) strongly agree b) agree c) uncertain d) disagree e) strongly disagree

OPINIONS I (See Special Scoring Instruction Sheet.)

A   1   2

| a b c d e | a b c d e | a b c d e | a b c d e | a b c d e | a b c d e | a b c d e | a b c d e |
| 3 | 4 | 5 | 6 | 7 | 8 | 9 | 10 |

TEST 2

OPINIONS II (See Special Scoring Instruction Sheet.)

a b c d e	a b c d e	a b c d e	a b c d e	a b c d e	a b c d e	a b c d e	a b c d e
1	2	3	4	5	6	7	8
9	10	11	12	13	14	15	16
17	18	19	20	21	22	23	24

TEST 3

OPINIONS III (See Special Scoring Instruction Sheet.)

a b c d e	a b c d e	a b c d e	a b c d e	a b c d e	a b c d e
1	2	3	4	5	6
7	8	9	10	11	12	13	14

TEST 4

MEMORY (See Special Scoring Instruction Sheet.)

Y N	Y N	Y N	Y N	Y N	Y N	Y N	Y N	Y N	Y N	Y N	Y N	Y N	Y N
1	2	3	4	5	6	7	8	9	10	11	12	13	14
15	16	17	18	19	20	21	22	23	24	25	26	27	28

TEST 5

OPINIONS IV (See Scoring for Test 1, Opinions I)

a b c d e	a b c d e	a b c d e	a b c d e	a b c d e
1	2	3	4	5
6	7	8	9	10

---

6 COMMON ANNOYANCES Sum of scores on items ÷ No. done

Example: A. Windows that stick when you try to close them.
a) very annoyed   b) a little annoyed   c) not at all annoyed

A   3 2 1

| 3 2 1 | 3 2 1 | 3 2 1 | 3 2 1 |
| 1 | 2 | 3 | 4 |

| 3 2 1 | 3 2 1 | 3 2 1 | 3 2 1 | 3 2 1 | 3 2 1 | 3 2 1 | 3 2 1 | 3 2 1 | 3 2 1 | 3 2 1 | 3 2 1 |
| 5 | 6 | 7 | 8 | 9 | 10 | 11 | 12 | 13 | 14 | 15 | 16 |

7 HUMAN NATURE I Sum of item scores ÷ No. done

Example: A. Most teachers are really interested in helping their students learn.
a) strongly agree   b) agree   c) uncertain   d) disagree   e) strongly disagree

A   a b c d e

5 4 3 2 1	5 4 3 2 1	1 2 3 4 5	5 4 3 2 1	1 2 3 4 5
1	2	3	4	5
6	7	8	9	10	11	12	13

| 5 4 3 2 1 | 5 4 3 2 1 | 5 4 3 2 1 | 1 2 3 4 5 | 5 4 3 2 1 | 5 4 3 2 1 | 1 2 3 4 5 | 5 4 3 2 1 |

NAME

IPAT
© 1971, IPAT

U.I. 20 SCORE SUMMARY SHEET

Test No.	Performance Score Number	T Number / MI Number	Psychologist's Title (Examinee's Title)	Derived Raw-Score Formula	(1) Derived Raw Score	(2) Mean of Derived Raw Scores m	(3) (1) minus (2)	(4) Weight w	(5) Special Subtest Standard Score (3) multiplied by (4) = z'
1	1	10b(1) 34	Insecurity of Opinion (Opinions I) See Special Scoring Instruction Sheet No. 1 for details of scoring.	$\dfrac{\Sigma(\text{Test }5 - \text{Test }1)}{\text{No. pairs}} =$		1.14		.1	
2	2	9g 65	Less Logical Consistency of Attitude (Opinions II) See Special Scoring Instruction Sheet No. 2 for details of scoring.	$\dfrac{\Sigma\lvert A_i + B_j - 2C_i\rvert}{\text{No. of complete clusters}} =$		2.67		.2	
3		9bj(1) 38	Not scored as such, but in relation to Test 4, following (Opinions III)	No score here					
4	3	9bj(2) 38	Ratio Consonant/Dissonant Recognition (Memory) See Special Scoring Instruction Sheet No. 3 for details of scoring.	$\dfrac{AY - AN + 15}{DY - DN + 15} =$		.74		.01	
5		10b(2) 34	Not scored as such, but already used in relation to Test 1 (Opinions IV)						
6	4	38a 211a	More Susceptibility to Annoyances (Common Annoyances) Note: Sum refers to a sum of item values, where a = 3, b = 2, c = 1.	$\dfrac{\Sigma \text{ item scores}}{\text{No. done}} =$		2.04		.04	
7	5	16b 100b	More Pessimistic Insecurity (Human Nature I) Note: Items No. 3, 5, 9, and 12 score a = 1, b = 2, c = 3, d = 4, e = 5. All other items score in the opposite direction, i.e., a = 5, b = 4, c = 3, d = 2, e = 1.	$\dfrac{\Sigma \text{ item scores}}{\text{No. done}} =$		2.8		.8	
	6	10b(1) 9 9bj(1) 152b	Tendency to Agree See Special Scoring Instruction Sheet No. 4 for details of scoring.	$\dfrac{\Sigma \text{MI } 152b}{\text{No. done}} =$		3.58		.4	
	7	10b(1) 9 9bj(1) 67a	Extremity of Response See Special Scoring Instruction Sheet No. 4 for details of scoring.	$\dfrac{\Sigma \text{MI } 67a}{\text{No. done}} =$		2.20		3.0	

Sum = Factor Score

To get the factor score in z-score form for each subject, obtain the "derived score" (Col. 1) according to formula for each subject, subtract the appropriate "m" value (Col. 2) from Col. 1 score, multiply the difference (Col. 3) by the appropriate "w" value (Col. 4). This procedure gives the special subtest standard score, z' (Col. 5). Add Col. 5 to get the factor score in "z-score" form for the subject.

180

T10b(1) and T10b(2), Test 1 and Test 5 in U.I. 20 booklet (MI 34) Insecurity of opinion

The rationale for this test is that persons taking the two sets of items, identical except for the influencing statement in parentheses at the end, will be insecure in their opinions to the extent that they shift in the direction of persuasion.

Each item in Test 1 is paired with the same numbered item in Test 5, so the difference between item values (as usual, $a = 5$, $b = 4$, $c = 3$, etc.) is an index of shift of opinion, that is, of change of opinion on the two occasions.

However, a higher score on the second occasion is a persuasion shift on items 1, 2, 3, 8, and 10, whereas a lower second score is a persuasion shift on 4, 5, 6, 7, and 9. To use the scheme below, enter the numerical value of response for each item in Test 1 and Test 5. Subtract the Test 1 value *from* the Test 5 value, and enter the remainder in the column to the right, leaving it with the same sign in 4, 5, 6, 7, and 9, and changing the sign to the opposite in 1, 2, 3, 8, and 10 (change of sign questions noted by shaded "difference" boxes). *If one item in the pair was not marked in either test, do not count that pair.*

Add up (algebraically) all the values in the column at the right, and divide the total by the number of completed pairs. The result is the derived score for MI 34.

Formula:
$$\frac{\Sigma\,(T_5 - T_1)}{\text{No. pairs}}$$

Where   Test 1_i is the value for a response to an item on Test 1,
Test 2_i is the value for a response to an item on Test 2,
Number done refers to the number of completed pairs.

Scoring scheme: To quantify responses, let $a = 5$, $b = 4$, $c = 3$, $d = 2$, $e = 1$

Item number	Test 5	Test 1	Difference	Corrected Direction of Difference
1				+ −
2				+ −
3				+ −
4				
5				
6				
7				
8				+ −
9				
10				+ −

SUM = [   ]

÷

No. of Pairs = [   ]

=

Derived
Raw Score
For U.I. 20 = [   ]
Test 1

181

T9g, Test 2 in U.I. 20 booklet   (MI 65) Less logical consistency of attitude

Items representing attitudes, formulated so that they are clusters of three sentences in quasi-syllogistic form, are scrambled throughout this test. Persons who agree with the two premises might be expected to agree with the attitudinal conclusion. Scoring is such that if responses to the three in a cluster are not prima facie consistent, the person gets a higher score.

To use the scoring scheme below, put the item response values in the places indicated, double the value for the third response as shown, do the addition and subtraction, and enter the result as an absolute number in the column to the right. Then add that column and divide by the number of triads completed, where a triad is taken to be a complete quasi-syllogism consisting of the three items in the cluster.

Formula:

$$\frac{\sum_{i=1}^{8} |A_i + B_i - 2C_i|}{\text{Number of complete clusters}}$$

Where A_i is a numerical value for a response to the first item in a cluster,
B_i is a numerical value for a response to the second item in a cluster,
C_i is a numerical value for a response to the third item in a cluster.
Summed for the number of completed clusters or triads.

Scoring scheme:
(a = 5, b = 4, c = 3, d = 2, e = 1, except for items 2, 8, 20, 23, for which a = 1, b = 2, c = 3, d = 4, e = 5)

Cluster Number	A plus	B minus	2 C	Cluster Absolute Score
1	item 1 _____	+ item 3 _____	— item 14 _____	=
2	item 4 _____	+ item 6 _____	—item 17 _____	
3	item 7 _____	+ item 9 _____	— item 20 _____	
4	item 10 _____	+ item 12 _____	— item 23 _____	
5	item 13 _____	+ item 15 _____	— item 2 _____	
6	item 16 _____	+ item 18 _____	— item 5 _____	
7	item 19 _____	+ item 21 _____	— item 8 _____	
8	item 22 _____	+ item 24 _____	— item 11 _____	

Sum =
÷

Number of
Complete Clusters   =

=

Derived Raw Score

182

U.I. 20 Special Scoring Instruction Sheet (No. 3): (For Tests 3 and 4 together)

T9bj(1) and T9bj(2), Test 3 and Test 4 in U.I. 20 booklet   (MI 38) Ratio of consonant to dissonant recognition

This variable is a ratio of correctly recognized phrases under two conditions: that the phrases were agreed with on a previous test, or disagreed with. Of the 28 recognition items in Test 4, 14 actually occurred in Test 3. Of these 14 which did occur, the subject will presumably have agreed with some in Test 3, disagreed with others. The 14 which did not occur in Test 3 but did in Test 4 are "padding," with which we are not concerned.

To use the scoring scheme below, first mark each item in Test 3 column either A for agree (if the subject marked A or B) or D for disagree (if the subject marked D or E), i.e., there is no 1-5 scoring here. Then mark the selected items in the Test 4 column, Y if the subject responded "Y" or N if the subject responded "N". Each row is then either an "AY", "AN", "DY", or "DN". Count the number of each type of row and proceed to the following.

Formula:
$$\frac{AY - AN + 15}{DY - DN + 15}$$

Where   AY is the number of rows correctly recognized in Test 4 to which the subject agreed in Test 3
AN is the number of rows not recognized in Test 4 to which the subject agreed in Test 3,
DY is the number of rows correctly recognized in Test 4 to which the subject disagreed in Test 3,
DN is the number of rows not recognized in Test 4 to which the subject disagreed in Test 3.

The value 15 is added simply to improve distribution properties.

Scoring scheme:

U.I. 20 Test 3 Item Number	Agree or Disagree	U.I. 20 Test 4 Item Number	Right or Wrong
1		1	
2		2	
3		4	
4		8	
5		10	
6		12	
7		13	
8		17	
9		19	
10		21	
11		22	
12		23	
13		25	
14		26	

No. of AY rows _____

No of AN rows _____

No. of DY rows _____

No. of DN rows _____

(count only complete rows)

AY _____ — AN _____ + 15 = _____
DY _____ — DN _____ + 15 =

MI 38 Derived Score for U.I. 20 [   ]

**T10b(1), T9g, T9bj(1), Test 1, Test 2, and Test 3 in U.I. 20 (MI 152b) Tendency to agree, (MI 67a)
Extremity of response**

These are not particularly complicated to score, but represent one instance in which more than one variable is obtained from a set of responses. The original use of these two scores as personality measures (Cattell, 1948; Cattell & Gruen, 1955) was later developed in "response style" literature (Cronbach, 1946; Messick & Ross, 1962; Wardell & Royce, 1975).

Both variables are calculated by taking the numerical sum of quantified responses, and dividing by the number done to adjust for response speed, but while the values for MI 152b are the usual (a = 5, b = 4, c = 3, etc.), the values of responses for MI 67a give greater weight to extreme responses (a = 3, b = 2, c = 1, d = 2, e = 3).

To use the scoring scheme below, first count, in Tests 1, 2, and 3, the number of "a" responses, "b" responses, etc. Then multiply the number of responses by the appropriate value *for each MI (variable)*. Sum each column, and do the divisions indicated.

Scoring scheme:

	Test 1 T10b(1)	Test 2 T9g	Test 3 T9bj(1)	Total Tests 1, 2, & 3	MI 152b	MI 67a
Number of "a" responses					x 5 =	x 3 =
Number of "b" responses					x 4 =	x 2 =
Number of "c" responses					x 3 =	x 1 =
Number of "d" responses					x 2 =	x 2 =
Number of "e" responses					x 1 =	x 3 =
			Number Done =		Sum =	Sum =

$$\text{Performance Score 6} = \frac{\Sigma \text{ MI 152b}}{\text{Number Done}} = \underline{\hspace{3cm}} = \boxed{}$$

(Tendency to Agree)

$$\text{Performance Score 7} = \frac{\Sigma \text{ MI 67a}}{\text{Number Done}} = \underline{\hspace{3cm}} = \boxed{}$$

(Extremity of Response)

184

Scoring

for

U.I. 21

Exuberance

Eight Subtests

Scoring Materials

1. Instructions for Scoring All on Score Summary Sheet

   Eight Subtests All in Expendable Booklet

No answer sheet or Special Scoring Instruction Sheets involved

U.I. 21   SCORE SUMMARY SHEET

					Numerical Columns			
				(1)	(2)	(3)	(4)	(5)
Test No. on Ans. Sht	T Number MI Number	Psychologist's Title (Examinee's Title)	Derived Raw-Score Formula	Derived Raw Score	Mean of Derived Raw Scores m	(1) minus (2)	Weight w	Special Subtest Standard Score (3) multiplied by (4) = z'
1	411d 335b	Faster Marking Speed (Following Directions Quickly)	Number done		15.11		.05	
		Note: Simply count the number of boxes marked, whether they are correct or not.						
2	43a 271	Higher Ideational Fluency (Ideas)	Number done (2 pages)		44.40		.07	
		Note: Count number of words or ideas on the two pages of the test. If in doubt of a word or phrase, count it so long as it starts with the correct letters. Any idea is accepted.						
3	88a 853	More Concrete Drawing Completion (Drawings I)	Number named (2 parts)		5.90		.04	
		Note: After drawing figures, subjects are asked to write in names of the ones that are real things. Count the total number of drawings named on both pages, accepting even questionable cases.						
4	164a 699	More Garbled Words Guessed (Can You Hear the Word?)	Number done		11.30		.07	
		Note: Count the number of words written.						
5	2d 7	Faster Speed of Gestalt Completion (Incomplete Pictures)	Number done (2 parts)		12.00		.06	
		Note: Count the number of pictures named on the two pages.						
6	3 8	Higher Frequency of Alternating Perspective ("In and Out")	Number marked (2 parts)		45.70		.01	
		Note: Count the number of marks on the "MARK HERE" line on both pages. Some subjects will mistakenly mark on the double line near the top of the page. These should be counted.						
7	51 28b	Greater Dynamic Momentum: Dictation (Listening and Writing)	Number words written (2 parts)		57.10		.02	
		Note: Count the number of words written on the two pages.						
8	136a 264	Faster Speed of Tapping (Tapping)	Number of blocks marked (2 parts)		62.20		.01	
		Note: Scan the blocks to see that there are in general 4 dots per block, or 4 largely in each block. Then count the blocks done. If examinee repeatedly drops below 4 to a block, do not count blocks with less than 4 dots.						
								Sum = Factor Score

To get the factor score in z-score form for each subject, obtain the "derived score" (Col. 1) according to formula for each subtest, subtract the appropriate "m" value (Col. 2) from Col. 1 score, multiply the difference (Col. 3) by the appropriate "w" value (Col. 4). This procedure gives the special subtest standard score, z' (Col. 5). Add Col. 5 to get the factor score in "z-score" form for the subject.

Scoring

for

U.I. 23

Mobilization-vs-Regression

Eight Subtests

Scoring Materials

1. **Keyed Answer Sheet (for 7 tests)**

2. **Score Summary Sheet**
    Note: Scoring for 8th test, in Expendable Booklet, given
    on Score Summary Sheet

3. **One Special Scoring Instruction Sheet**

PRINT YOUR NAME IN THE BOXES PROVIDED, THEN BLACKEN THE LETTER BOX BELOW WHICH MATCHES EACH LETTER OF YOUR NAME.

YOUR LAST NAME   YOUR FIRST NAME   MI

Use pencil only.

Be sure each mark is black and completely fills the space.

Erase completely any answer you wish to change.

IDENTIFICATION NUMBER

AGE — To Nearest Year

GRADE

TODAY'S DATE

HSOA 23

TEST 1

Example: **ANNOYANCES**

A. Toys that break easily.
a) very much b) a little c) not

See Special Scoring Instruction Sheet.

1 2 3 4 5 6 7 8
9 10 11 12 13 14 15 16 17 18 19 20

TEST 2

COMPARING LETTERS

No. right ÷ No. done (both parts added)

1 2 3 4 5 6 7 8
9 10 11 12 13 14 15 16 17 18 19 20 21 22 23 24
25 26 27 28 29 30 31 32 33 34 35 36 37 38 39 40
41 42 43 44 45 46 47 48
49 50 51 52 53 54 55 56 57 58 59 60 61 62 63 64
65 66 67 68 69 70 71 72 73 74 75 76 77 78 79 80

3

WHERE DO LINES CROSS?

Example: A. 1B — DC

No. right − ¼ No. wrong ÷ No. done

1 2 3 4 5 6 7 8
9 10 11 12 13 14 15 16

4

WHICH WOULD YOU RATHER DO?   No. right ÷ No. done

1 2 3 4 5 6 7 8 9 10 11 12 13 14 15 16

5

ASSUMPTIONS II   No. right ÷ No. done

Example: A. Bossie is contented because she is a cow.

ONE 1 2 3 4 5   TWO 6 7 8 9 10
THREE 11 12 13 14 15   FOUR 16 17 18 19 20

WHAT DO YOU SEE?

1 3 6 9 12
13 15 16 19
22 24 26 29 30 32
34 36 37 40

MATCHING WORDS   No. right ÷ No. done

1 2 3 4 5 6 7 8 9 10 11 12

IPAT

NAME

© 1971, IPAT

188

U.I. 23 SCORE SUMMARY SHEET

Test No.	T Number / MI Number	Psychologist's Title (Examinee's Title)	Derived Raw-Score Formula	(1) Derived Raw Score	(2) Mean of Derived Raw Scores m	(3) (1) minus (2)	(4) Weight w	(5) Special Subtest Standard Score (3) multiplied by (4) = z'
1	38b / 242	Higher Ratio Social/Nonsocial Annoyances (Annoyances)	$\dfrac{\Sigma \text{ odd}/\text{No. done odd}}{\Sigma \text{ even}/\text{No. done even}} =$ See Special Scoring Instruction Sheet for details of scoring.		1.05		.2	
2	44c / 120b	Higher Ratio Accuracy/Speed in Letter-Number Comparison (Comparing Letters)	$\dfrac{\text{Number right}}{\text{Number done}} =$ (2 parts) Key: DSDDS SDSSS SDDDS SDDDS SDSDD SSSSD SDDSD DDSDD SDDSD SSDDS DDSDS DDSDS		.88		1.0	
3	112 / 609	Higher Perceptual Coordination (Where Do Lines Cross?)	$\dfrac{\text{No. right} - \frac14 \text{ wrong}}{\text{No. done}} =$ (2 parts) Key: aebd edcb bdae bcbc		.70		1.8	
4	197 / 401	Less Preference for Competitive Associations (Which Would You Rather Do?)	$\dfrac{\text{Number right}}{\text{Number done}} =$ Key: aabb abba abbb bbab		.71		1.5	
5	11b / 36	High Ability to State Logical Assumptions (Assumptions II)	$\dfrac{\text{Number right}}{\text{Number done}} =$ (2 parts) Key: FFTFF TTFFF TFFFF FFTFF		.70		4.0	
6	20b / 105	Fewer Threatening Objects Seen (What Do You See?)	$\dfrac{\text{Number right}}{\text{Number done}} =$ Key: Consider only the following items: 2, 4, 5, 7, 10, 11, 14, 17, 18, 20, 21, 23, 25, 27, 28, 31, 33, 35, 38, 39. The total among these marked N is the right score. The number of these marked N or Y is the number done.		.65		.2	
7	224b / 714	Fewer Rhyming and Alliterative Words Chosen (Matching Words)	$\dfrac{\text{Number right}}{\text{Number done}} =$ Key: abcba cbacc cc		.87		.02	
8	1a / 2a(1)	Lower Rigidity: Backward Writing (How Fast Can You Write?)	$\dfrac{\Sigma \text{Part III}}{\Sigma \text{Part I}} + \dfrac{\Sigma \text{Part IV}}{\Sigma \text{Part II}} =$ Note: This test is from the expendable booklet. In the formula above, the "Sum" refers to the number of letters written in each part. Do not count any words accidentally spelled backwards in getting the four sums.		.20		.2	
							Sum = Factor Score	

To get the factor score in z-score form for each subject, obtain the "derived score" (Col. 1) according to formula for each subtest, subtract the appr... "m" value (Col. 2) from Col. 1 score, multiply the difference (Col. 3) by the appropriate "w" value (Col. 4). This procedure gives the special subtest si... score, z' (Col. 5). Add Col. 5 to get the factor score in "z-score" form for the subject.

189

T38b (MI 242) Higher ratio of social to nonsocial annoyances

The rationale for this test is that some persons are more annoyed by social inconveniences than by nonhuman sources of irritation.

To use the scoring scheme below, first get the four subtotals, find the values S and N, then do the final division; i.e., divide the item sum by the number done for social annoyance items, divide the item sum by the number done for the nonsocial annoyance items, then divide the first quotient by the second.

Formula:

$$\frac{\dfrac{\text{Item Score Sum Social Items}}{\text{Number done social items (odd items)}}}{\dfrac{\text{Item Score Sum Nonsocial Items}}{\text{Number done nonsocial items (even items)}}}$$

Where   Sum social items is a usual item sum (a = 3, b = 2, c = 1), taken only on the odd (1, 3, 5, etc.) items.

Other subtotals are similar.

Scoring scheme:

Item sum for odd items	ΣO _____	⟶	$\dfrac{\Sigma O}{\text{NOD}}$ = S	_____
Number done for odd items	NOD _____	⟶		
Item sum for even items	ΣE _____	⟶	$\dfrac{\Sigma E}{\text{NED}}$ = N	_____
Number done for even items	NED _____	⟶		

$$\frac{S}{N} = \underline{\quad\quad}$$

Test 1. MI 242 = ☐

190

Scoring

for

U.I. 24

Anxiety

Eight Subtests

Scoring Materials

1. Keyed Answer Sheet

2. Score Summary Sheet

3. One Special Scoring Instruction Sheet

No Expendable Booklets involved.

U.I. 24 KEYED ANSWER SHEET

PRINT YOUR NAME IN THE BOXES PROVIDED, THEN BLACKEN THE LETTER BOX BELOW WHICH MATCHES EACH LETTER OF YOUR NAME

YOUR LAST NAME

YOUR FIRST NAME

MI

IDENTIFICATION NUMBER

AGE Nearest Year

SEX

Use pencil only.

Be sure each mark is black and completely fills the space.

Erase completely any answer you wish to change.

TODAY'S DATE

HSOA 24

HUMOR TEST
Sum of item scores ÷ Number done

DO YOU SOMETIMES? Sum ÷ Number done

WHAT'S YOUR COMMENT?
Number right ÷ Number done

PUTTING UP WITH THINGS
See Special Scoring Instruction Sheet

WHAT BOTHERS ME
Sum of item scores ÷ Number done

FAVORITE TITLES Number right ÷ Number done

If

© 1971, IPAT

IPAT

NAME

192

U.I. 24 SCORE SUMMARY SHEET

Test No. on Ans. Sht	T Number / MI Number	Psychologist's Title (Examinee's Title)	Derived Raw-Score Formula	(1) Derived Raw Score	(2) Mean of Derived Raw Scores m	(3) (1) minus (2)	(4) Weight w	(5) Special Subtest Standard Score (3) multiplied by (4) = z'
1	430 / 2404(2)	Preference for Outright Humor (Humor Test). Note: Before computing the sum of item values, set the *even* item responses to a = 4, b = 3, c = 2, d = 1, coding, and the *odd* item responses to a = 1, b = 2, c = 3, d = 4.	$\dfrac{\text{Sum of item scores}}{\text{Number done}} =$		3.04		.04	
2	27b / 117b	Less Alertness to Highbrow Tastes (How Do You Like . . . ?). Note: Before computing the sum, set the "highbrow" items (items 1, 4, 6, 8, 9, 11, 12, 14, 16) to a = 1, b = 2, c = 3, d = 4, e = 5. All other item values are a = 5, b = 4, c = 3, d = 2, e = 1.	$\dfrac{\text{Sum of item scores}}{\text{Number done}} =$		3.40		.4	
3	41a / 219	More Common Frailties Admitted (Do You Sometimes . . . ?). Note: Even items set to a = 1, b = 2, c = 3, etc. Odd items set to a = 5, b = 4, c = 3, etc.	$\dfrac{\text{Sum of item scores}}{\text{Number done}} =$		2.89		.7	
4	36 / 205	More Emotionality of Comment (What's Your Comment?) Key: bbcbc cc	$\dfrac{\text{Number right}}{\text{Number done}} =$		0.29		.7	
5	187a / 218	More Willingness to Play Practical Jokes (Jokes and Tricks). Note: 'Y' is counted right for all items.	$\dfrac{\text{Number right}}{\text{Number done}} =$		0.62		1.5	
6	163a / 1370	Less Compliance (Putting Up With Things). Note: See Special Scoring Instruction Sheet for details of scoring.	$\dfrac{\text{Sum of item scores}}{\text{Number done}} =$		2.28		.06	
7	38c / 211b	Higher Susceptibility to Annoyances Involving Ego Threats (What Bothers Me). Note: Item values are a = 3, b = 2, c = 1.	$\dfrac{\text{Sum of item scores}}{\text{Number done}} =$		2.15		.7	
8	25 / 321	Book Preferences: More Questionable Taste Preferences (Favorite Titles). Key: aaaab abaaa aa	$\dfrac{\text{Number right}}{\text{Number done}} =$		0.70		.7	

Numerical Columns

Sum = Factor Score

To get the factor score in z-score form for each subject, obtain the "derived score" (Col. 1) according to formula for each subtest, subtract the appropriate "m" value (Col. 2) from Col. 1 score, multiply the difference (Col. 3) by the appropriate "w" value (Col. 4). This procedure gives the special subtest standard score, z' (Col. 5). Add Col. 5 to get the factor score in "z-score" form for the subject.

U.I. 24   Special Scoring Instruction Sheet

T163a(MI 1370) Less compliance, from Test 6.

Q 1-12	Y	N	Q 13-24	a	b	c	d	e
Q1			Q13					
Q2			Q14					
Q3			Q15					
Q4			Q16					
Q5			Q17					
Q6			Q18					
Q7			Q19					
Q8			Q20					
Q9			Q21					
Q10			Q22					
Q11			Q23					
Q12			Q24					
Sum # Done								
				x 1	x 2	x 3	x 4	x 5
					+	+	+	+	=	Sum of Item Scores

Enter Y or N for Q1-12.

Sum the N column = Sum # Done.

For all *'NO'* response questions, *continue* by entering a tally in the appropriate box for the answer given on the answer sheet.

Count the # of tallies for column "a", "b", etc.

Multiply # of tallies by value given below each column and write in the box below.

Add the bottom row of values to obtain sum of item scores.

$$\frac{\textbf{Sum of Item Scores}}{\textbf{Sum \# Done}} \;=\; \underline{\hspace{3cm}} \;=\; \underline{\hspace{3cm}}$$

Scoring

for

U.I. 25

Realism-vs-Tensidia

Seven Subtests

Scoring Materials

1. Keyed Answer Sheet (Two Sides)

2. Score Summary Sheet

No Expendable Booklets or Special Scoring Instruction Sheets involved.

PRINT YOUR NAME IN THE BOXES PROVIDED, THEN BLACKEN THE LETTER BOX BELOW WHICH MATCHES EACH LETTER OF YOUR NAME

YOUR FIRST NAME MI

YOUR LAST NAME

Use pencil only.

Be sure each mark is black and completely fills the space.

Erase completely any answer you wish to change.

IDENTIFICATION NUMBER

AGE   Nearest Year

SEX

HSOA 25 - Side 1

TODAY'S DATE

HUMAN NATURE II   Sum of item scores ÷ No. done

MEMORY   No. right ÷ No. done

MEMORY FOR NUMBERS   No. right ÷ No. done

BEST WORD TO FIT   No. right ÷ No. done

MEMORY   No. right ÷ No. done

NAME

© 1971, IPAT

196

PRINT YOUR NAME IN THE BOXES PROVIDED, THEN BLACKEN THE LETTER BOX BELOW WHICH MATCHES EACH LETTER OF YOUR NAME.

YOUR FIRST NAME

YOUR LAST NAME

MI

Use pencil only.

Be sure each mark is black and completely fills the space.

Erase completely any answer you wish to change.

IDENTIFICATION NUMBER

AGE — TEST, Nearest Year

SEX — G (GRADE)

TEST 7

HSOA 25 - Side 2

TODAY'S DATE

COUNTING LETTERS AND NUMBERS   No. right ÷ No. done

1 2 3 4 5 (repeated for items 1–80)

1 ... 2 ... 3 ... 4 ... 5 ... 6

7 ... 8 ... 9 ... 10 ... 11 ... 12 ... 13

14 ... 15 ... 16 ... 17 ... 18 ... 19 ... 20

21 ... 22 ... 23 ... 24 ... 25 ... 26

27 ... 28 ... 29 ... 30 ... 31 ... 32 ... 33

34 ... 35 ... 36 ... 37 ... 38 ... 39 ... 40

41 ... 42 ... 43 ... 44 ... 45 ... 46

47 ... 48 ... 49 ... 50 ... 51 ... 52 ... 53

54 ... 55 ... 56 ... 57 ... 58 ... 59 ... 60

61 ... 62 ... 63 ... 64 ... 65 ... 66

67 ... 68 ... 69 ... 70 ... 71 ... 72 ... 73

74 ... 75 ... 76 ... 77 ... 78 ... 79 ... 80

NAME

1971, IPAT

197

U.I. 25   SCORE SUMMARY SHEET

Test No.	T Number / MI Number / Psychologist's Title (Examinee's Title)	Derived Raw-Score Formula	(1) Derived Raw Score	(2) Mean of Derived Raw Scores m	(3) (1) minus (2)	(4) Weight w	(5) Special Subtest Standard Score (3) multiplied by (4) = z'
1	16b / 100b — Less Pessimistic Insecurity (Human Nature II)	$\dfrac{\text{Sum of item scores}}{\text{Number done}} =$		2.6		.5	
2	9bk / 2411 — Better Immediate Memory (Memory)	$\dfrac{\text{Number right}}{\text{Number done}} =$		0.87		3.0	
3	431 / 2408 — Greater Accuracy in Digit Span (Memory for Numbers)	$\dfrac{\text{Number right}}{\text{Number done}} =$		0.89		2.5	
4	31 / 144 — Agreement with Homely Wisdom (Wise Statements)	$\dfrac{\text{Number right}}{\text{Number done}} =$		0.63		.2	
5	224a / 714 — Fewer Alliterative, Rhyming Choices (Best Word to Fit)	$\dfrac{\text{Number right}}{\text{Number done}} =$		0.80		.2	
6	118a / 249 — Better Memory, Proper Nouns (Memory)	$\dfrac{\text{Number right}}{\text{Number done (2 parts)}} =$		0.31		6.5	
7	49c / 120h — More Accuracy, Ideomotor (Counting Letters and Numbers)	$\dfrac{\text{Number right}}{\text{Number done}} =$		0.93		4.5	

Test 1 Note: Items 3, 5, 9, and 12 score a = 1, b = 2, c = 3, d = 4, e = 5. All other items score in the opposite direction, i.e., a = 5, b = 4, c = 3, d = 2, e = 1.

Test 2 Key: NYYNY YNNYN YNNYN NYNNN N

Test 3 Key: bbaba aabba abba

Test 4 Key: 'a' is scored correct for all items

Test 5 Key: cacaa aabca bbcaa b

Test 6 Note: Only the following items (proper nouns) are scored:

```
Item   2  4  7  8  9 11 12 14 15 16 18 20 21 22 23 24
Key:   Y  Y  Y  Y  N  N  N  Y  N  N  Y  N  N  Y  N  Y  N
      25 28 30 31 33 34 35 37 39 40 42 43 44 46 47 48
       N  Y  Y  N  N  N  Y  Y  Y  Y  Y  N  Y  Y  Y  N
       N  Y  Y  N  N  N  N  Y  Y  Y  N  Y  Y  N  Y  N
```

Test 7 Key: 35123 14223 13545 31224 51325 32141 35542 12524
13545 31224 31445 51235 35542 12534 11425 35432

Sum = Factor Score

To get the factor score in z-score form for each subject, obtain the "derived score" (Col. 1) according to formula for each subtest, subtract the appropriate "m" value (Col. 2) from Col. 1 score, multiply the difference (Col. 3) by the appropriate "w" value (Col. 4). This procedure gives the special subtest standard score, z' (Col. 5). Add Col. 5 to get the factor score in "z-score" form for the subject.

198

Scoring

for

U.I. 28

Asthenia

Seven Subtests

Eight Performance Scores

Scoring Materials

      1. **Keyed Answer Sheet**

      2. **Score Summary Sheet**

      3. **One Special Scoring Instruction Sheet**

No Expendable Booklets involved.

PRINT YOUR NAME IN THE BOXES PROVIDED. THEN BLACKEN THE LETTER BOX BELOW WHICH MATCHES EACH LETTER OF YOUR NAME

YOUR LAST NAME / YOUR FIRST NAME / MI

Use pencil only.
Be sure each mark is black and completely fills the space.
Erase completely any answer you wish to change.

IDENTIFICATION NUMBER

AGE Nearest Year

SEX / GRADE

OPINIONS V Score 1 (Agree) With Test 6. See Special Scoring Instruction Sheet
Score 2 (Guilt) Items 11-20. Sum of items + Number done
Score 3 (Institutional) Items 21-33. Sum of items + Number done

HUMAN NATURE III
Sum of item scores ÷ Number done

HOW LONG WILL IT TAKE?
Sum of item scores ÷ Number done

WHAT WILL HAPPEN?
Number right ÷ Number done

WHAT DOES IT TAKE? (Sum 2/No. done 2) + (Sum 3/No. done 3) + Sum 1/No. done 1

End Part 1

End Part 2

End Part 3

Scored with Test 1 above: See Special Scoring Instruction Sheet.

LONGER OR SHORTER?
(Sum − No. done) + No. done

HSOA 28

TODAY'S DATE

NAME

IPAT

© 1971, IPAT

200

U.I. 28 SCORE SUMMARY SHEET*

Test No.	Performance Score	T Number / MI Number	Psychologist's Title (Examinee's Title)	Derived Raw-Score Formula	(1) Derived Raw Score	(2) Mean of Derived Raw Scores m	(3) (1) minus (2)	(4) Weight w	(5) Special Subtest Standard Score / (3) multiplied by (4) = z'
1	1	9c(1) / 152b	Tendency to Agree (Opinions V) — Note: See Special Scoring Instruction Sheet for details of scoring. This MI is from items 1-10, Test 1, and items 1-10, Test 6.	$\dfrac{\text{Sum 1}}{\text{Done 1}} + \dfrac{\text{Sum 6}}{\text{Done 6}} = \underline{\quad} + \underline{\quad} =$		6.30		.4	
	2	9ek / 116	Lower Severity and Guilt (Opinions V) — Note: This MI is from items 11-20, Test 1. Let response values be a = 5, b = 4, c = 3, etc.. except for items 15, 17, 18, 19, where a = 1, b = 2, c = 3, etc.	$\dfrac{\text{Sum}}{\text{Number done}} = \underline{\quad}$		2.80		1.0	
	3	9d / 125	More Institutional Values (Opinions V) — Note: This MI is from items 21-33, Test 1. Response values are a = 5, b = 4, c = 3, etc., except for items 30 and 31, for which a = 1, b = 2, c = 3, etc.	$\dfrac{\text{Sum}}{\text{Number done}} = \underline{\quad}$		2.60		.8	
2	4	16a / 100	More Cynical Pessimism (Human Nature I) — Note: Response values are a = 5, b = 4, c = 3, etc., for items 1, 8, 12, 13, 14. For remainder, a = 1, b = 2, c = 3, etc.	$\dfrac{\text{Sum}}{\text{Number done}} = \underline{\quad}$		3.00		.08	
3	5	19 / 192	Longer Estimates of Time To Do Tasks (How Long Will It Take?) — Note: For all items, a = 1, b = 2.	$\dfrac{\text{Sum}}{\text{Number done}} = \underline{\quad}$		1.59		.6	
4	6	149 / 364	Preference for External Control (What Will Happen?) — Key: abbab baa	$\dfrac{\text{Number right}}{\text{Number done}} = \underline{\quad}$		0.40		1.5	
5	7	96 / 1160	More Skepticism About Success (What Does It Take?) — Note: Item response patterns are a = 5, b = 4, c = 3 for all questions. Part I is comprised of items 1-18; Part 2 items 19-36; Part 3 items 37-54.	$\left(\dfrac{\text{Sum 2}}{\text{Done 2}} + \dfrac{\text{Sum 3}}{\text{Done 3}}\right)\Big/\dfrac{\text{Sum 1}}{\text{Done 1}} = \left(\underline{\quad} + \underline{\quad}\right)\Big/\underline{\quad} =$		1.69		.6	
6		9c(2) / 152b	Scored as part of MI 152b, from Test 1 above.						
7	8	76 / 97	Longer Estimates of Waiting Period Time (Longer or Shorter?) — Item scores are a = 4, b = 3, c = 2, d = 1.	$\dfrac{\text{Sum item scores} - \text{No. done}}{\text{No. done}} = \underline{\quad}$		2.49		.4	
							Sum = Factor Score		

*In this battery there are seven subtests and eight performance scores, one of the latter being a contrast between two of the former (Tests 1(a) and 6).

To get the factor score in z-score form for each subject, obtain the "derived score" (Col. 1) according to formula for each subtest; subtract the appropriate "m" value (Col. 2) from Col. 1 score, multiply the difference (Col. 3) by the appropriate "w" value (Col. 4). This procedure gives the special subtest standard score, z' (Col. 5). Add Col. 5 to get the factor score in "z-score" form for the subject.

T9c(1) Test 1, Opinions V   (MI 152[b]) Tendency to agree

This concerns itself only with the first 10 items in Test 1, Opinions V, and the corresponding items 1 through 10 constituted by Test 6, Opinions VI. To "hide" the structure from the examinee the items begin differently as shown below.

	Test 1		Test 6
	Item		*Item*
	1 _____		2 _____
	2 _____		3 _____
	3 _____		4 _____
	4 _____		5 _____
	5 _____		6 _____
	6 _____		7 _____
	7 _____		8 _____
	8 _____		9 _____
	9 _____		10 _____
	10 _____		1 _____
	Sum _____		Sum _____
	No. done _____		No. done _____

In both parts, responses score a $= 5$, b $= 4$, c $= 3$, d $= 2$, e $= 1$. Enter these values in table as given, add to totals at bottom, and calculate

$$\left(\frac{\text{Sum of item scores in Test 1}}{\text{No. done in Test 1}} \quad + \quad \frac{\text{Sum of item scores in Test 6}}{\text{No. done in Test 6}} \right)$$

Scoring

for

U.I. 32

Exvia-vs-Invia

Eight Subtests

Scoring Materials

1. **Keyed Answer Sheet**

2. **Score Summary Sheet**
   (Scoring Instructions for three of the Tests in Expendable Booklet are on Score Summary Sheet)

3. **One Special Scoring Instruction Sheet given for one remaining test using an Expendable Booklet ("Can You Hear the Word?")**

HSOA 32

Print your name in the boxes provided. Then blacken the letter box below which matches each letter of your name.

YOUR LAST NAME | YOUR FIRST NAME

Use pencil only.
Be sure each mark is black and completely fills the space.
Erase completely any answer you wish to change.

IDENTIFICATION NUMBER

AGE — To Nearest Year

SEX / GRADE

TODAY'S DATE

JUDGING LINES Number done (Ignore whether correct or incorrect)

L S E columns for items 1 through 80

WHICH IS MORE?
Number done
(Ignore correct or incorrect)

A B for items 1 through 20

QUALITIES
Number right

a b c d e for items 1 through 80

CRIME AND PUNISHMENT
Sum of odd item scores/Number of odd items done
Sum of even item scores/Number of even items done

5 4 3 2 1 for items 1 through 14

© 1971, IPAT

NAME

IPAT

204

U.I. 32 SCORE SUMMARY SHEET

Test No.	T Number / MI Number	Psychologist's Title (Examinee's Title)	Derived Raw-Score Formula	(1) Derived Raw Score	(2) Mean of Derived Raw Scores m	(3) (1) minus (2)	(4) Weight w	(5) Special Subtest Standard Score (3) multiplied by (4) = z'
1	45 / 309	Quicker Line Length Judgment (Judging Lines)	Number done		47.80		.05	
2	62b / 737	Willingness to Risk Decision on Vague Data (Which Is More?)	Number done		12.91		.09	
3	142a / 356a	More Correct Attribute Naming (Qualities) Key: cbaec abdce adbde bedac bdabe abdce aecdc dabce badec ecdba dbeca decab cadbe dceba	Number right (4 parts)		19.91		.03	
4	97 / 1169	Assignment of Punishment: Less Influenced by Extenuating Circumstances (Crime and Punishment)	$\dfrac{\Sigma \text{odd item scores}/\text{No. odd done}}{\Sigma \text{even item scores}/\text{No. even done}} =$		0.79		1.6	
5	13a / 763a	More Fluency Concerning People's Characteristics (What People Are Like)	Number of characteristics		14.00		.04	
6	164b / 2412	Garbled Words Heard As Family Words (Can You Hear the Word? II)	Number of *family* words written		0.40		.4	
7	121 / 15	CMS: More Circles Used (Obstacles)	Number of circles used		25.30		.01	
8	1d / 2a	Lower Motor Rigidity (Writing Signatures)	$\dfrac{\text{No. of lines in pts I(b) and II(b)}}{\text{No. of lines in pts I(a) and II(a)}} =$		0.40		3.5	

Sum = **Factor Score**

Note (Test 4): Odd numbered items contain extenuating circumstances, so that the ratio of severity of punishment with those conditions to severity without those conditions (even items) is the variable tapped with this MI. Item responses are a = 5, b = 4, c = 3, etc.

Note (Test 5): This is the first test in the expendable booklet. To score it, simply count the number of characteristics listed.

Note (Test 6): A list of acceptable family words is given on the Special Scoring Instruction Sheet attached. Ignore all other words.

Note (Test 7): Simply count the number of circles drawn on the two pages of the test. If the subject does *more* than 99 circles, assign a score of 99.

Note (Test 8): Count the number of times examinee's name is written in Parts I(b) and II(b) (the sum of the two), divide by sum of names written in Parts I(a) and II(a). Count in (b) only those obviously written backwards, and if more than half a name is done call it one. Printing is allowable.

To get the factor score in z-score form for each subject, obtain the "derived score" (Col. 1) according to formula for each subtest, subtract the appropriate "m" value (Col. 2) from Col. 1 score, multiply the difference (Col. 3) by the appropriate "w" value (Col. 4). This procedure gives the special subtest standard score, z' (Col. 5). Add Col. 5 to get the factor score in "z-score" form for the subject.

U.I. 32   Special Scoring Instruction Sheet

T164b   (MI 2412) Garbled words heard as family words, from Test 6 in the U.I. 32 Expendable Booklet.

The following are acceptable as home and family words:

Mother	Moma	mom	mommy	husband
father	dad	dada	papa	pop
daddy	uncle	aunt	ant	auntie
anti	brother	sister	grandma	grandmom
grandpa	bad boy	ma	be good	I'm home
don't	Hi, ma	daughter	bring home	m-no
home	baby	family	parent	

Scoring

for

U.I. 33

Discouragement-vs-Sanguineness

Seven Subtests

Scoring Materials

    1. Keyed Answer Sheet

    2. Score Summary Sheet

No Expendable Booklets or Special Scoring Instruction Sheets.

PRINT YOUR NAME IN THE BOXES PROVIDED, THEN BLACKEN THE
LETTER BOX BELOW WHICH MATCHES EACH LETTER OF YOUR NAME.

YOUR FIRST NAME   YOUR LAST NAME   MI

Use pencil only.

Be sure each mark is black and completely fills the space.

Erase completely any answer you wish to change.

IDENTIFICATION NUMBER

AGE

PERFORMANCE ESTIMATES
Sum of item scores ÷ Number done

HOW MANY FRIENDS?
Sum item scores ÷ Number done

WHAT IS FUN?
Number right ÷ Number done

MY FEELINGS
Sum of item scores ÷ Number done

CHANCES OF SUCCESS
Sum of item scores ÷ Number done

OPINIONS VII
Sum of item scores ÷ Number done

HOW WOULD EVENTS AFFECT YOU?
Sum of item scores ÷ Number done

TODAY'S DATE

HSOA 33

NAME

© 1971, IPAT

208

U.I. 33   SCORE SUMMARY SHEET

Test No. on Ans. Sht	T Number / MI Number	Psychologist's Title (Examinee's Title)	Derived Raw-Score Formula	(1) Derived Raw Score	(2) Mean of Derived Raw Scores m	(3) (1) minus (2)	(4) Weight w	(5) Special Subtest Standard Score (3) multiplied by (4) = z'
1	22b 108	Less Confidence in Unfamiliar Situation (Performance Estimates) Note: For this sum, let a = 1, b = 2, c = 3, d = 4, e = 5	$\dfrac{\Sigma \text{ item scores}}{\text{Number done}} =$		3.22		.4	
2	64b 473	Fewer People Who Appreciate One As a Friend (How Many Friends?) Note: For this sum, let a = 3, b = 2, c = 1	$\dfrac{\Sigma \text{ item scores}}{\text{Number done}} =$		1.39		.1	
3	40c 2413	Less Willingness to Participate Actively (What Is Fun?) Key: 'N' is scored correct for all items.	$\dfrac{\text{Number right}}{\text{Number done}} =$		0.34		.2	
4	156b 1245	More Depression (My Feelings) Note: For this sum, let a = 1, b = 2, c = 3, d = 4, e = 5	$\dfrac{\Sigma \text{ item scores}}{\text{Number done}} =$		2.35		.01	
5	39 212	Less Belief in Attainability of Goals (Chances of Success) Note: For this sum, let a = 1, b = 2, c = 3	$\dfrac{\Sigma \text{ item scores}}{\text{Number done}} =$		2.00		.8	
6	9e1 116a	More Severe Pessimistic Superego (Opinions VII) Note: For this sum, let a = 1, b = 2, c = 3, d = 4, e = 5 for all items *except* 10, 12, 13, 14, 16, 17, 18. For those seven items, let a = 5, b = 4, c = 3, d = 2, e = 1	$\dfrac{\Sigma \text{ item scores}}{\text{Number done}} =$		2.83		.1	
7	24 112	Greater Expectation of Negative Consequences (How Would Events Affect You?) Note: For this sum, the usual weights, a = 5, b = 4, c = 3, d = 2, e = 1, are used.	$\dfrac{\Sigma \text{ item scores}}{\text{Number done}} =$		3.14		1.6	

Sum = Factor Score

To get the factor score in z-score form for each subject, obtain the "derived score" (Col. 1) according to formula for each subtest, subtract the appropriate "m" value (Col. 2) from Col. 1 score, multiply the difference (Col. 3) by the appropriate "w" value (Col. 4). This procedure gives the special subtest standard score, z' (Col. 5). Add Col. 5 to get the factor score in "z-score" form for the subject.

9
Second- and Third-Stratum Personality Factors and the Use of Depth Psychometry

The next step beyond the obtained standard factor scores of the last chapter is ordinarily to proceed to their use in diagnosis and prediction. But we shall temporarily postpone that to take stock of second-order factors, which are also derivable from the O-A Kit, and which complete the view of the scores obtainable. The usefulness of second-order factors is often overlooked by those unfamiliar with the meaning of factor structure. For example, in using the 16 PF or CAQ, psychologists sometimes forget that they can simultaneously obtain the basic second-order scores. (Indeed, they have been known to add to the testing time, for example, Eysenck's P, E, and N scales, which only contribute in any case three among the eight secondaries already scorable from the 16 PF, HSPQ, or CAQ already given.) However, in the case of the O-A primaries the second strata do not yet have their meanings extended by criterion experiments, so their use for a while is likely to be mainly in research. For that reason we have included their definition and their scoring in the present chapter, in separation from the primary trait definitions and scoring instructions.

Consideration of second-order factors and of the correlations among primaries are different aspects of the same thing. Even in ordinary use of the primaries one needs to know these mutual correlations, though one may not need to use second-order factors. For example, when one has found the correlations of several primaries with some criterion and wishes to find the best weights to give to them, one must use R_f, the matrix of correlations among the primaries, in the familiar formula which we have presented in correct form for primaries elsewhere (p. 131). For the weights to get secondaries, one calculates for a given secondary:

$$\mathbf{W}_c = \mathbf{R}_f{}^{-1}\mathbf{V}_c \tag{9.1}$$

where $\mathbf{W}_c$ is a 10 x 1 column vector of weights to apply to the primary scores, $\mathbf{R}_f$ is a 10 x 10 of the primary intercorrelations, as just stated (with 1's in the diagonal) and $\mathbf{V}_c$ is a 10 x 1 column vector of the empirically discovered correlations of the 10 source traits with the given second-order factor.

Parenthetically, a better term for these broader (but shallower) "factors among factors" than "second order" is "second stratum." The reasons for using terms to bring out this difference of concept are given elsewhere (Cattell, 1973b), but essentially it is that "order" applies only to a given matrix, whereas "stratum" refers to a mapping stabilized over many experiments, in which factors have been located in their correct strata in a hierarchy of primaries, secondaries, tertiaries. The higher strata factors are best considered broad influences, each of which acts on several lower stratum factors. They are not, however, usually as psychologically predictive as the primary-strata traits.

There is, of course, theoretical as well as practical interest in knowledge about strata. The hierarchy tells us something important about the structure of personality. Among other things, the exploration of strata has shown the way to solving the vexed question of whether the same personality structures are being revealed through the three possible media of observation and measurement, namely: L-data (life behavior, usually rated by onlookers); Q-data (from introspection in questionnaires); and T-data (from behavioral tests as in the O-A Battery). We know from the recent Cattell, Pierson, and Finkbeiner study (1976) that questionnaire (Q-data) responses and observer ratings (criterion or L-data) in everyday life, indeed occupy largely the same "factor space" and yield trait structures that correspond mutually, e.g., A, affectia; C, ego strength; F, surgency; and so on for a dozen or more factors. That is, they are largely predictable one from the other and present pictures, in different dress, of the same "instrument-transcending" personality factors. An early attempt to investigate the overlap of these L-Q factors with T-data (objective tests) by Saunders (Cattell & Saunders, 1954) and the present writer showed substantial overlap, but stopped short of specific matches because methodology was then inadequate. The recent study of Goldberg, Norman, and Schwartz (1972) confirms, however, that T-data is at least as good as Q-data in predicting real life ratings. It is not surprising, therefore, that today good factor alignment of T- and Q-data trait patterns can be found. However, somewhat to the surprise of investigators, who had looked for matches of primaries in T-data with primaries in L- and Q-data, the alignments so far discovered are of *second-stratum* factors in L- and Q- with *first* stratum (primaries) in T-data (Cattell, 1955a, 1957a; Wardell & Yeudall, 1976). Table 9.1 shows the alignments from joint factorings in two media.

It should be stressed that though three cases of T-primaries with L-Q secondaries are relatively firmly supported, those of two others— U.I. 19 and U.I. 22—are still in need of further careful checking.

The theory of *instrument-free personality factors* (Cattell, 1973b; Cattell, Pierson, & Finkbeiner, 1976) leads us to expect that these matchings will be extended, since it says that the same personality structures should be reached, in somewhat different "expressive dress," across all three media of observation. However, the important thing to note about these matchings in Table 9.1 is that L-Q data on the one hand and T-data factors on the other come out at different levels, presumably because of the greater breadth or lower "density" of the variables in the T-data. Thus what we are now approaching as second-stratum factors in T-data should be the equivalent of third stratum in the questionnaire field,

Table 9.1

MATCHES OF O-A PRIMARIES WITH SECOND-STRATUM
QUESTIONNAIRE MEDIA PERSONALITY FACTORS

O-A Primary Trait		Questionnaire Secondary
*U.I. 17 Control	Matched with	Q VIII Good Control and Restraint $(G+, Q_3+, F-)$
U.I. 19 Independence	Matched with	Q IV Independence $(Q_1+, E+, M+, L+, Q_2+)$
*U.I. 22 Cortertia	Matched with	Q III Cortertia $(I-, A-, M-)$
U.I. 24 Anxiety	Matched with	Q II Anxiety $(Q_4+, C-, O+, L+, Q_3-, H-)$
U.I. 32 Exvia-Invia	Matched with	Q I Exvia-Invia $(F+, Q_2-, A+, E+, H+)$

The questionnaire factors are indexed in Roman numerals as consistently used in Cattell (1973b) and elsewhere. In parentheses below each are the primaries on which they are significantly loaded, and by which they have long been recognized, arranged in descending order of loadings.

*In Extended Kit only.

and presumably—though this is beyond present knowledge—third-stratum T's would be fourth-stratum Q's.

Despite the fact that 20 T-data factors are known to exist, not this many Q-data second-stratum factors have been verified (Cattell, 1973). Supporting this difference we find that only five or six *third*-stratum Q-data have appeared, against seven to nine *second* stratum in T-data (also presumably on the same level). Consequently, we are forced to the conclusion that T-data is in some way covering a wider span of the total personality behavior than Q-data. This is at first a little surprising in view of the determined attempts that have been made to cover the realm of personality exhaustively and systematically in L- and Q-data (Cattell, 1946, 1973b; Goldberg, 1975; Norman, 1967) by the *personality sphere* concept and techniques, not to mention the general confidence among questionnaire users that by their choices of items they can cover all behavior. But good reasons can be offered for some limitations in questionnaire data, such as

213

that we are not fully conscious of all our behaviors or that we are not capable of assessing our position relative to that of others on more obscure and private forms of behavior. This is one more argument for using objective tests instead of questionnaires wherever possible, despite the greater care and time they require.

Without further inquiry into the reasons for the "fault line" in the strata we can tentatively accept that in starting at the primary factor level in the O-A we are starting at the second stratum in Q- and L-data. Now second-order factors are factors found from factoring the correlations among primary factors. Accordingly, we begin here with a matrix of correlations among the 20 primaries found in the largest and most recent study, by Cattell, Schuerger, Klein, and Finkbeiner (1976). Table 9.2 presents, for economy, only that section of the **R** matrix which deals with the 10 traits in the O-A Main Kit, plus U.I. 17 and 26 from the Extended Kit; but the analysis which follows was performed on the larger (19 x 19) matrix for methodological completeness. These values are from the largest sample yet gathered, namely, the N = 2522 males (around 15-16 years of age) in the Cattell, Schuerger, Klein, and Finkbeiner study (1976). Other matrices are available (N = 394) in Cattell and Klein (1975), and in the ASIS microfilms for Cattell, Knapp, and Scheier (1961) which collated five studies on air force and navy personnel. The matrices are visibly similar and the second orders from them even more so. But there are also differences which appear to be systematic, notably between the two recent studies on 15-16-year-olds and the older studies on men in their 20s. There are, of course, also some differences between the T's for literal battery scores and those for pure factors. Table 9.2 correlations are for pure factors as reached at the unique simple structure position. Hopefully, a task force of researchers will soon provide us with more exact knowledge of the systematic modifications of the second- and third-strata factor patterns with age, sex, and cultural sampling.

Five earlier researches on second-order T-data personality source traits exist. Four were based on the pure factor cosines found at the simple structure position (Cattell, 1955a, 1955b; Cattell & Scheier, 1958a, 1958b, 1959) and one on direct correlations among the primary batteries (Cattell, Knapp, & Scheier, 1961). Their agreement has been examined closely (Cattell, Knapp, & Scheier, 1961) and found to be good. They agreed (1) on seven secondary factors being required, and (2) on the patterns of these factors; but with some weakness of definition on Factors V and VI. The most readily accessible setting out of patterns inferred prior to the present O-A Kit data is to be found in Table 19-5 in Nesselroade and Delhees (1966), but also in Cattell, Knapp, and Scheier (1961). The present results, from the larger sample of 2522 in Table 9.2, agreed with earlier studies in finding seven factors by the scree test, with patterns as shown in Table 9.3. The agreement with the *consensus* of the earlier studies is good

Table 9.2

CORRELATIONS AMONG PURE FACTORS AT SIMPLE STRUCTURE

Factor Number	U.I. No.	1 (16)	2 (19)	3 (20)	4 (21)	5 (23)	6 (24)	7 (25)	8 (28)	9 (32)	10 (33)	11 (17)	12 (26)
1	16		.19	.10	.25	.20	−.07	.16	.10	.14	−.16	.04	.10
2	19	.36		.14	−.13	.16	−.24	.37	−.14	.03	.10	.01	.14
3	20	−.23	−.29		.01	.19	−.20	.13	−.04	−.11	−.01	−.17	−.14
4	21	.31	.11	−.18		−.01	.08	−.03	.19	.16	−.18	.11	.13
5	23	.24	.41	−.33	.12		−.19	.05	−.09	−.02	−.07	−.08	−.00
6	24	−.19	−.37	.03	−.08	−.26		−.21	.17	−.15	−.21	.20	−.13
7	25	.29	.38	−.24	.22	.23	−.12		.11	.12	.14	.12	.14
8	28	−.19	−.36	.01	−.12	−.30	.31	−.31		−.08	−.07	.10	−.12
9	32	.12	−.18	−.12	.31	−.06	.21	.08	.07		−.17	.21	.45
10	33	−.08	.16	−.06	−.22	.10	−.05	.05	−.10	−.28		−.13	−.04
11	17	.01	.12	−.03	−.01	.07	−.08	.05	−.05	−.05	−.01		.25
12	26	.14	.13	−.13	.06	.16	−.09	.10	−.20	−.01	.15	.05	

The upper right is from Cattell and Klein (1975) on N = 394 14-16-year-olds. The lower left is from Cattell, Schuerger, Klein, and Finkbeiner (1976), N = 2522.

215

Table 9.3

SECOND-STRATUM FACTOR PATTERNS FROM THE LARGEST (Male) SAMPLE (N = 2522)

Second-Stratum Source Traits

			T I	T II	T III	T IV	T V	T VI	T VII	h²
Primaries	U.I. 16	1	−0.01	0.35	0.67	−0.08	−0.06	0.11	−0.06	.47
in	U.I. 19	2	−0.40	−0.41	0.26	0.04	0.04	−0.12	−0.11	.62
Main	U.I. 20	3	0.59	0.04	−0.03	0.41	−0.08	−0.06	−0.02	.54
Kit	U.I. 21	4	−0.03	−0.13	0.54	0.01	0.02	0.04	−0.02	.37
	U.I. 23	5	−0.47	0.16	0.05	−0.03	0.16	0.17	−0.15	.40
	U.I. 24	6	0.01	−0.05	−0.05	0.00	0.01	0.01	0.74	.41
	U.I. 25	7	−0.42	0.05	0.40	0.24	−0.09	−0.21	0.28	.68
	U.I. 28	8	0.44	−0.01	−0.22	−0.69	0.00	−0.16	−0.08	.43
	U.I. 32	9	−0.00	−0.34	0.38	0.02	0.07	0.05	0.26	.23
	U.I. 33	10	−0.37	0.10	−0.34	−0.03	−0.31	0.05	0.05	.35
Not	*	11	−0.43	0.02	−0.10	0.05	−0.09	0.26	0.30	.24
in	*	12	0.03	−0.12	0.03	0.08	0.34	0.02	0.04	.16
Main	*	13	−0.04	−0.09	0.40	−0.03	−0.40	−0.05	−0.08	.30
Kit	U.I. 17	14	−0.04	0.09	−0.02	0.07	0.21	−0.15	−0.02	.07
	*	15	−0.05	−0.48	0.00	−0.02	−0.08	−0.03	−0.10	.21
	*	16	−0.06	−0.38	−0.09	0.03	0.08	0.11	0.02	.17
	*	17	0.01	0.01	0.00	0.36	−0.03	−0.60	0.12	.44
	U.I. 26	18	−0.30	−0.02	0.06	−0.03	−0.31	0.36	−0.05	.26
	*	19	0.16	−0.28	0.13	−0.01	0.12	0.19	0.16	.34

As usual, h² is the communality.

*These factors are not yet adequately interpreted and named.

Note U.I. 33 was used with loading only on one previous study. Its loadings on I, III, and V are treated as only suggestive.

Loading here confirms in sign and significance the earlier studies

Loading significantly here but not in the earlier studies

and we have therefore preserved continuity with the earlier titles, with slight modifications in response to emphases in the present findings.

Brief descriptions of the natures of these factors follow in Table 9.4, and there one will see listed the main primaries involved (setting aside in brackets the factors that are from the Extended Kit).

Scoring of Second Orders

By a decision based on the loading of each primary averaged across the latest research (Table 9.3) and the earlier researches, the primaries are separated in Table 9.4 into those deserving a weight of 1 and those whose consistently higher loadings indicate the need for a weight of 2. To obtain a person's score on the secondaries, therefore, the primaries should first be produced in standard scores (which will have positive and negative values) and then added as indicated, i.e., the scores for those on the right just as they stand and for those on the left with doubled weight. No norms are yet available by which to translate the total "raw" scores thus obtained, but they will stand symmetrically around a score of zero and have a sigma, for TI and TIII, for example, of about 3. The psychologist will probably decide to bring the raw scores to a sigma of 1, in relation to his own group, in order to deal conveniently in standard scores, centiles, or stens.

Elsewhere (Cattell, 1973*b*), it has been pointed out that the meanings of higher strata factors may cease to be purely psychological and may refer to influences operating in sociological or physiological domains. What we have labeled pathological predisposition (TI) in Table 9.4 could, for example, represent a complex of genetic, physiological, temperamental endowments predisposing to general pathology, while the polite self-restraint in TV might represent the imprint of an upper socio-educational status. By the same argument that higher orders represent analyses into more remote influences, TIII, irrepressible ardor, and TVII, high sympathetic excitability to environment, could represent purely genetic and physiological contributors operation in the formation of primary traits.

Although full interpretation of these factors is not immediately possible from loading patterns themselves, it behooves us to pursue precision in the loading patterns and scoring of higher strata factors as far as we can, in order that their scores may be tried out against various criteria. Parenthetically, while they are in this limbo of temporary and largely descriptive naming, it is important to hold on vigilantly to identification by a noncommittal but reliable basic indexing system. The system proposed uses U.I. 1, 2, 3, etc., for objective test primaries, U.I. I, II, III, etc., in roman for the secondaries, and U.I. α, β, and γ, using Greek symbols for the tertiary traits. The problem always arises that rotations need to be pursued so tirelessly and thoroughly if the factor correlations are to reach accuracy that adequate accuracy is rarely attained. Whatever

Table 9.4

THE NATURE AND SCORING OF THE O-A SECONDARIES

T I Pathological Predisposition

Scoring:

Weight by 2
U.I. 19−, 20+, 25−, 28+

Weight by 1
U.I. 23−, 32−, 33− (and 26− if using the Extended Kit)

This is tentatively interpreted as a pattern with some genetic determination, since U.I. 19, 20, 25, and 32 are among factors with higher heredity. The combination of subduedness, evasiveness, ambivalence, tensidia, asthenia, and restriction of the ego is noticeably similar to the first discriminant function separating clinical cases from normals on p. 253-254.

T II Independent Ego-Id Expression-vs-History of Comparative Failure

Weight by 2
U.I. 16+, 19+

Weight by 1
U.I. 21+, 25+, 32− (36+ if using the Extended Kit)

This pattern shows some discrepancy between the earlier, older age groups and the present (Table 9.2) respecting U.I. 23 and U.I. 32. The above scoring rests on the weights that agree, except for U.I. 32, which accepts the latest.

The high-T II individual shows many aspects of an ego strength that has succeeded (note intelligence loading in Cattell, Knapp, & Scheier, 1961) in giving expression to many id needs, particularly for self-assertion. The build-up of the self-sentiment fits this explanation. It suggests "the loser syndrome" at the negative pole, and is tinged with hypomanic qualities at the positive pole.

T III Irrespressible Ardor of Temperament-vs-Susceptibility to Inhibition

Weight by 2
U.I. 16+, 19+, 21+

Weight by 1
U.I. 20+, 32+, 33−

Since a distinctly high heritability applies to the primaries most involved—19, 21, 20—and since low susceptibility to inhibition could contribute to all of them, this suggests an inheritable *temperament* factor. As (low) *susceptibility*, it should be distinguished from T I, which is concerned with the actual degree of heavy-handedness of the cultural impress.

Table 9.4 (Continued)

T IV   Alert Self-Concerned Realism

Weight by 2
U.I. 25+, 28— (18+, 22+, and 36+ if using the Extended Kit)

Weight by 1
U.I. 20+ (30+ if using the Extended Kit)

As stated, this factor depends largely on the five previous researches, having only 25, 28, and 33 as possible matches, correct by sign. Its nature is one of alertness (see the high U.I. 22 loading), but also of self-concern and realism possibly all rooted in early insecurity and finishing in an alert build-up of the self-sentiment.

T V   Self-Restraint

Weight by 2
U.I. 23+ (17+ if using the Extended Kit)

Weight by 1
U.I. 33—, 25— (26— if using the Extended Kit)

As with T IV, the match is not strong and the use of the factor must be tentative. The psychological sense of the combined earlier and later patterns is, however, convincing. The high-T V individual has the indicators of a good, disciplined upbringing (U.I. 17, 23), including restraint on narcism (U.I. 26). It seems to center on a family atmosphere of training in self-restraint, and perhaps concern for others.

T VI   Narcistic Self-Expression

Weight by 2
(U.I. 26+ if using the Extended Kit)

Weight by 1
U.I. 25— (27+, 34+ if using the Extended Kit)

The match again rests on few markers and requires the Extended Kit for a good score estimate. The autism and apathy of U.I. 34 and 27 fit the general sense of a narcistic ego (U.I. 26 being most prominent) with low reality contact (U.I. 25—).

T VII   Sympathetic Excitability

Weight by 2
U.I. 24+, 25+

Weight by 1
U.I. 32+, 23— (18+, 30+ if using Extended Kit)

This is a well-defined factor of anxiety (U.I. 24) and over-reactivity (U.I. 18 and 30), along with good reality contact. It suggests either a temperamental sympathetic nervous system excitability, as in D and Q_4 in the anxiety second order in Q-data, or a marked effect of environment insecurity, with search for security in extraversion. It might characterize (if the regression in U.I. 23— becomes extreme) manic psychotics.

219

Table 9.5

CORRELATIONS AMONG HIGHER STRATA FACTORS AND THE PATTERNS OF THIRD-STRATUM FACTORS

Correlations of Second-Stratum Factors

a-1) Pawlik and Cattell (1964)

	T I	T II	T III	T IV	T V	T VI	T VII
T I		—.10	—.06	—.17	.19	—.18	.07
T II			.01	—.07	—.17	.07	.12
T III				—.18	—.14	.38	—.14
T IV					—.08	—.06	.05
T V						—.08	—.07
T VI							—.04
T VII							

b-1) Cattell, Schuerger, Klein, and Finkbeiner (1976)

	T I	T II	T III	T IV	T V	T VI	T VII
T I		—.28	—.30	—.02	—.05	.17	.36
T II			—.26	.19	—.24	—.17	—.19
T III				—.17	.21	—.02	—.15
T IV					—.22	—.01	—.40
T V						.13	.06
T VI							.18
T VII							

Table 9.5 (Continued)

Patterns of Third-Stratum Factors

a-2) Pawlik and Cattell (1964)

		Oblimax Rotated Factor Pattern			Maxplane Rotated Factor Pattern		
		α	β	γ	α	β	γ
Pathological Predisposition	T I	−.03	.46	.04	−.03	.47	−.11
Independent Ego-Id Expression	T II	.04	.02	.59	.05	.01	.63
Irrepressible Temperament	T III	.70	.08	−.02	.70	.07	−.07
Alert Self-Concerned Realism	T IV	−.40	−.56	−.27	−.40	−.55	−.09
Self-Restraint	T V	−.08	.23	−.17	−.08	.24	−.25
Narcistic Self-Expression	T VI	.44	−.09	.01	.44	−.09	.03
Sympathetic Excitability	T VII	−.16	−.00	.20	−.16	−.00	.22

6-2) Cattell (in press)

	Rotoplot Rotated Factor Pattern		
	α	β	γ
T I	−.19	.67	.03
T II	−.55	−.65	.27
T III	.64	−.05	−.22
T IV	−.61	−.42	−.62
T V	.42	.21	−.02
T VI	.09	.31	−.05
T VII	.14	.62	.44

Correlations of Third-Stratum Factors

a-3) Pawlik and Cattell (1964)

	Oblimax			Maxplane		
	α	β	γ	α	β	γ
α	1.00	−.34	.03	1.00	−.35	.05
β	—	1.00	−.36	—	1.00	−.05
γ	—	—	1.00	—	—	1.00

b-3) Cattell (in press)

	Rotoplot		
	α	β	γ
α	1.00	−.35	.02
β	—	1.00	−.13
γ	—	—	1.00

α = Immature Demandingness   β = Pathological Withdrawal   γ = Controlled Assertiveness

221

is common in the verdict of two or more researches is therefore our best resort. Table 9.5 puts side-by-side Pawlik and Cattell's 1964 analysis based on a composite of five second-order studies, and Cattell's 1978 analysis based on the large sample (N = 2522) averaging 15 years of age. This data came from the Cattell, Schuerger, Klein, and Finkbeiner (1976) study.

The agreement of two different rotation methods on the factors is excellent, but that of the adult student and schoolboy pattern only moderate. One cannot, without further experiment, conclude whether the differences are due to age or other causes, but there is substantial agreement that α loads TIII (+) and TIV (−), that β loads TI (+), TIV (−), and TV (+), and that γ loads TII (+), TIV (−), and TVII (+). There is also agreement that the α - β correlation is negative, the β - γ correlation is negative, and the α - γ correlation is practically zero. Interpretation of the tertiaries must be highly tentative, pending criterion and other ancillary evidence, but to hold the hypothesis in view, α has been named immature demandingness, β pathological withdrawal, and γ controlled assertiveness. Pawlik accepted a Freudian interpretation as id, superego, and ego, respectively, but the more complete present determination of patterns makes this unlikely.

The utility of higher strata factors is both theoretical—offering by depth psychometry further psychological understanding of personality structure—and practical, in that scores on them *can* be used in criterion prediction—though the criterion relations will not be known until secondary and tertiary scores get more widely tried out.[1]

As one might expect from these tentative interpretations of the secondaries, neurotics are found to be very significantly higher in social conformity and self-restraint, though lower in independent ego. The sociopathic pattern is different, showing greatest difference by reduced realism, reduced restraint, and reduced ego expression, along with high narcistic self-expression. The third difference—reduced ego expression (TII−)—is

---

[1] Secondaries may be scored by adding the scores first worked out for primaries, either simply as standard scores or with the weights provided for computer synthesis scoring.

Although few may be interested in the more complex procedures of estimating higher order scores directly from the subtest standard scores, it can be done if one has the first-, second-, and third-order factor matrices. In the case of three strata, assuming that one wishes to score third orders, first one has to get the factor pattern matrix of the third order directly on the variables which is given by:

$$\mathbf{V}_{fp \cdot \text{III} \cdot v} = \mathbf{V}_{fp\text{I}} \cdot \mathbf{V}_{fp\text{II}} \cdot \mathbf{V}_{fp\text{III}} \qquad (9.2)a$$

by the Cattell-White formula where $\mathbf{V}_{fp\text{I}}$ is the $n \times k$ first order, $\mathbf{V}_{fp\text{II}}$ is the $k \times p$ second order on primaries and $\mathbf{V}_{fp\text{III}}$, the $p \times m$ third order on secondaries (Cattell, 1978). $\mathbf{V}_{fp \cdot \text{III} \cdot v}$ gives the loadings of the m tertiaries on the n variables. To convert this to a $\mathbf{V}_{fe}$, factor estimation matrix, i.e., weights of the variables to give factor scores, one computes:

$$\mathbf{V}_{fe\text{III} \cdot v} = \mathbf{R}_v{}^{-1} \mathbf{V}_{fp \cdot \text{III} \cdot v} \mathbf{R}_{f \cdot \text{III}} \qquad (9.2)b$$

where $\mathbf{R}_v$ is the unreduced correlation matrix among variables and $\mathbf{R}_{f \cdot \text{III}}$ is the correlation among the tertiary factors.

surprising unless we interpret TII with more emphasis on pure ego strength. In that case we may understand the sociopath as one whose ego strength is actually lower than that of the neurotic to the point that he is unable to maintain control of his impulses. In any case, a good discriminant function for practical use is indicated by Table 11.4 for separating neurotics from sociopaths and from normals.

There has been some tendency among testers to regard primaries and secondaries as if they were alternative sets of measurements, with some rivalry as to their relative utility. Eysenck's EPI, for example, has confined itself to secondaries, stating that these are the large factors in the diagnostic picture. It is certainly attractive to some psychologists to treat personality as if it were simpler than it really is, and such wishful thinking will incline one to secondaries, for, of course, one will always find decidedly fewer secondaries than primaries.[2] However, a true perspective is gained only if one recognizes, first, that the primaries from any domain are *always* psychometrically capable of predicting more of a criterion than the secondaries can do. Hence, if it were a question of staying *with one or the other*, one would stay with primaries. But the personality theorist knows that *psychological meaning*, at least in what has been called the Stratified Uncorrelated Determiners (SUD) model (Cattell, 1978a, b), requires one to recognize that primaries and secondaries could have different properties, e.g., genetically, on age curves, in regard to learning influences, and so on. Knowledge of these properties gives one power to extend prediction beyond immediate statistical predictions. Consequently, the best use will employ both, in what Cattell (1973b) has called "depth psychometry."

The theory of depth psychometry has already been briefly described here. It recognizes that personality structure is hierarchical, or, more precisely, that it consists of *stratified uncorrelated determiners* as in the *SUD model* (Cattell, 1978). The SUD can be illustrated by exvia and anxiety. The questionnaire primaries A, affectia, F, surgency, H, parmia, and Q2—, low self-sufficiency, in exvia must be regarded as partly due to a development peculiar to themselves (specifics to primary factors in the second-order factor analysis) and partly to the contribution of the second-order exvia factor (QI). All five are mutually uncorrelated—hence *uncorrelated determiners*—but the higher stratum exvia, by its contribution to all, causes the actual scales for A, F, H, and Q2 to be correlated.

---

[2]Nevertheless, the evidence is now indubitable (Cattell, 1973b) that in the Q-medium the 35 primaries (as in the CAQ and the 16 PF with a seven-factor extension) yield at least nine secondaries in the "normal" area and at least four known in abnormal behavior (notably general depression and general psychosis), giving at least 13 important secondaries. Consequently, the EPI and other questionnaires which offer three or four secondaries such as exvia, anxiety, neuroticism, and psychoticism are far short of a coverage of the personality sphere for adequate prediction and diagnosis. For a psychologist using depth psychometry it is most convenient to score both primaries and secondaries from the 16 PF itself; but if he wishes to resort to a set of secondary scales, then Barton's work on a *Core Trait-State Kit* might be of interest (see Professor Keith Barton, Department of Applied Behavioral Sciences, 140 Walker Hall, University of California, Davis).

223

Table 9.6

CRITERION RELATIONS OF SECOND-STRATUM TRAITS
TO CLINICAL DIAGNOSES

Secondary (as scored in positive direction)	t-Ratios,* with Sign Showing Direction of Difference from Normals	
	("Typical" Neurotics)	("Sociopathic" Neurotics)
T I Pathological Predisposition	+ 4.06	+ 2.64
T II Independent Ego-Id Expression	— 4.44	— 6.61
T III Irrepressible Temperament	+ .80	+ 2.34
T IV Alert Self-Concerned Realism	— .32	— 3.86
T V Self-Restraint	+ 2.33	— 2.80
T VI Narcistic Self-Expression	— .27	+ 5.63
T VII Sympathetic Excitability	— .40	— .74

NOTES: This table shows the deviations of means of neurotics and of sociopaths from the normal group, expressed as t-ratios directly. Primary objective test scores compounded into secondary scores as described in Cattell and Scheier (1961), p. 78. Titles of secondaries slightly modified in meaning in accordance with advance of theoretical interpretation.

*A t-ratio of 2.00 is significant at the 5 per cent level while a value of 2.67 is significant at the 1 per cent level.

Similarly, C—, ego weakness, O+, guilt proneness, Q3—, poor self-sentiment, and Q4+, ergic tension, found in the anxiety secondary are jointly subject to enhancement by anxiety, QII. Acceptance of the SUD model which best fits the facts at present leads to an alternative to a simple primary behavioral specification equation. In this alternative, the behavior or the symptom in question is explained and predicted partly by the primary "stubs" (best estimated by the existing primary scales) and partly by the independent secondaries (or even tertiaries). Thus, we can proceed by the Schmid-Leiman formula (see Cattell, 1973b, p. 108) to write the prediction (estimation) of a criterion in a specification equation that contains *side-by-side* the first orders (as "stubs") and the secondaries, thus:

$$C_j = b_{j1}T_1 + \cdots + b_{jn}T_n \left(+ b_jT_j\right) + b_{jI}\mathbf{T}_I + \cdots b_{j\pi}\mathbf{T}_\pi \qquad (9.3)$$

Here the i subscripts for the individual are omitted; the specific factor is in parentheses to indicate it is unscorable; the n primaries, T_1 through T_n, are in italics to remind us they are actually the "stubs" of the original primaries (Cattell, 1977a). These stubs can be scored with just the same relative weights of subtests as used in each of the original primaries; and the π secondaries, $\mathbf{T}$I through $\mathbf{T}_\pi$, are scored from the weights of primaries on the secondaries derived from Table 9.4 above. The b's for secondaries come from the Schmid-Leiman calculation. Both primaries and secondaries must be entered as standard scores.

The above equation is given here primarily for the theoretical completeness of understanding of trait structure and depth psychometry. It is correct, but practicable only to the degree to which the higher strata factors are defined. And as we have seen in Table 9.5, there are degrees of error by the time we reach the tertiary stratum which suggest that in practice one would best keep to the primaries or, at most, the secondaries. Since, however, personality theory now calls for basic research on meaning and origin of the secondaries and tertiaries, the pioneering psychologist will need to score them, and for this the weighting matrix in footnote 1 above would be most apt.

The practicing psychologist may also wish to explore their predictive power—in terms of using the seven secondaries together—against various criteria. in that case the matrix, computer handling of the calculation for the best weights for predicting a criterion x proceeds as follows. If $\mathbf{C}_x$ is a column vector of correlations of the secondaries with the criterion and $\mathbf{R}_{f\mathrm{II}}$ is the $\mathbf{R}$ matrix of correlations among secondaries from Table 9.5(b)1, the weight matrix $\mathbf{W}$ is obtained by:

$$\mathbf{W} = \mathbf{R}_{f\mathrm{II}}^{-1}\mathbf{C}_x \tag{9.4}$$

If one wishes to find out what the predictive power of all seven secondaries is on the given criterion, then we calculate the multiple correlation, R, as:

$$R^2 = \mathbf{W}'\mathbf{C}_x \tag{9.5}$$

The above calculations may be put to use only by a few, but the theoretical perspective of depth psychometry is important to all. What we are saying is that where we happen to reach the same score for two profiles on exvia or anxiety, it can nevertheless be reached in a different way by these individuals. In one, exvia may go along with the large endowment in the warmhearted quality of affectia, A, in the other with the low inhibition of surgency, F. And in anxiety, one may explain one case of anxiety with more ego weakness, C—, and another with more guilt proneness, O+. Where it is practicable to obtain simultaneously scores on primaries and secondaries, the insight of depth psychometry will be valuable to the clinician and the broader specification equation and give more dependable prediction into the future for the industrial and educational psychologist. In the domain of the O-A Kit, however, some years are likely to elapse before the psychological character and natural history of the secondaries are sufficiently understood to make direct statements with regard to their meaning and probable life courses.

10

Criterion Relations: I. Arranged Under Individual Source Traits

Compared to the extensive research on criterion relations of questionnaires, that on the O-A is as yet new and developing. Nevertheless, in proportion to the number of studies seeking criterion predictions, the O-A Kit almost certainly has a better percentage of significant relations than questionnaires and most other personality tests. The account of these improved diagnostic and predictive resources presented here is most helpfully given by an approach from two angles:

1) an account *by single source traits* of criterion associations found, which is given in this chapter, and

2) a consideration, in the next chapter, of the practitioner's diagnostic and predictive needs *classified by areas of practice* rather than by source traits, with an indication of which choice of factor batteries from the Kit would be most useful for each area, and what specification equations for all factors are available for a given area of criterion and practice. Let us proceed with 1).

Criterion Relations for Individual Source Traits

A preliminary indication of several of these relations has already been given in the initial account of the psychological nature of the traits in Table 3.1; so there will be some slight repetition here. The statistical significances of the associations are necessarily reported in different statistical forms in different studies and are on different samples, so they cannot always be exactly comparably reported here. But frequently we have expressed them as "t-values. (These have been roughly averaged and rounded, since no Bonferroni procedure is yet justified. But this has been done only where all instances from experiment are significant.) A t-value probably gives the simplest view of comparability, since it can be taken that with the range of sample sizes here in research studies a t-value of 2.5 means at least a $P < .05$ significance. Separate clinical, educational, and occupational and social adjustment (delinquency) relevancies will generally be given for each factor. The summaries will be shortened by use of "telegraphese" style, as follows.

U.I. 16. Ego Standards. — Ego scores are decidedly ($t = 7.0$) lower in schizophrenics (both paranoid and simple) than normals (Tatro, 1968). This finding is supported at $t = 2.3$ by Schmidt (1975) who, with others, found it lower also in general psychotic groups. It is lower in involutional depressives and in neurotic depressives, but less so than other pathologies. Lower in neurotics generally ($t = 6.5$; Cattell & Scheier, 1961). Cartwright, Tomson, & Schwartz (1975) found delinquents lower than normals. These decided negative relations of U.I. 16 with virtually all kinds of psychopathology support the interpretation of either ego strength, or some form thereof, involving control, competition, and self-assertion. Criminals are higher than neurotics but lower than normals (Knapp, 1965).

It has positive association with higher school performance (over and above intelligence and other factors, of course). Minimum r of $+ .23$ ($P < .01$) with grade point average (Schuerger, Dielman, & Cattell, 1970). Among main questionnnaire scale associations, Knapp (1960) found positive relations to ascendance, general activity, thinking introversion, literary, and feminine interests.

Occupationally, Sells found that U.I. 16 is higher in flyers with better pilot adjustment rating (Cattell, 1955b) and with higher aviation qualification test grades (Knapp & Most, 1960). It relates significantly negatively, however, with peer approval rating (other data suggest "ego assertiveness" tends somewhat to unpopularity, and Knapp's r of .52 with frequency count of military sick bay visits suggests narcism or fussiness). It shows a positive, .23 and .22 (significant), relation with pass-fail criterion and class standing in submarine training (Knapp, 1962). Reuterman, Howard, and Cartwright (in press) found a correlation of $+ .60$ with social status, and found it higher in members of adult-sponsored, respectable boys' clubs than in delinquent street gangs of the same age ($P < .01$). Negative r's were found in two studies with scores on the MMPI Lie scale. Laboratory results show high U.I. 16 with better resistance to frustration and to distraction, and with more "higher education in home" and "upper class" tastes. Nature-nurture research (Cattell, Stice, & Kristy, 1957; Cattell & Klein, in preparation) shows decidedly larger environmental than genetic determination.

U.I. 16 has also some significant somatic and neural associations: with body size, longer and thicker bones and muscles, higher systolic blood pressure, and better endurance of physical tensions, but correlates with below average performance on voluntary treadmill run to exhaustion. On the EEG, frontal-motor parietal-alpha phase length and amplitude are *negatively*, and frequency *positively*, related to U.I. 16 (Pawlik & Cattell, 1965).

U.I. 19. Independence. — The independence source trait is lower in psychotics generally than normals ($t = 6.1$; Tatro, 1968). It is specifically lower than normal in schizophrenics ($t = 4.5$; Tatro, 1968). The relation is supported by Schmidt (1975) ($t = 2.2$) and by Killian (1960) for both paranoid and nonparanoid schizophrenics ($t = 3.4$). Patrick, Cattell, and Price (in press), however, found for hospitalized depressives a t-value of 4.70 ($P < .0001$), again pointing to a *general* psychotic association, i.e., with both schizophrenia and depression (though not necessarily mania).

Lower in neurotics (than normals): Cattell, Schmidt, and Bjerstedt (1972, $t = 3.0$). Same finding by Cattell and Scheier ($t = 2.5$, 1961).

In school achievement it is positively related to performance in several subjects, but particularly the scientific and mathematical areas. Independent studies show it significantly related to general school grade (Pawlik, 1974). It was found to correlate $+ .26$ ($P < .01$) with grades (8th grade) by Schuerger, Dielman, and Cattell (1970). In questionnaires it is related to low lie scale score (MMPI), general activity and thoughtfulness (G-Z), and to Factor E, dominance, on the 16 PF. These questionnaire relations are best understood as the already confirmed relation to second-order questionnaire factor Q IV), independence (primaries A—, E, M, Q_1, and Q_2).

Occupationally, Knapp (1961b) found in submariners an r of .15 with pass-fail and .27 with class standing. Wardell and Royce (1975) relate it in cognitive performance to Witkin's field independence, to an analytic, independent, rational style, and high "field articulation."

Ustrzycki (1974) found U.I. 19 significantly negatively related to actual behavior problem checklist scores on the scale for "unsocialized psychopathic" and "subcultural unsocialized" (Quay and Peterson scales). On the other hand, Hundleby and Loucks (1974) found U.I. 19 *within* a delinquent 12-15-year-old training group *positively* related to more "daring" activities (alcohol and drugs, sex offenses, $+ .27$ to $+ .34$). However, in a comparison of delinquent and nondelinquent groups ($N = 143$ and 196; age 12-13), U.I. 19 correlated $+ .43$ ($P < .01$) with being in the nondelinquent group.

The independence source trait is thus one powerfully correlated with mental health, good use of available abilities in performance, and, in a "good" society, with positive social values, but, in an "inverted," delinquent society, with delinquent initiative.

It is among the most substantially inherited of source traits (Cattell, Stice, & Kristy, 1957) and is evidently a temperament factor favoring vigor, independence, initiative, and self-sufficiency.

U.I. 20. Evasiveness. — This is a subtle personality trait which, until grasped, seems to present paradoxes. Its effects are mainly not in the pathological realm, but rather in undependability and delinquency. The results (Cattell, Schmidt, & Bjerstedt, 1972; Tatro, 1968) show no differences of schizophrenics and neurotics from normals, though Patrick, Cattell, and Price (in press), in a study with carefully diagnosed depressives (hospitalized), found them significantly higher ($t = 3.42$, $P < .01$) than normals. Others have found substantial relations with emotional instability, lack of objectivity, psychopathic, rhathymic, and hypomanic tendencies, as measured by common questionnaire scales, for U.I. 20. An association with the manic-depressive temperament is indicated. If a longer label could be used, the old one of "sociable, emotional evasiveness" and undependability (Hundleby, Pawlik, & Cattell, 1965) would be ideal, for it stresses the curious combination of sociability with emotional instability, manic-depressive states, low correlation with moral dependability, and high evasiveness of reality and responsibility.

Ustrzycki (1974) found r's of .26 to .46 (N = 252) with three questionnaire scales of diverse delinquent tendencies, but barely significant relations to actual degree of legal violations. There is (in an industrial school group) some correlation with belonging to teams and number of girl friends. However, the industrial school group as a whole was actually *lower* on U.I. 20 than the normal controls, and Knapp and Most (1960) found the lie scale score also lower on U.I. 20. There are thus paradoxes, at the child level particularly, suggesting a subtle pattern not yet understood. For example, two psychiatrists (see Cattell & Scheier, 1961) rated higher U.I. 20s as significantly lower in "characterological anxiety," yet Knapp and Most found positive r's of .25 and .35 with anxiety (QII) and guilt (O) on the 16 PF. Cattell and Scheier (1961), however, found it *slightly* negatively related to *neurotic* anxiety. We are left with the impression that U.I. 20 (+) persons have an emotionality which causes them to overrate themselves (relative to the psychiatric and school observer) on anxiety, guilt, and delinquent tendencies.

The significant relation to depressive tendencies is interesting in the above connection. U.I. 20 shows *higher* than normal scores for involutional and neurotic depression but lower than normal for situational and cyclic depressions, thus offering diagnostic help among the depressions (Schmidt, 1972).

In adults U.I. 20 has some positive relation to practical performance (Knapp on helicopter pilots), but slightly negative ($-.13, P < .05$) with school grades at 8th-grade level. Reuterman, Howard, and Cartwright (in press) found in street gangs higher U.I. 20 in those living closer together ($r = .55$) and lower ($r = -.75$) in areas with greater family and neighborhood disorganization. First nature-nurture results show definitely high heredity on U.I. 20, suggesting the whole pattern is a temperamental volatility and "irresponsibility."

U.I. 21. Exuberance. — Substantial clinical relations with *low* neuroticism (Cattell & Scheier, 1961, $t = 4.2$; Schmidt, 1975, $t = 3.0$). Lower scores than for normals also in general psychotics, in paranoid and nonparanoid schizophrenics ($t = 4.0$) and *all* depressives—general, involutional, neurotic.

In questionnaires Knapp (1960) finds exuberance related on G-Z scales to general activity, ascendance, and to low agreeableness. No relation has been found to measured anxiety, but a negative relation to *psychiatrists'* anxiety ratings exists. Wardell and Royce (1975) mention enthusiasm, dominance, energy, and excitability in high-U.I. 21 persons.

School performances show differences best interpreted in terms of the degree of creativity in the performance scored. Getzels and Jackson

(1962) used some U.I. 21 tests (which may almost certainly be added to a single U.I. 21 score) in extensive creativity studies which point to its relation to (a) creativity in the sense of resourcefulness and imagination and (b) some unpopularity on sociometric counts. With adults Knapp (1961a) found significant positive relationship to class standing (grades), negative relationship to peer ratings of popularity, and positive relationship to life record data on number of sick bay calls. Dielman, Schuerger, and Cattell (1970) confirmed relation to grade point average with an r of .31, but in a very rigid school environment a low negative was found by Gruen (Cattell & Gruen, 1955). Wardell's (1976) analysis found socially oriented fluency less central than straight fluency, speed of judgment, and "future associations," indicating a socially unconcerned irrepressibility in U.I. 21, which may help explain the above indications of social unpopularity.

Cartwright, Tomson, and Schwartz (1975) found delinquent youths lower than controls, but that individuals in gangs who were high on U.I. 21 engaged in more street fighting and in more property offenses. "Respectable" boys' clubs average higher than gangs generally ($P < .01$) for U.I. 21. All criteria fit the "exuberance" interpretation and the "Churchill factor" label well, pointing to an energetic, imaginative endowment which disturbs associates and may come out well or ill according to (a) the needs of the situation and (b) the level of control by other source traits such as U.I. 16, 17, and 25. U.I. 21 has very substantial hereditary determination and is theoretically best conceived so far as a temperamental quality of mental energy probably associated with some cortical chemical pacemaker.

U.I. 23. Mobilization-vs-Regression. — Through the work, particularly of Dielman, Eysenck, Hundleby, Knapp, Meredith, Scheier, Schmidt, and Tatro, this source trait is rich in criterion associations.

In the clinical field it was first noted by Eysenck (1961) to be low in neurotics. Cattell and Scheier (1961) confirmed this ($t = 4.8$) but found (a) other clinical pathological syndromes equally low and (b) other factors equally low in neurotics, as also did Schmidt (1972). Psychotics, examined over diagnostic categories extending from schizophrenics (paranoid and nonparanoid) ($t = 4.0$) to manics ($t = 6.0$ approximately), fall as low as or lower than neurotics. But Schmidt's results, in particular, show an interesting trend of manics being more regressive and unable to mobilize than depressives (psychotic or neurotic). Tatro's (1965) results also show the score coming near to yielding a significant distinction of nonparanoid from paranoid schizophrenia, the former being lower. Many neurotic symptoms statistically examined individually are found to be well predictable from a low U.I. 23 score.

In educational achievement, mobilization correlates positively with grades, though it also correlates with intelligence (see Table 11.1). Its effect on grades, however, is significant apart from the intelligence association. Some results on the Kuder Interest Test (Knapp, 1960) point to a curious split in which computational and artistic interests are positively (22 and .24), and literary and scientific interests are negatively ($-.25$ and $-.22$) correlated with mobilization. This is interpretable, perhaps, as due to the former requiring immediate decisiveness. Dielman, Schuerger, and Cattell (1970) confirm the above relation to school performance with a .23 correlation with grade point average (8th grade).

In occupational observations Knapp (1961a) found U.I. 23 correlating significantly positively with popularity as evident in peer ratings of pilot proficiency, officer-like qualities, and social acceptability ($P < .01$), and with final flying grades (0.35). In the astronaut program low U.I. 23 was found associated with fainting under stress, while other results also suggest some "physical fitness" correlations. However, the challenge of a stress situation (treadmill run threat) seems to give a slight but significant rise in U.I. 23. Although there is appreciable hereditary influence, neither heredity nor environment shows any clear predominance in determining the level.

In the area of delinquency there are significant relations, adult offenders being below normals, but well above neurotics. Negative correlation is similarly found with lie scales on the MMPI and EPI. Mobilization-regression is a measure which has been found to change very significantly, in the theoretically expected upward direction, through therapy (see Table 11.5). As the name now given to it indicates, it is best conceived as the capacity of the individual to mobilize his resources—his skills, motives, memories, and interests—in an integrated way to meet whatever demands the environment makes for adjustments. At the regression pole there is lack of this capacity and regression of normal interests from their objectives. It is seemingly more environmentally than genetically determined in its level at any time, and prolonged mental conflict or other deep fatigue inducers could be largely responsible for its reduction from a normal, healthy level.

U.I. 24. Anxiety. —This is a clear-cut, and now uniquely determinable, factor, previously perceived and described clinically and in everyday life as anxiety, in its various normal and pathological manifestations. The correlational evidence clearly shows this identity, and that this single factor accounts for *most* of a wide range of anxiety manifestations. Thus, alike in factor-analytic examination of ratings and questionnaires, in situational stimulus effects, and in physiology, U.I. 24 stands as the essence of anxiety. The separate studies of Tatro (1968), Killian (1960), and Cattell, Schmidt, and Bjerstedt (1972) find no significant difference of schizophrenics from normals. They, and Cattell and Scheier (1961), found, on the other hand, neurotics significantly above normal but not as much ($t = 1.8$ and 2.2) divergent as they are on U.I. 16 or 21. Thus, it may well be, as Freud said, that anxiety is "central to the neuroses," but modern experiment shows it is not the sole factor or even the most crucial differentiator in neuroses. It has an appreciable appearance in normal, healthy dynamics in relation to realistic situational provokers of anxiety. Results on psychotics, other than schizophrenics, show no common trend: involutional depressives were not significantly higher and manics were lower than normals. General depressives and some other psychotics seem above normal, though not significantly so. Some results do not show them above normal at all. The relation of U.I. 24 to questionnaire anxiety scales is very high, and Wardell and Yeudall (1976) confirm the findings of Cattell and Scheier (1961), and others, of appropriate correlations with the second-order components, C−, G−, O+, Q₃−, and Q₄+ scales in the 16 PF, i.e., the identity of U.I. 24 with Q II.

As is well known from extensive literature, the relation of anxiety to school achievement depends on age and grade level, type of learning, and situation. With autonomic conditioning rates, the U.I. 24 relation is positive (Cattell & Scheier, 1961; Taylor, 1951). At the 7th and 8th grade, Cattell and Butcher (1968) found an r of .2 with success, but in other areas, generally zero or negative correlations. Brogden's (1940) and Gruen's (see Cattell & Gruen, 1955) early studies at younger ages in school also showed positive relations. But in college groups, *negative r's* have been fairly consistently found (Scheier & Cattell, 1958) with achievement. One may reconcile these results with the generalization that in simpler, earlier learning, and reflex or autonomic learning, U.I. 24 predicts positively, but in more complex and later learning (other than emotional learning), anxiety distracts and impedes cognitive learning. However, the negative relation of achievement to anxiety in adolescence and later could be *partly* due to the reverse direction of action, i.e., low achievement causing anxiety, as shown in Tsushima's experiment (see Cattell & Scheier, 1961). Knapp (1962) with naval candidates found a significant r of .26 on U.I. 24 with pass-fail success measures and .12 with class standing. Since this is a low-anxiety group, the result points to *milder* anxiety increases being beneficial for achievement. Sarason (1966) has suggested a curvilinear relation, and, as we have indicated, since university students were higher on anxiety than Knapp's submariners, it is likely that in low-anxiety groups U.I. 24 correlates positively and in high anxiety, negatively with achievement. Pawlik (1974) with students found lower U.I. 24 scores in high and overachievers than in low and underachievers, consistent with the main trend over higher ranges being negative between anxiety and achievement.

Cartwright, Tomson, and Schwartz (1975) found no difference in mean U.I. 24 score between "good" boys' clubs and street gangs, which fits the usual lack of raised anxiety found in "acting-out" disorders. However, in regard to fighting behavior, their results point to a curvilinear relation with U.I. 24 resembling that to achievement! In general, they

233

found a correlation of —.76 between anxiety and fighting, but "in certain gangs those engaging in more conflict were actually the more anxious boys." Knapp (1963) found adult offenders above average ($t = 8.2$) on U.I. 24, yet not so deviant as neurotics. Ustrzycki (1974) found significant positive relation of U.I. 24 to use of alcohol and drugs, which is extensively supported by relations to the corresponding anxiety questionnaire factor, QII (Cattell, Eber, & Tatsuoka, 1970). They found a slight negative relation to being a juvenile delinquent ($-.13$, $P < .05$). The relation of anxiety to delinquency is thus, in general, slight and changing in direction according to the situation and age of the offender. With adult offenders, on less gross crime and *actually convicted cases*, Knapp's (1965) finding of higher anxiety seems more typical.

Occupationally, airmen, firemen, Olympic athletes, etc., are below average, and editorial workers, bank clerks, etc., score above average (see lists in Cattell & Scheier, 1961). Knapp (1961b) found popularity in a group correlatimg —.26 with U.I. 24, and other results suggest the same direction (but probably through association of anxiety with neuroticism).

As the work of Rickels (see Table 11.5), Bartlett, Hunt, and others (see Cattell, Rickels, et al., 1966; Hunt, et al., 1959; Rickels & Cattell, 1965) indicates, U.I. 24 measures are sensitive to therapeutic action, on the one hand, and to situational threats on the other. Sells (in Cattell, 1955b) found scores up on flyers on hazardous missions; Tsushima found it raised by news of failure in an exam. Rickels found significant reductions on U.I. 24 (QII) with therapy and chemotherapy. Cureton (1963), Ismail and Young (1977), and others have found it to drop with physical exercise courses.

Numerous physiological criteria have been firmly related to the U.I. 24 score, such as higher systolic blood pressure, lower electrical skin resistance, faster respiration, faster pulse, greater production of saliva, higher hippuric acid, and 17 OH ketosteroids in the urine (see summary in Cattell & Scheier, 1961). Proneness to anxiety was found by Eysenck and Prell (1951) and also by Cattell and Klein (in press) to have quite appreciable heritability.

The question of state and trait relations in anxiety is discussed in the next section. But one must question here the tendency to give U.I. 24 other names, such as neuroticism (Eysenck, 1961), emotionality, impulsivity (Kagan, 1966), impulse instability (Wardell & Yeudall, 1976). "Neuroticism" is gravely misleading because there is a demonstrated multifactor determination of neuroticism (Cattell & Scheier, 1961) in which, as seen above, U.I. 24 is seemingly not even as important in association as other personality factors. The notion of considering U.I. 24 to be emotionality and impulsivity is often tied to neurological approaches, which take anxiety to be located in the limbic system. Our own theory is that anxiety is largely elicited as an autonomic expression from the hypothalamus and both control and provocation thereof come through the limbic system from the frontal lobes, e.g., frustration information creating anxiety comes that way. The careful factor-analytic separation of source traits places emotionality, and much of impulsivity, squarely on the C factor (negative pole), well-named *ego-strength* in its positive aspects. The connection of anxiety with the 16 PF Factor C, which is an ingredient in QII, is accurately established, but the confusion of C and U.I. 24 can do nothing but retard a clear grasp of factor meanings in this area.

U.I. 25 Realism-vs-Tensidia (The latter is *"psychoticism"* in Eysenck's interpretation [1968]).—Realism is lower in nonparanoid schizophrenics than normals (Tatro (1968): $t = 2.6$; Killian (1960): $t = 2.5$) and, to a lesser degree, lower in depressives (with regard to whom Patrick, Cattell, & Price [in press] found $t = 1.98$, $P < .05$). It is also lower in psychotics generally, but not so low, or so specific to psychosis, as to justify Eysenck's label of "psychoticism" for this dimension. Low U.I. 25 is more a disregard of and weakness in adjusting to realities than it is any particular psychotic defect. Thus it is low in character disorders ($t = 2.9$; Killian, 1960), in general neurotics ($t = 3.0$; Schmidt, 1975) and neurotic depressives (Schmidt, 1975), and even somewhat low in severe society-withdrawn TB patients (Killian, 1960). Schmidt found low U.I. 25 especially characteristic of schizophrenics ($t = 4.0$). Wardell and Yeudall (1976), finding tensidia related to lower intelligence and extraversion simultaneously, suggest U.I. 25 is related (negatively) to "disinhibition" and reduction of reality contact after frontal lobe damage or lobotomy.

Knapp (1963) finds it significantly negatively related to delinquency almost to the same extent as U.I. 16. Sociopaths score below normal, and delinquents below sociopaths. Cartwright, Tomson, and Schwartz (1975) agree in finding this one of the best factors distinguishing "good" boys' club members from gang group members ($P < .01$). In gang and other groups, they found U.I. 25 higher on groups of higher group cohesion ($r = .52$) and higher communality of attitudes ($r = .54$). The tense inability to think calmly shown in tensidia (U.I. 25—) is evidently very important in the "hysteria" of crowds noted by many from LeBon to McDougall and Freud.

Occupationally, Knapp (1962) found in both pilot and submarine groups that better performance went with higher U.I. 25.

All in all, the available analyses fit very well the theoretical interpretation of U.I. 25 as capacity for self-controlled behavior and good contact with reality, as shown by avoidance of delinquent difficulties, of neurotic and psychotic withdrawal from reality testing, and by good performance where "common sense" realism is important. Indications at the neural level suggest its identification with effective frontal lobe action (though not including superego connections). It belongs among the six

235

higher factors for hereditary influence but its still appreciable environmental determination suggests learning as primary, with neural frontal
lobe adequacy as only a limiting condition.

U.I. 28. Asthenia-vs-Self-Assurance. — Unlike several previous
factors, this seems to have few useful clinical associations, as confirmed in
the work of Tatro (1968), Schmidt (1974), and others. The only significant
relation has been a tendency to higher U.I. 28 scores in depressives,
neurotics, and psychotics. Scheier, Cattell, and Horn (1960) found all kinds
of neurotics a little (but significantly) above normal. Its association with
pathology is thus slight but pervasive.

In questionnaires it shows some steady positive relations to
16 PF Factors L, M, Q_1, H, and Q_4—, and in the G-Z questionnaires to lack
of objectivity, low agreeableness, and low cooperativeness. This general
pattern of autism, asthenia, negativism, and radicalism has been theoretically interpreted by Cattell (1964a) as a reaction against initial early
dependence on dominant parents and premature enforcement of superego
standards. Consistent with this view of U.I. 28 as the product of broad
early inhibition is the finding (Cattell and Klein, in press) that genetics
plays very little part in determining its level. Despite the "surly" autism,
high U.I. 28 behaves like inhibition in being associated with neurosis, while
its opposite, low U.I. 28, is associated with delinquency, drug addiction,
and alcoholism (Scheier, Cattell, & Mayeske, 1960). Cartwright (1974),
however, reports no significant delinquent gangs-vs-boys' club differences.
Knapp (1965) found a small (significant) positive correlation with class
standing, in military training, but in school children Pawlik (1974) found
this insignificant. In terms of criteria yet tried, its general predictive
usefulness is at present not great, but there is a special contribution to
separating neurotics from delinquents, and manics from depressives.

U.I. 32. Exvia-vs-Invia. — Though a normal temperament
dimension, U.I. 32 has clinical associations. Neurotics are more inviant ($t =$
3.0; Cattell & Scheier, 1961; $t = 2.1$, Schmidt, 1974; see also Eysenck,
1961). This is supported as far as may be by various studies using less pure
measures of "extraversion-introversion." That schizophrenia is far from
being merely simple introversion is shown by schizophrenic scores on
introversion not being really extreme. The differences from normals *are* in
the inviant direction, but vary from barely significant to $t = 4.0$ values
(Schmidt). Tatro (1968) found definite indications that nonparanoid (simple)
schizophrenics are lower, i.e., more inviant, than paranoid schizophrenics.
This fits other evidence and the concept of process schizophrenia. However, the finding that not only involutional depressives (excluding ordinary
depressives) *but also manics* are significantly more introverted than
normals (about $t = 4.0$; Schmidt, 1974) introduces some new theory
regarding the structure of these disorders.

236

The relation of U.I. 32 to school performance is significant, but of a different form according to the age of students and the mode of instruction. Probably the most extensive data in personality source-trait terms at the high school level is that of Cattell and Butcher (1968), using QI for U.I. 32, and that of Barton, Dielman, and Cattell (1972), using other tests, while at earlier levels Cattell and Howarth (1964), Cattell and Damarin (1968), and Cattell and Gruen (1955) offer evidence in strictly O-A measures. On a questionnaire basis the relation of exvia to school achievement has been analyzed by Eysenck (1977) and his associates, and by Cattell and Butcher (1968). The general agreement is that in the earlier years and in a social, classroom situation, exvia is moderately positively related to achievement. At college, and later (Knapp [1962] found an r of $-.12$ [significant] between U.I. 32 and class standing in the military), and, with more scope for private study, higher achievement is more strongly and significantly related to invia.

More emphatic is the relation of invia to *creativity*, as distinct from routine grade gains. Invia is not the *whole* story of creativity, since other personality factors are important (Drevdahl & Cattell, 1958; Cattell & Butcher, 1968), but in *real-life creativity situations* (as distinct from test situations), there can be no doubt that the inviant temperament, with its inhibition of superficial response and relative disregard of social approval-disapproval, conduces strongly to original and realistic invention.

The evidence on relation to delinquency is also complex, not entirely supporting the present writer's and Eysenck's simpler hypothesis of delinquents differing from neurotics in being primarily more exviant. True, psychopaths are unquestionably more exviant (see pattern in Cattell, Eber, & Tatsuoka, 1970), but delinquency is not one pattern, and the several subforms differ in regard to the role of exvia-invia. In lesser, impulsive delinquencies, particularly at earlier ages, the exviant shows up as more prone to defy inhibitory rules; but much has yet to be found regarding exvia-invia effects on types of crime in adult life.

As regards occupation interests, substantial differences have been found using questionnaire scales (see Cattell, Eber, & Tatsuoka, 1970), but not yet checked on U.I. 32 batteries. In interests, U.I. 32 has positive relations (Knapp, 1960) of .21 with artistic interest and $-.33$ with clerical interest, as measured on the Kuder. Other scales support this general direction of distinction and show U.I. 32 negatively correlated with scientific interests. As discussed in Chapter 3, air pilots, athletes, military cadets, stewardesses, and salesmen score high on U.I. 32 and accountants, scientists, religious teachers, and farmers, low.

Associations are accumulating at the physiological level (Duffy, 1962; Eysenck, 1961; Hundleby, Pawlik, & Cattell, 1965), though the discovered greater autonomic threat reactivity of inviants must be considered to reside largely in the Factor H—, threctia, component of invia. The other components (F excepted) have low hereditary determination, consistent with the finding of Cattell and Klein (in press)—though not with Eysenck and Prell (1951)—that environment is rather more important than heredity in determining the exvia-invia balance. In the EEG indicators of activation, one finds, in the resting condition, no relation to exvia-invia, but in activities such as calculating, the amount of α index, and the α frequency and phase length are positively correlated with U.I. 32 (which, interestingly enough, is *opposite* to the relation to U.I. 16 and U.I. 22) (Pawlik & Cattell, 1965).

Some of the above associations rest more definitely on questionnaire, Q-data, but the association of U.I. 32 with QI, loading the primaries A, affectia-vs-sizia, D, excitability, F, surgency-vs-desurgency, H, parmia-vs-threctia, and Q2—, group action-vs-self-sufficiency, is so well confirmed that the inferences are justifiable. Parenthetically, in view of the central historical importance of Jung's "extraversion-introversion" concept, it is surprising that psychology has taken so long to discover objective tests approaching the questionnaires in validity and reliability.

U.I. 33. Discouragement-vs-Sanguineness. — Both Schmidt (1974) and Tatro (1968) found a moderate tendency ($t = 2.3$) for schizophrenics to be higher than normals on this factor. On the other hand, these studies agreed in finding no relations to neuroticism. The questionnaire associations of U.I. 33 with the G-Z questionnaires are with low ascendancy (—.26), low cooperativeness (—.31), low confidence, low calmness, high social introversion, and high depression. In interests, U.I. 33 is negative with Kuder "persuasive" interests, and positive with "clerical" (Knapp, 1960).

As a predictor of school achievement or military occupational performance, this factor has no role, the results showing essentially zero r's.

Although Reuterman, Howard, and Cartwright (in press) found no differences between gang and boys' club members, Knapp (1965) found adult delinquents significantly below normals, i.e., more sanguine. Reuterman, Howard, and Cartwright found better physique correlated with sanguineness (U.I. 33—), centering on .60 for height and .59 for weight. (These values are across group means and higher, therefore, than for individuals.) Also, "those with higher levels of U.I. 33 came from lower socioeconomic class neighborhoods ($r = -.56$)." It would seem that the best present theory about the U.I. 33 pattern is that it is a form of inhibition and depression based on accumulated experience of frustration and deprivation. Consistent with this is the finding (Cattell & Klein, in press) that its level is largely a product of environment. Its importance is likely to be greatest in the analysis of depression, and the recent work of Patrick, Cattell, and Price (in press) supports this by showing statistically significant ($P < .05$ and $P < .01$) differences of hospitalized and outpatient depressive from normal controls in the hypothesized direction.

Since rapidly increasing numbers of criterion researches with the O-A are anticipated, the practicing psychologist may expect appreciable augmentation of the above predictive resources and of theoretical clarification of the nature of the source traits in the near future. A summary of these will be given in an IPAT bulletin at the appropriate stage of replication of findings.

11

Criterion Relations: II. The O-A Kit Organized Under Educational, Socio-Occupational, and Clinical Uses

In practice, through the first 60 years of this century, psychologists tended to fashion different kinds of batteries, with different principles and concepts, separately for work in clinical, educational, industrial, and other areas. Naturally, some adaptations of central concepts of psychology, in personality and ability, to the convenience of particular fields is desirable and is indicated by suggested subsets from the O-A Kit. But the *ad hoc* test developments just described spring more from a vacuum in central concepts than adaptations. In the face of this parochial thinking the personality theorists today must reassure the "practical" man that, when all is said, the same personality, with the *same* capacities, desires, and conflicts, is still being measured in the individual who enters a school or a clinic, or seeking a job appointment. Consequently, we should be viewing this human being as a whole and using the best available diagnostics and assessment instruments for understanding the total personality and ability picture, regardless of the field of applied psychology concerned. Naturally, the fund of *criterion relations* and programmatic knowledge developed within these areas will be relatively specialized, but the basic temperament, ability, and dynamic traits will be the same, and the personality theory will employ the best model for the total action of personality in all its situational settings. Since the backbone of our multivariate experimental approach to personality theory is the behavior specification equation, let us repeat it here for ensuing discussion. This time, let us remember that our personality factors, P's (z of them in formula 11.1 below), are operating also with a series of traits from the other two modalities: abilities and dynamic (motivation) traits. However, because we are not concerned here with details of abilities we will enter them in the equation as a single term for the summed effect of the person's m abilities ($\Sigma b_x A_{xi}$) and similarly for his n dynamic traits, using ($\Sigma b_y D_{yi}$). In deriving a_{hijk} for the particular performance to be predicted by the behavioral equation we set out the personality modality, however, in the separate z personality scores, P_{1i}, P_{2i}, etc.

$$a_{hijk} = \Sigma\, b_{jx}\, A_{xi} + b_{j1}P_{1i} + b_{j2}P_{2i} + \cdots + b_{jz}P_{zi}$$

$$+ \Sigma b_{jy}\, D_{yi} \qquad (11.1)$$

Here A_{xi} is the individual's i score on the ability trait A_x, and similarly for the other traits, and the b's are weights, obtained from correlations, showing the given trait's involvement in the act (performance

241

or symptom) a_{hij}. The h and k remind one that the b value is also dependent on the total situation, as given by the focal stimulus h and the ambient situation k. Thus, h and k are properly subscripts for every one of the b's, but in order not to clutter up the equation for the reader we have not included them to the right of the equal sign.

We wish here to indicate particularly how the personality scores are brought in, and so initially we shall neglect the A's and D's, but, of course, our degree of prediction and understanding of the behavior of symptom a_{hijk} will be lower until they are brought in also.

Now the behavior specification equation can be looked at forwards or backwards. What we may call the forward direction is when one has the individual's trait scores and is estimating how well he may be expected to do in college or in a job. This use supposes we also have the b weights, i.e., "behavioral indices" for the given behavioral situation, such as doing well on a given job. What we may call the backward, or diagnostic, approach is when we have the individual's performance, a, and wish to analyze how and why it is done to the extent that it is. For example, we might be puzzled by a case where the performance is an underachievement relative to a student's apparent intelligence. By looking at the general specification equation (the b's), we see at once which factors other than intelligence have significant loadings in achievement and can examine the individual's score levels on these personality and motivation traits to discover the sources of the discrepancy.

The preceding chapter has examined the psychological meaning and predictive value of source traits *individually*, factor by factor. The present chapter, orienting to the specification of particular behaviors, will necessarily overlap with it as do the warp and woof of a fabric. For it will examine the factors now *as organized about the practical purposes and specific predictions of psychologists*, severally in educational, occupational, and clinical psychology. It will restate and extend some criterion relations already given under individual factors, but in the context of relevance to these areas of applied psychology, beginning with education.

Application in Educational Psychology

As regards sheer relevance, it will be evident, from a perusal of the relation of educational criteria to individual factors in the last chapter, that very significant associations are found for achievement with the following source traits:

	Source Traits	Direction of action on school achievement
U.I. 16	Ego Standards	+
U.I. 19	Independence	+
U.I. 23	Mobilization	+
and U.I. 25	Realism	+

The correlations now reported with these factors are significant, but seemingly not large, namely, about 0.2 to 0.3. However, one must remember they were found with less finished forms of the O-A and that with correction for attenuation (for "shortness unreliability") they rise, in the case of U.I. 16 and 19, to the 0.3 to 0.4 level. Further, the statistically minded psychologist will perceive at once the difference implied here between such correlations with random scales, often highly mutually correlated, and correlations with relatively pure factor batteries essentially independent. In the latter case, b weights (essentially correlations) for achievement of 0.5 with intelligence, and of 0.3 with each of the above four personality factors, would yield a multiple correlation of 0.78. If one considered also such correlations as have been found with motivation strength factors in the School Motivation Analysis Test (SMAT), contributing 20% of achievement variance, the combined battery could yield a correlation of .90 of the predictors with school achievement. It is therefore obvious that in the nature of things, with several personality, motivation, and ability factors as independent predictors, we should not expect significant correlations of single personality traits, as such, to be above about 0.3 in order to get substantial predictions from the total personality measurements.

Lesser correlations with school achievement, significant in certain populations and school conditions, have been found for:

U.I. 21 Exuberance, positive with *creative* performance only;

U.I. 20 Evasiveness, mainly negative;

U.I. 24 Anxiety, mainly negative;

U.I. 32 Exvia, negative at university level;

U.I. 33 Discouragement, mainly negative, but smaller.

Some of the most systematic research on educational performance prediction from the O-A Kit has been done by King (1976), who used all 10 primaries and an intelligence test. Noteworthy correlations are shown in Table 11.1. Here and elsewhere, some special predictive power for mathematics has been noted in U.I. 19.

In agreement with the first results cited above, U.I. 16 (ego standards), 19 (independence), 23 (mobilization), and 25 (realism-vs-tensidia) now prove to have the most powerful effects. The very slight positive relation with exvia (U.I. 32) agrees with conclusions quoted above,

Table 11.1

SCHOOL PERFORMANCE ESTIMATED FROM INDIVIDUAL PRIMARY PERSONALITY TRAITS IN THE KIT

	Universal Index (U.I.) Numbers of Traits									
	16	19	20	21	23	24	25	28	32	33
Freshman Grade Point Average	15	33	—20	04	30	—25	30	—23	06	—07
Sophomore Grade Point Average	16	32	—16	06	25	—20	33	—22	08	—05
Reading Comprehension	34	52	—18	07	54	—28	29	—40	18	—04
Mathematical Reasoning	41	53	—21	04	47	—15	38	—28	13	—16

N = 105

NOTES: The math and reading scores are independent experimentally of the Grade Point Average, though, of course, matched by similar measures in the total grades.

The Freshman and Sophomore values are given separately to show the considerable consistency of the year-to-year action of the personality factors.

e.g., Cattell and Butcher (1968), and supported by Eysenck's recent data, that in junior high school years extraversion operates moderately in a positive direction. But here we must point out that, contrariwise, *invia*, not exvia, is related positively at the university level. The consistent negatives for anxiety (U.I. 24) agree with our generalization that except for high anxiety groups, or learning of an autonomic reflex kind, poorer performance goes with anxiety.

A curious finding by King (1976) is that appreciable prediction of *intelligence test performance*, on both crystallized and fluid (culture-fair) tests, can be given by personality primaries U.I. 19, 23, and 25, reaching indeed to 0.5 in some populations in the case of U.I. 19. Does this mean that performance on these personality test batteries has sufficient demand on cognitive abilities to be contaminated with intelligence? Or, conversely, are we to conclude that *performance* on intelligence tests, as distinct from the intelligence factor (g_f or g_c) itself, depends partly on personality factors which help the individual effectively to organize his intelligence in actual test-taking situations? Probably improved psychometry will need in the future to take notice of both "contaminations." Thus, in measuring U.I. 19, independence, improvements should result from

244

balancing out the closure and spatial abilities performances (prominent in Witkin's "field independence" measures) by sensory approaches other than the visual one to expressions of independence.

The magnitude of ultimate prediction of school achievement from the 10 factors in the Kit, alone and with one general ability factor, intelligence, added, are worked out by King (1976), as shown in Table 11.2.

The combinations in the 2nd, 3rd, 4th, 7th, 8th, and 9th rows are those found by stepwise regression to be the effective necessary combinations. Combinations with no decided predictive value are not entered with R's. Pending fuller exploration with other groups, these values suggest an economical use of one, two, or three well-chosen factors from the Main Kit for educational performance prediction purposes. (The uniformly higher values for the universal, standardized reading and math tests in Table 11.1 point perhaps to these criteria being more reliable than the grade average in the King sample from one class teacher.) If we take .26 and .48 (the means of the 2 years) as correlations, respectively, from intelligence alone and intelligence plus personality, the fraction of achievement variance predicted goes from 13% to 23%. That is to say, there is a 77% increase when personality measures from the O-A are added. This is in line with other findings on increase of prediction from personality measures being added (Cattell & Butcher, 1968). If we take the evidence (Cattell, 1972) that traditional intelligence tests are already contaminated with school achievement, as such (and therefore some personality too), and switch to the Culture Fair Intelligence Test, the full impact of the personality measures becomes more clear. For the IPAT Culture Fair correlates about .32 to .38 with school work. Taking $r = .32$, the gain from bringing in personality in the O-A is now from 10% to 23%, i.e., an increase of 130%. What these results point to is that in the prediction of school performance, as Cattell and Butcher (1968) found with questionnaire measures of personality, the addition of personality measures to intelligence measures typically just about doubles the precision of estimate. If this is so in academic performance, one can surmise that in performances less dependent on sheer cognitive abilities, e.g., athletics or leadership, the efficacy of personality measures would be even more important.

In terms of *understanding* how the total personality operates, one should give attention to the traits listed above beyond the statistically powerful predictors U.I. 16, ego standards, U.I. 19, independence, U.I. 23, mobilization, and U.I. 25, realism-vs-tensidia. Evasiveness, U.I. 20, anxiety, U.I. 24, asthenia, U.I. 28, and discouragement, U.I. 33, also have real, though slighter, influences, and all in a negative direction, while U.I. 21 has a positive influence, particularly in creativity. These results fit very well the theory about the nature of these source traits. However, had the source traits with hypothesized superego qualities, U.I. 17, and U.I. 29, as well as cortertia, U.I. 22, with its prediction of flying school performance, been entered in school research, one may reasonably hypothesize that the

Table 11.2

MULTIPLE *R*'s PREDICTING SCHOLASTIC ACHIEVEMENT FROM THE WHOLE KIT,
WITH AND WITHOUT INTELLIGENCE

	Freshman G.P.A.	Sophomore G.P.A.	Reading Comprehension	Math Reasoning
All Ten Primaries	.45	.43	.66	.62
U.I. 23 and 25 only		.38		
U.I. 19, 23, 28—, and 32 only			.65	
U.I. 16, 19, and 23 only				.61
Intelligence alone	.38*	.34*	.67	.68
Intelligence and 10 primaries	.50*	.46*	.74	.74
Intelligence and U.I. 23	.42		.70	
Intelligence and U.I. 25		.41		
Intelligence and U.I. 33—				.70

*Averages of .36 and .48 from this table are reported in the text of this chapter.

school performance prediction would be still further improved through small positive correlations with them. Those source traits are in the Extended Kit.

In regard to predicting creativity, as distinct from academic achievement in examinations, Getzels and Jackson (1962) have found the tests of U.I. 21 positively important, while U.I. 19 (positively) and U.I. 32 (negatively) have been predictive in unpublished work on small samples. This refers to creativity in the life situation, not "creativity" in tests in an examination situation. (The latter, though often called the criterion, is only fluency, or "divergent thinking" in Guilford's definition.) The findings agree with findings in creativity from measures of the same personality factors in questionnaires (Cattell & Drevdahl, 1955; Drevdahl, 1961) when they overlap.

Analyses and remedial work with individuals essentially begins with fitting the individual's factor scores into the specification equation implied by any row of Table 11.1. Incidentally, we say "implied" because these were left by King (1976) as correlations and one would normally use weights—which statistically are likely to be a little different. However, regarding *b*'s and *r*'s, since the correlations among factors are moderate and changeable, correlations and weights are close, and one may well in practice use the *r*'s as weights. By looking at the 10 products (correlation size multiplied by the person's standard score on factors) on the right of the specification equation, one can see where the biggest negative values are, and ask, insofar as the natural history of each factor is known, how far and in what way the defect of personality or motivation may be remedied. In this educational field, as in all fields, the above statistical analysis has to be illuminated further by the "clinical" skills of the psychologist. Some instructive illustrations of the combined use of factor measurement with general psychological principles are available in Karson and O'Dell (1976), though they apply them to the 16 PF factors, but these, after all, include, at the second order, our U.I. 17, 19, 24, and 32.

Application in Occupational and Social Psychology

The source traits effective in occupational performance have so far been examined mainly in military and air pilot callings. The significant relations appear to some extent in the same personality areas as in student performance. Obviously, as research proceeds, important differences will be found among occupations, but at present one sees mainly operative the factors in "general competence." These are, in the positive weighting direction, U.I. 16, 19, 21, 23, and 25, while U.I. 24 weights positive or negative according to low or high mean of the group, but largely negatively. Of these, U.I. 16, 19, 21, and 23 are at present best substantiated, and might be given a .4 weight relative to $\pm$ .2 for U.I. 24 and 25, respectively.

In situations where the job performance criterion can be objectively evaluated as well as rated by peers or others, some differences have been noted not previously clearly seen in questionnaires. For example, Knapp and Most (1960) note that the pilot adjustment qualification test correlates 0.37 with U.I. 16, which agrees with other competence relations to U.I. 16; but ratings of proficiency as a pilot by peers in training give an r of —.39! (See "popularity" below.) Knapp (1962) found evaluation of Navy submarine personnel positively and significantly related to U.I. 16, 19, 25, just as in air pilots, indicating the generality of the effect of these personality traits despite different specific ability requirements.

In regard to occupational areas, artistic, personal contact, and "persuasive" occupations, e.g., salesmen, have been found predictable when measured as interests (Kuder artistic 0.2, clerical and scientific —0.3), and as actual activities, from U.I. 32, exvia-invia measures. Air pilots, athletes, military cadets, actors, airline stewardesses, and salesmen have been found higher on U.I. 32, either here or in its QI equivalent. On the other hand, accountants, scientists, creative writers, religious leaders, and farmers are inviant (low U.I. 32). One other factor already recognized as useful in this area is U.I. 33, which correlates positively with clerical and negatively with salesmen and related interests.

Turning from occupations per se to broader social roles and positions, we note certain relations to social status, most clearly of U.I. 16 and U.I. 33—, but also of U.I. 19, 21, as well as 22 and 26 (the last two in the Extended Kit). These, in certain instances (U. I. 16 and 33—), relate to other elements in the social status complex (education of parents and larger physique).

As regards sociability and popularity in groups, the latter (including military ratings of social acceptability) is predicted by U.I. 16 (ego standards) negatively, U.I. 21 (exuberance) negatively, U.I. 24 (anxiety) negatively, and U.I. 26 (self-sentiment) positively. There are suggestions of U.I. 19 and 20 negatively and U.I. 32 positively. As noted earlier, it is intriguing that U.I. 16 and 21, contributing to competence and creativity, should also contribute to unpopularity. A possible explanation is given by Knapp's finding that U.I. 16, 21, and 26— relate to frequency of sick bay visits, and since this is the pattern above in unpopularity, it may be a narcistic quality in the individual rather than envy in peers which generates this social distance.

Sociability, as contact-making, is positively related to U.I. 20 and 32 and negatively to U.I. 24. Reuterman, Howard, and Cartwright found higher average U.I. 25 in members positively related to total group cohesiveness. That objectivity and sanity should aid group functioning makes sense. They found leadership (but in the sense of popularity, carefully sociometrically estimated) negatively related to U.I. 21, 24, and 33, as well as positively to U.I. 17, good upbringing and restraint, as described in the Extended Kit. U.I. 21, strangely, varied with groups. These findings on adolescents fit those above on adults, including the finding that U.I. 21, which contributes to enriching group ideas, is negatively related in small groups to the acceptance and popularity of the individuals concerned.

Clinical Pathology and Delinquency

The use of the O-A Battery is fortunately well advanced in the clinical area, through extensive and statistically adequate studies over the last 15 years by Bjerstedt, Brengelmann (related tests), Cattell and Rickels, Eysenck, Killian, Knapp, Patrick, Price, Scheier, Schmidt, Schuerger, Tatro, Wardell and Yeudall, and others. Thus, profiles or specification equations for diagnosis, prognosis, and the monitoring of therapeutic progress already exist. Nevertheless, to use these statistically well-replicated relations with full effect requires increase in our knowledge of the psychological role and natural history of these source traits. One needs to become familiar, moreover, with the existing evidence, e.g., on U.I. 24 as anxiety, as summarized in Cattell and Scheier's *Meaning and Measurement of Anxiety and Neuroticism* (1961), on U.I. 23 as regression (Rickels & Cattell, 1965), and the numerous comparisons in Schmidt (1975) and Cattell, Schmidt, and Bjerstedt (1972), which enrich the meaning of U.I. 16, 19, 20, 21, 24, 25, and other source traits. On the basis of these meanings, set out individually in Chapter 3 and augmented by the clinical associations here, the clinician should feel free to carry his interpretations of the factor scores into insightful diagnosis and prognostic anticipations.

The experimental and quantitative work in the clinical field with primary personality factors as measured by the O-A (and the Clinical Analysis Questionnaire [CAQ], for that matter) gives, in some respects, a new and different perspective on the pathologies from that of psychoanalytic and other pre-metric theories. Although the O-A Kit is capable of finer discrimination—as shown objectively by multiple discriminant functions—between syndromes than has been demonstrated by any other instrument, it indicates more features in common among the pathologies than has been recognized by older clinical theories. For example, neurotics and schizophrenics (and, for that matter, most other psychoses) agree in diverging from normals in lower U.I. 19, 21, 23, and 25 (at the $P < .01$ and $P < .001$ levels). That is to say, they share the higher inhibition of U.I. 21—, the subduedness of U.I. 19—, the regression and incapacity to mobilize of U.I. 23—, and the poor contact with reality of U.I. 25—. We must conclude that the term "pathological" means something in *general* personality features and that the degree of this total severity of pathology in individual cases can be measured by these three factor batteries from the Kit.

Amidst this general pathology there are, as shown first by the Q second orders in the CAQ and now by the O-A, more precise factor dimensions of general anxiety, general psychoticism, and general depression, which additionally offer scores contributing to the differentiation of neurotics and psychotics, as well as character disorders and psychopaths or sociopaths, etc. A rationale explaining these differences has been proposed by Cattell and Scheier (1961), in terms of separating associations due to (a) *pathology-contributing* factors, i.e., those predisposing toward maladjustment; (b) *pathological process* factors which represent the growth in the individual of actual disease processes; and (c) *residual condition* factors which represent traits likely to persist for some time after therapy as a consequence of the conflict and disease processes. Thus, the association of neuroticism with U.I. 16—, ego weakness, is due to the latter's predisposing the individual to poor handling of emotional problems; the statistical association with U.I. 24, anxiety, is part of the pathological conflict process; and the association with U.I. 23—, regression, is a persisting exhaustion consequence or residual. The fact (see summary of researches in Table 11.3) that neurotics are high in anxiety and schizophrenics are not, whereas schizophrenics show more regression (U.I. 23—), significantly less somindence (U.I. 30), and significantly greater detachment from reality (U.I. 25—) suggests that the former have an arrested disease

249

Table 11.3

SIGNIFICANCE OF SOURCE-TRAIT DIFFERENCES OF NEUROTICS AND PSYCHOTICS (SCHIZOPHRENICS) FROM NORMAL CONTROLS: t VALUES OF DIFFERENCES OF MEANS

(a) Neurotics. From diagnostic samples in the U.S.A., North and South, and Canada.

	Factor Title (Positive Pole)	Universal Index Number	(Toronto) 30 Normals 24 Neurotics N = 54	(Illinois) 32 Normals 25 Neurotics N = 57	(Tennessee) 19 Normals 5 Neurotics N = 24	(Illinois) 49 Normals 49 Neurotics N = 98
Noteworthy	Cortertia	U.I. 22	−2.62*	−8.33†	−3.31*	
Differences	Over-reactivity	U.I. 29	−5.62†	−7.95†	.33	
	Ego Standards	U.I. 16	−4.47†	−8.73†	.52	
	Mobilization-vs-Regression	U.I. 23	−3.60†	−5.73†	.45	−2.85*
	Intelligence test	U.I. 1	−4.12†	−3.67†	X	
	Independence	U.I. 19	−3.87†	−1.04	−1.27	
	Exuberance	U.I. 21	−4.53†	−3.68†	1.20	
	Anxiety	U.I. 24	2.01*	1.34	.15	
	Exvia-vs-Invia	U.I. 32	−2.10*	−3.94†	.42	
	Realism-vs-Tensidia	U.I. 25	−.54	−2.17*	.22	
	Inconautia	U.I. 34	X	5.75†	X	
	Asthenia	U.I. 28	3.06*	−4.03†	−.55	
	Control	U.I. 17	1.82	−3.24†	.14	
Inconsistent	Hypomania Temperament	U.I. 18	.92	−.45	.66	
or	Evasiveness	U.I. 20	1.07	.23	−.42	
Slight	Narcism	U.I. 26	−2.68*	.27	1.77	
Differences	Discouragement	U.I. 33	−.21	.20	X	

NOTES: An X means that the test was not used in that sample. Data from Cattell and Scheier (1961). It is to be noted that wherever differences of descriptions and diagnosis of neuroticism exist across these cultural areas the consensus is definite enough to permit a characteristic profile to emerge on most source traits. U.I. 16−, 21−, 22−, 23−, and 29+ are most prominent in the profile.

* Significant at $P < .05$; † significant at $P < .01$.

250

Table 11.3 (Continued)

(b) Compared on Two Population Samples

(*P* values in parentheses)

Factor	Schizophrenics		Neurotics	
	Former Group	Recent Group	Former Group	Recent Group
U.I. 16 +	—	—(.05)	—	—(.05)
U.I. 17 +	+	ns	ns	ns
U.I. 19 +	—	—(.05)	—	—(.01)
U.I. 20 +	ns	ns	ns	ns
U.I. 21 +	—	—(.001)	—	—(.01)
U.I. 22 +	ns	ns	—	ns
U.I. 23 +	—	—(.001)	—	—(.01)
U.I. 24 +	ns	ns	+	+ (.05)
U.I. 25 +	—	—(.001)	ns	—(.01)
U.I. 28 +	ns	ns	+	ns
U.I. 29 +	ns	ns	—	ns
U.I. 30 +	—	(—)ns	ns	ns
U.I. 31 +	ns	ns	ns	ns
U.I. 32 +	ns	—(.001)	—	—(.05)
U.I. 33 +	+	(+)ns	ns	ns

NOTES: A — shows the group lower than normal controls; a + , higher. Occasionally, signs are put in even when nonsignificant (ns). *"P"* is omitted before the probability signs.

The "former group" is from Tatro (1968), Cattell and Scheier (1961), and Killian (1960) (see also Cattell & Killian, 1967). The "recent group" is that studied by Cattell, Schmidt, and Bjerstedt (1972).

process, whereas the latter have passed through it to obstinate residual conditions shown in the diagnostic scores on U.I. 23, 25, and 30.

Regarding the diagnosis of *neurosis,* the highest trait associations, in sheer statistical terms (as checked by two to four independent researches), are, in the Main O-A Kit, with:

U.I. 16— Low ego standards strength,
U.I. 19— Low independence, subduedness,
U.I. 21— Suppressibility, inhibition,
U.I. 23— Regression,
U.I. 24 Anxiety.

The last association, though significant variously at *P* < .05 and *P* <.01, does not support the view that it is "central to neuroses" (Freud) or Eysenck's calling it *the* neuroticism factor in his Q scales. The theory which Cattell has stated, in other discussions, is that, in fact, characterological

251

weaknesses (visible in U.I. 16, 19, 21, etc., scores) are more important, in sheer variance contribution, than the anxiety from the particular conflict, and that it is misleading to consider neuroticism a single factor (as in Eysenck's N) identical with anxiety. Besides the above, there are significant but slighter associations of neuroticism with U.I. 20+, evasiveness, U.I. 25—, tensidia, and U.I. 32—, invia, and (usually insignificant) with U.I. 28, asthenia. In the Extended Kit there are very significant associations with U.I. 17—, low control, U.I. 22—, pathemia, and U.I. 29—, low will strength, wherefore Hundleby is proposing to standardize the tests for these in a clinical supplement. Our present theoretical analysis, liable to revision, would therefore place U.I. 16, 19, 21, 22, and 32 as predisposing contributory factors; U.I. 24 and 25 as disease process; and U.I. 21 (again), 23, and 32 (again) as residual condition traits. A summary of statistical significances is given in Table 11.3.

As to schizophrenics, the number of factors differentiating them from normals with substantial significance is such as to permit a highly diagnostic weighted composite. They are:

U.I. 16—,
U.I. 19—
U.I. 21—
U.I. 23—,
U.I. 25—,
U.I. 30— Somindence direction (not in Main Kit),
U.I. 32—,
U.I. 33.

It will be noticed that 16, 19, 21, 23, and 32 are shared with neuroticism, and constitute, in the first four, our "general pathology." But, as the Cattell, Schmidt, and Bjerstedt (1972) analyses show, there are differences of schizophrenics and neurotics (and general psychotics and neurotics) even on these. The U.I. 21— difference from normals is less, the U.I. 25— is greater, U.I. 28 is absent, U.I. 33 is here but not in the neurotic pattern, while there is no U.I. 24 (anxiety) deviation here at all. From the above, Schmidt (*op. cit.*) has worked out a discriminant function to apply to the O-A scores, giving virtually complete separation of schizophrenics and neurotics as shown in Table 11.4.

The studies before the Cattell-Schmidt discriminant function analyses (Figure 11.1) agree very well in showing certain O-A factors very potent in separating neuroses and psychosis. From the whole extended pattern of differences substantial diagnostic separation can be achieved. Cattell and Schmidt found neurotics relative to psychotics to be significantly more anxious (U.I. 24), more controlled (U.I. 17), lower on cortertia (U.I. 22), more deviant from normal on inability to mobilize (regression, U.I. 23—), decidedly less detached from reality (U.I. 25), more asthenic (U.I. 28), and not deviating as psychotics do on U.I. 30— and U.I. 33. They

Table 11.4

DISCRIMINANT FUNCTION WEIGHTS IN DIFFERENTIATING SEVEN GROUPS

	Factor	1	2	C*
	U.I. 16	−.04	−.30	.04
	U.I. 19	.55	−.16	.40
	U.I. 20	−.09	−.21	.07
	U.I. 21	.51	.07	.38
	U.I. 23	.50	.31	.37
	U.I. 24	−.10	.54	.09
	U.I. 25	.27	−.26	.20
	U.I. 28	−.19	.29	.14
	U.I. 32	−.10	.04	.07
	U.I. 33	−.08	.15	.05
Not	U.I. 17	−.01	.01	.01
in	U.I. 22	.01	−.24	.02
Main	U.I. 29	.07	−.26	.06
O-A	U.I. 30	.06	.36	.05
Kit	U.I. 31	.04	.00	.03

NOTES: Columns 1 and 2 are the first two of six possible discriminant functions concerned with maximizing the separation of seven clinical groups. These are listed, except for brain damaged, in Table 11.7.

It is rare in practice to use more than the first function (see Lawlis & Chatfield, 1974), but here by a vector combining the first two from rotating the maximum patient-nonpatient separation, we give C as the most generally useful. The meaning is that if we want to combine factor scores (as standard scores) with a single score that alone will give best separation of patients into groups (by closeness to the means of these groups on the composite), the C composite is indicated. The purpose is to both separate patients from normal controls and to separate clinical types among the patients. However, in practice a psychiatric diagnostic conference may chiefly be concerned with two, e.g., is the patient compulsive neurotic or an incipient schizophrenic, and, in that case, the differentiators set out in the text for those syndromes should be the guide.

*The weights of the functions 1 and 2 have been combined as follows:
  (1) multiplication of the weights by the amount of variance for which a function accounts;
  (2) square of the weights;
  (3) adding the squared weights;
  (4) square root of the sum for each factor.

Figure 11.1

SEPARATION OF CLINICAL GROUPS AND NORMALS
BY TWO DISCRIMINANT FUNCTIONS

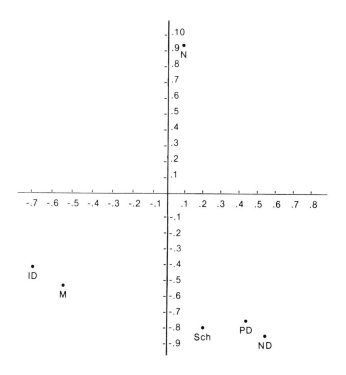

First discriminant function is vertical axis.

N = Normal controls

ID = Involutional depressives

M = Manics

Sch = Schizophrenics

PD = Psychotic depressives

ND = Neurotic depressives

deviate toward U.I. 32—, invia, though some psychotics, schizophrenics, and manics do the same. Relative deviation of neurotics from normality is also less on ego strength standards (U.I. 16—), independence (U.I. 19—), and evasiveness (U.I. 20). By combining these score deviations clinicians should now be able to get even more complete diagnostic separation than the high degree obtained in the Cattell and Schmidt study (1972, Table 11.5 below).

Turning to differentiation among varieties of psychoses, we find as yet relatively few studies. The character disorders have been found to have a fairly definite pattern of deviation from normality in reduced realism (U.I. 25—), some invia (U.I. 32—), higher apathy (U.I. 27), a significant but slight rise in anxiety (U.I. 24), and, very curiously, a higher level of control (U.I. 17).

Schizophrenics, as shown by the extensive studies of Tatro (1968), Schmidt and Cattell (1977), and Killian (1960) are also, as would be expected, significantly more inviant (U.I. 32—) than other psychotics, decidedly higher on "discouragement" (U.I. 33), lower on independence (U.I. 19—), cortertia (U.I. 22—), and higher on apathy (U.I. 27), and loss of reality contact—tensidia (U.I. 25—).

Among the deviations which thus significantly differentiate schizophrenics from normals, namely, on 16—, 19—, 21—, 23—, 25—, 32—, and 33, it will be noticed that 16, 19, 21, 23, and 32 are shared with the diagnosis of neuroticism, but that 25— is stronger here, 21— is weaker, 28 is absent, and there is no difference of psychotics and normals on 24, anxiety, which peculiarly distinguishes neurotics. As Schmidt's discriminant functions show, these latter have weights that are the discriminators of schizoid psychosis from neurosis.

As between paranoid and nonparanoid schizophrenics, though both are particularly marked by low 16 (ego standards) and 19 (independence), simple, hebe-phrenic, and catatonic schizophrenics together differ from paranoid by lower 23 (regression) and by more marked invia (low 32).

The statistically inclined psychologist may decide, instead of handling these factors separately, to use discriminant function methods. Several functions would finally be needed, but we may illustrate by taking the first worked out by Schmidt and Cattell (1972) and labeled No. 1 in Table 11.4. This happens to be the function producing the first major separation of the psychoses among themselves. We find that this combination of lower U.I. 19, lower U.I. 21, and lower U.I. 23 separates involutional depressives (ID's) and manics (M's) from psychotic depressives generally (PD's) and neurotic depressives (ND's). This combination of factors is evidently important, particularly in the affective psychoses, though a third and fourth discriminant function should be worked out and should prove very effective, as more O-A source-trait evidence becomes available for clinicians. The nature of separation by two functions only is shown in Figure 11.1.

Some provocative evidence arises from the O-A Battery with regard to manics, in the first place by the startling fact that they score more inviant (U.I. 32—) than normals and depressive but not schizophrenic psychotics. Unless this comes from two odd samples it suggests that what has been customary facile classification of their behavior as extreme "extraversion" is theoretically quite misleading. If we turn to the questionnaire domain to see how the lower order components of exvia (Q I) behave, we see results consistent with the present, namely (see Cattell, Eber, & Tatsuoka, 1970), that in both manic and depressive phases of manic-depressive disorders the scores on Q_2, self-sufficiency, are above normal, and Q_2 is, of course, an *inviant* component on the exvia-invia dimension. Of the other three exvia-invia components, A, affectia, is non-diagnostic, and F, surgency, and H, parmia, are exviant in the manic and markedly inviant in the depressive phase. The low score of manics on U.I. 21, exuberance, is at first a puzzle, unless we recognize mania not as an increase in fluency but a decrease in inhibition. Their significantly lower scores on U.I. 23, mobilization versus regression, fits earlier work interpreting "overwroughtness" as U.I. 23—, as well as the very high ergic tension scores (Q_4 on the questionnaire). Certainly, the manic syndrome takes on a new direction and new qualities in the light of the O-A source-trait pattern.

Among depressives, the deviations on 16—, 19—, 21—, 23—, and 25— common to psychoses generally prevail along with higher 20, 28, 24, and 33. However, some interesting differences of neurotic and, especially, involutional depressives exist. The latter are lower on U.I. 16 and higher on U.I. 20. U.I. 25 is lower in neurotic depressives than others. Schmidt's (Cattell, Schmidt, & Bjerstedt, 1972) results show manics differentiating from depressives by being much lower on U.I. 23 and also lower on anxiety, U.I. 25. It is noteworthy that Cattell, Schmidt, and Bjerstedt (1972) found manics as well as depressives significantly inviant, i.e., low on U.I. 32.

Recent work by Patrick, Cattell, and Price (in press) on psychotic depressives shows especially large differences in the direction of U.I. 19—, subduedness ($t = 4.7$, $P < .0001$) and U.I. 20+, evasiveness ($t = 3.44$, $P < .001$), but also some interesting differences close to significance in the direction of U.I. 25—, tensidia ($t = 1.98$, $P < .05$), and U.I. 30+ ($P < .05$). (The last factor is somindence, not in the Main O-A Kit but No. 17 in the Extension).

A survey of the above studies, some restricted to particular factors and particular diagnostic groups, supports the verdict, in its various parts, of the comprehensive study of Cattell, Schmidt, and Bjerstedt (1973, p. 72), namely, that the full Kit is capable of yielding discriminant functions that will separate the chief psychotic and neurotic groups up to the full reliability of the psychiatric conference diagnoses.

As theoretical advances are made in the interpretation of the unitary personality traits, a valuable function of the O-A measures will be to monitor the course of change under therapy. As discussed in the next chapter, personality theory can thus make therapy more nearly an exact science while still needing the skills of an art. For example, we know there is a distinctly high hereditary determination of U.I. 19, independence, and U.I. 21, exuberance, so these must be taken into account like intelligence, as among the relatively fixed resources and causes, but anxiety (U.I. 24), regression (U.I. 23), and others show low nature-nurture ratios and are open to therapeutic manipulation.

Accordingly, a well-designed course of therapy must take stock, as with a clinical thermometer, of the changes occurring on these dimensions of mental health. Cattell and a team of psychiatrists have investigated the changes, specifically on U.I. 23 and 24, on a substantial sample of private patients in New York and Philadelphia undergoing both psychotherapy and chemotherapy (action of tranquilizers). Significant reductions occurred both on the anxiety (U.I. 24) and the regression (U.I. 23—) batteries as shown in Table 11.5. Other, smaller sample research has shown a rise on U.I. 16, ego strength standards, through the same combined psychotherapy and tranquilizer action as in the above. A program of physical exercise has also been shown significantly to reduce U.I. 24. A psychometrically valuable by-product of this research was the demonstration that the verbal questionnaire measures of the anxiety factor (QII) behaved in just the same way as the objective test battery (U.I. 24), which requires both that there be an *instrument-transcending* source trait (Cattell, Pierson, & Finkbeiner, 1976) *and* that the subjects have no temptation to fake on questionnaires, which is generally true of patients. It is time that the nature of therapeutic change be explored and demonstrated on the whole spectrum of source traits in the O-A.

Crime, delinquency, psychopathy, and sociopathy. These phenomena are brought into the clinical section rather than the social psychological, since the emphasis here is on personality analysis. The essential conceptual and methodological point must be made at the outset that this behavioral domain includes far more than one type, and is probably less uniform even than "psychosis." Another difficulty for ANOVA designs is the lack of clear psychiatric agreement on definition of such groups as sociopaths, psychopaths, character disorders, acting-out types, and so on. Nevertheless, as culled from substantial research by Knapp (1963, 1965), Nesselroade and Delhees (1966), Reuterman, Howard, and Cartwright (in press), Schuerger (1977), Wardell (1976), and more sporadic studies, we conclude that high evasiveness (U.I. 20) seems common to most types as also does low reality contact (U.I. 25—) and higher exvia (U.I. 32), while low U.I. 30 has been noted in sociopathic groups. Reuterman, Howard, and

Table 11.5

MEASURABLE CHANGES IN U.I. 23, MOBILIZATION-vs-REGRESSION, AND U.I. 24, ANXIETY
PRODUCED BY THERAPY

Comparison of Anxiety and Regression Change Under Therapy
On Questionnaire and Objective Test Measures[a]

	Initial Score (1)	Final Score (2)	Change (2) — (1)
IPAT Verbal Anxiety			
(N = 46) Patients	46.09	43.02	—3.07[c]
(N = 53) Controls	26.13	26.77	0.64
O-A Anxiety Battery			
Patients[b]	0.361	0.198	—0.163[c]
Controls	—0.361	—0.472	—0.111
O-A Regression Battery			
Patients	0.440	0.114	—0.326[d]
Controls	—0.458	—0.611	—0.153[c]

NOTE: Results from Cattell, Rickels, and others (1966).

[a]N = 46 patients, 53 normal controls.
[b]Numerical agreement of these two initial values for patients and controls is accidental. All scores are raw scores and have no comparability immediately from objective to questionnaire values, being unstandardized.
[c]Significant at $P < 0.05$.
[d]Significant at $P < 0.001$.

Cartwright found U.I. 25 averaging lower in delinquent gang groups than good boys' clubs (controlled for same age).

Situational factors and types of crime are important. Convicted criminals in prison have repeatedly been shown to score higher on anxiety (U.I. 24) than noncriminals and lower on U.I. 23 and U.I. 33. These do not characterize Knapp's "sailors in the brig" for lesser offenses (Table 11.6). Certain kinds of sociopaths, particularly drug addicts, likewise score higher on U.I. 24.

If we look next for the personality traits specifically separating the "acting-out" criminal from the clinical neurotic and psychotic, we find the largest differences on U.I. 16, the delinquent having higher ego strength (though not higher than the normal control). We next find U.I. 28 and U.I. 32 throwing these two types on opposite sides of a normal profile—clinical cases being more inviant (U.I. 32—) and delinquents exviant (U.I. 32+), and clinicals higher on U.I. 28, while psychopaths and sociopaths are significantly lower than normals. Reuterman, Howard, and Cartwright (in press) found among young delinquents that fighting and property offenses were characteristic of high-U.I. 21 (exuberance) adolescents, and less fighting was recorded for high-anxiety (U.I. 24) individuals. Ustrzycki (1974) found negative correlations of U.I. 19 with total check list of offenses, but positive with more daring offense. It is evident that the general personality profile determines (with situations) the type of offense, but that certain traits are common to most poor stability or antisocial behavior.

Studying the character disorders in the clinical cases, we noted reduced U.I. 25 and 32 and raised U.I. 17, 24, and 27. In the related psychiatric category of personality disorders, Delhees and Cattell (1971) found low scores on U.I. 16 and 21 and high on U.I. 19. Significant differences were also observed on factors measured only in the Extension Battery here, namely, in the directions U.I. 17—, 27—, and 30+. Cattell and Scheier's (1961) study supports this only in part (but with no contradictions), showing higher U.I. 19 and U.I. 32 to be significantly involved in delinquency, and other studies pointed to delinquents showing U.I. 16—, 25—, and 33—. Eysenck (1960, 1961) has repeatedly argued for extraversion (Q I, U.I. 32) being related to delinquency, but others have questioned this. Our own conclusion is that the association with exvia is usually positive but so moderate that it will even change sign in some groups. Certainly it is a gross oversimplification to think of extraversion as a prime cause of delinquency. At least five other source traits have greater correlation with proneness to delinquency and personality disorders, as finally summarized in our estimated specification equation below.

A particularly valuable study is that of Knapp (1965) on delinquency in the armed forces, where environmental effects and situational determiners are more uniform. As Table 11.6 shows, five of the significant relations agree with those of the separate researches above; but two source traits—U.I. 26, narcistic personality, and U.I. 29, overresponsiveness—never tried before—appear with high significance ($P < .001$). The offenses are of a relatively minor "adult delinquent" nature, and this may explain the fact that U.I. 23 changes in its direction, for it is clear from the above that serious criminal behavior, especially of the impulsive kind, is associated with personality pathology, generally, in which U.I. 23—, regression, typically appears. In this connection, we note that the most statistically significant deviations for personality disorders, as well-diagnosed cases, were found by Cattell and Killian (1967) to be high U.I. 17 ($P < .05$), low U.I. 25 = ($P < .01$), and high U.I. 27 ($P < .05$), while in comparison with psychotics generally, these character disorders showed slightly raised anxiety, U.I. 24, and high U.I. 19, independence. Some of these suggest psychological conflict with high standards to be more evident in the personality disorders than in straight delinquency.

Table 11.6

TRAIT SCORE DIFFERENCES OF CONVICTED ADULT OFFENDERS
AND NONDELINQUENT CONTROLS IN A UNIFORM ENVIRONMENT

Main O-A Battery Traits	Offenders	Controls	F*	Direction in Delinquents
U.I. 16 Ego Standards	34.25	35.43	2.14	—
U.I. 19 Independence	25.60	24.60	2.24	+
U.I. 20 Evasiveness	40.54	38.48	9.12	+
U.I. 23 Mobilization	20.49	19.32	4.76	+
U.I. 24 Anxiety	31.18	29.14	8.42	+
U.I. 25 Realism	34.12	36.02	5.27	—
U.I. 33 Discouragement	14.61	15.40	2.84	—
Extended O-A Battery Traits				
U.I. 17 Inhibitory Control	35.60	34.12	4.35	+
U.I. 22 Cortertia	30.26	28.95	2.82	+
U.I. 26 Narcistic Ego	41.68	37.77	32.56	+
U.I. 29 Over-Responsiveness	31.29	28.05	22.06	+
U.I. 30 Dissofrustance	15.78	14.41	8.94	+

NOTE: In a Navy population this compares 92 men "in the brig" with 98 matched nonoffenders. 18 factors were measured by 68 subtests.

*The F values are for analysis of covariance with educational level and length of service held constant (see Knapp, 1965, from which this table is a simplified presentation). Traits in no way approaching a significance difference have been omitted.

Delinquency, of course, has its sociological and situational determiners, but as overwhelmingly shown elsewhere (Cattell, 1950), genetic features of personality have *some* role. By the age at which delinquency appears, however, environmental influences have already created some of the acquired source traits on which we find measurable differences. It is, therefore, useful to determine as reliably as possible the personality profile of the delinquent, initially for the most general and later for more specific delinquencies.

Cartwright, Tomson, and Schwartz's results suggest that a potent discriminant function could be written for likelihood of delinquency.

It would have the pattern U.I. 16—, 21—, 25— on the O-A, and also U.I. 26—, 18+, and 26— on the O-A Extension. If one seeks to condense the above evidence in an estimated specification equation, one would reach something like the following:

$$\text{Likelihood of delinquency} = .2 \, (\text{U.I.} \, 19 - \text{U.I.} \, 16 + \text{U.I.} \, 23 + \text{U.I.} \, 24 - \text{U.I.} \, 33) + .4 \, (\text{U.I.} \, 20 - \text{U.I.} \, 25) + .1 \, (\text{U.I.} \, 21) + .3 \, (\text{U.I.} \, 32) + [.4 \, (\text{U.I.} \, 26 + \text{U.I.} \, 29)]$$

The two values in square brackets are from the Extended Kit. With the nine traits from the Main Kit, the above might give an R with the criterion of about 0.7 to 0.8, possibly higher if U.I. 26, narcism, and U.I. 29, overresponsiveness, are brought in.

In this chapter our purpose has been to give the useful, practical, quantitative evidence on the nature of differences in personality in deviant groups, leaving theoretical insights and hypotheses about mode of action to the next chapter. Within the realm of diagnosis it is at least clear, as Schmidt says, that "the separation of clinical groups by objective tests is more emphatic than by questionnaires." Indeed, it treads so closely on the heels of the psychiatrists' diagnoses that one may wonder which really should count as predictor and which as criterion. Table 11.7, from discriminant functions, "places" patients in the categories agreed on in psychiatric case conferences.

A horizontal row shows how the patients placed by the O-A in that row category were disposed as to psychiatric categories. It will be seen at once that the large values are down the diagonal, which represent agreements, and, indeed, on the bottom right we see that 45 of 48 normal controls were correctly placed by the O-A (of the three misplaced, two were considered manics and one a depressive, but this much pathology could really exist in a "normal" group). It may well be doubted whether psychologists possess any other test to date that could give the diagnostic validity shown in Table 11.7. At any rate, the question can and should be put to the verdict of independent experiment.

Table 11.7

AGREEMENT OF DISCRIMINANT FUNCTION PLACEMENTS BY O-A BATTERY WITH PSYCHIATRIC DIAGNOSES

	Psychiatric Diagnoses						
Factors as Predictors	Involutional Depressives	Other Psychotic Depressives	Neurotic Depressives	Schizophrenics	Manics	(Anxiety Neurotics)	Controls
Involutional Depressives	8	0	0	0	2	0	0
Other Psychotic Depressives	1	7	2	3	0	1	1
Neurotic Depressives	0	2	5	0	0	0	0
Schizophrenics	0	2	2	8	1	1	0
Manics	2	0	1	1	7	1	2
Anxiety Neurotics	1	0	1	0	1	6	0
Controls	0	0	0	0	0	0	45
Total	12	11	11	12	11	9	48
% valid predictions	67%	64%	45%	67%	64%	67%	94%

NOTE: We will use the diagnosis of "manic" to illustrate the use of this table. Reading across the fifth row of the table, it can be seen that the O-A diagnosed 14 of the 48 subjects as manic. From the fifth column, it can be seen that the psychiatrists diagnosed 11 of the 48 subjects as manic. The two approaches (O-A versus psychiatric evaluation) were in agreement on 7 subjects. Of the remaining 7 subjects who had been diagnosed by the O-A as manics, psychiatrists diagnosed 2 as involutional depressives, 2 as neurotic depressives, 1 as schizophrenic, and 1 as an anxiety neurotic.

12

The Use of Personality Theory in Relation to the O-A Battery

Test Choice in Relation to Theory and Multiple Determination Principles

The signal advantage of tests built to correspond to personality structures, as previously revealed and checked by basic research, is that they can operate within a truly general personality theory. This means that knowledge of the natural history of these structures, e.g., their degree of genetic determination, their normal age curves, their effects upon and from adjustive life experiences, can be added to purely statistical estimates made with psychometric formulas. So far in this Handbook we have generally stopped at giving the incontrovertible psychometric evidence evaluating source-trait reliabilities, validities, and relevances, as they are required by the "hard-nosed" psychologist for his work. However, we did venture occasional asides on what the psychological causes of the connections might be. In the present chapter, we beg leave to speculate with hypotheses and testable theories that may enrich and explain the above relations. At the same time, we shall broaden the discussion of the general psychological setting and the possible range of other measures and tests with which the O-A Kit measurements can advantageously be combined.

First, some attention needs to be given to the interactions and relations of personality source traits with one another, and with ability, motivation, and state measures. The practicing psychometrist, in education and industry, has, at least, experience of objective tests in the field of abilities. (Elsewhere he has probably used questionnaires.) If he carries this experience over without regard for personality theory into the O-A, he may be misled because he is accustomed to an ability like intelligence, which *alone* can predict a large fraction of the variance in a chosen criterion, such as school achievement. He can also assume that the ability remains relatively fixed over time, partly because it has a high hereditary determination.

In personality, he needs to "change gear" in his implicit theoretical thought processes in both of the above respects. First, the criteria in clinic and job are likely to involve the *total* personality to a greater degree than the somewhat artificial or controlled classroom situation and, therefore, to involve a greater number of primary factors. It is not that intelligence is a "larger" factor than, say, ego strength, or extraversion, or anxiety—indeed, U.I. 1, intelligence, is a primary, falling in just the same stratum as U.I. 16, 17, or 32—but in scholastic achievement it happens to be predominant. However, since clinical and general life behavior will be multiply determined, no one monarchic source trait is likely to prevail, and so the psychologist will not expect, in a typical situation, that individual source traits will much exceed a 0.2 to 0.4 correlation with the criterion. He will usually, however, expect *more* of them to be operating. Lest the low criterion relevances just mentioned strike the educational psychologist as relatively trivial, he is to be reminded that 10 independent factors, each correlating 0.3, would yield a multiple R of 0.95, which is decidedly more than psychological practice today—or perhaps ever—can hope to actually reach in predicting real life behavior.[1]

Good strategy calls for initially trying out the whole spectrum of 10 source traits in the battery, because the chances are that *several* will be needed. This spread, and the time demanded, may be difficult in an applied situation, and in pure research the investigator may have a theory confining him to one or two factors. But a broad sweep, even to the 20 factors formed by including the Extended Kit, is worthwhile in the long run. Once it is made, the psychologist can confidently settle down to the two or three factors which he then knows contribute *most* of the predictable part of the criterion.

For example, creativity in scientific work might be predictable as far as is possible from U.I. 1, intelligence, U.I. 19, independence, and 32—, invia, while a diagnosis of varieties of depression might be largely made from U.I. 21, 23, 25, 28, and 33. As pointed out in the introduction, it is because such special selections need to be made that the O-A factors were put together as a Kit which the psychologist can place conveniently on his shelf of instruments, and from which he can take particular factor batteries according to his best estimate. Elsewhere (Cattell & Warburton, 1967; Cattell, 1973*b*), it has been pointed out that many psychologists trained in a prefactorial era of testing do not always make the best use, in terms of effective prediction, of the always-too-little time which they and the subjects have for testing. They may throw away an hour or more, over two or three apparently distinct tests (often with elaborate special names), which are largely a measure of only one factor, e.g., intelligence, fluency, or anxiety. They may then cram 10 other factors, equally important to the field, into the second hour, forcing each down to very dubious reliabilities and validities obtainable from only 6 minutes of testing.

Incidentally, if intelligence is to be measured as the "11th" O-A factor, we would recommend giving it no greater and no lesser length of testing than each of the personality factors—about 25 to 35 minutes—which is readily done by using the Culture Fair Intelligence Test. (*Note:* A traditional, crystallized intelligence measure, incidentally, contains already some contaminating and unknown personality measurement in its score. By

---

[1]It is three centuries since La Rochefoucauld wrote in his maxims, ''Nature gives us our qualities, but chance sets them to work.'' No matter how perfect our measurement of the individual, the prediction of a criterion is imperfect to the extent that we do not have knowledge of future situations, needed to be entered into our equations.

using a pure g_f fluid intelligence, measure we get clear separation of the ability and personality factors.)

There is thus no good argument for giving more time to an ability than to a personality factor measure in education, industry, and most fields of life prediction—especially clinical diagnosis and the selection of high level officers and executives. But there *is* good argument for giving more time to the regular testing session *as a whole* than most psychologists have hitherto accepted as a norm. They have drifted into the practice of restricting to a 1-hour session, due to managerial and popular pressures. We are not at a technical stage when we can do a thorough examination as quickly as can, say, medicine, and even a good medical examination requires an afternoon. If important decisions hang on the measurements, as they commonly do in clinical and vocational guidance work, then 3 to 5 hours, such as the full O-A Kit (plus intelligence or motivation measures) requires, surely is not too much time for the subject to give. In a well-planned test installation this would involve a technician's time and not that of the most highly trained psychologist, whose role is interpreting and putting together the obtained values. Parenthetically, this time is better spread over two sessions because of function fluctuation effects. Group mental health spot check surveys are, of course, another matter. For these situations IPAT has developed the special-purpose Neuroticism, Anxiety, and Depression Scales, each of 10 minutes' duration.

Alertness to Psychometric Principles Within Personality Theory

Sound psychometry is not the ultimate end, but it is certainly the necessary beginning of good psychological practice. Measurements, as indicated in the introduction to the O-A Handbook, initially need to be wisely chosen in the light of both psychological theory and psychometric technical knowledge. The former calls for knowledge of personality structure and development. The dependence of so many clinicians, for example, on drawings, Rorschach blots, handwriting, and open-ended projection tests, designed as *ad hoc* devices before personality structure had been psychometrically determined, has been repeatedly shown by experiment to be either a complete illusion or of decidedly poorer validity than can be reached by structured scales (Vernon, 1953).

However, the psychologist needs also to be aware of limitations and idiosyncratic properties of factored measures, and so we propose here a very brief excursion into some broader psychometric principles not covered in the earlier discussions of consistency and validity.

A first question is "How far can one depend on the structure of traits in the O-A holding up across cultures?" The O-A has been shown to have great stability of pattern across cultures chosen for diversity, namely, across the U.S.A., Austria, and Japan (Cattell, Schmidt, & Pawlik, 1973). Nevertheless, the *transferability coefficient* is not perfect, and some change of validity across subcultures, ages, sex, etc., is to be expected (Cattell, 1978b). This source of generally minor score error cannot be beaten until as many O-A Batteries are constructed and standardized as there are subcultures, and this would require an effort on an international scale.

A second psychometric caveat concerns the *fluctuation* (not the regular growth change to be considered later) of scores. Beginning with abilities, such as intelligence, psychologists have fallen into the habit of regarding their measures as relatively fixed. Possibly such stability exists also for personality traits, notably among those of high hereditary determination, such as U.I. 19, independence, U.I. 20, evasiveness, U.I. 21, exuberance, and, to some degree, U.I. 32, exvia. But this is not true of others, or of dynamic traits, as in the Motivation Analysis Test (MAT). There is now overwhelming evidence from what are called dR- and P-technique experiments (Cattell, 1973b; Nesselroade, 1966; Nesselroade & Bartsch, 1973), that for every trait pattern measured there is a closely corresponding *trait-change* pattern. Theory indicates that occasionally these are states, such as will be discussed below; but generally they are simply fluctuations in the level of a relatively fixed trait, occurring with change in situation and inner condition. According to the *trait-constancy* coefficients given in Table 5.1, which define the sigma of variations over occasions, one must make a score allowance, and, when the constancy is low, take an average of two or more measures over time to get a trait measure.

In some cases, notably anxiety, the trait and state patterns (not only the trait change factor pattern) are so similar that a problem arises in separating them. Progress is being made, particularly in anxiety (Cattell & Nesselroade, 1976; Curran, 1968; Nesselroade & Bartsch, 1973; Wessman & Ricks, 1966), in batteries capable of giving clearer separation (Curran & Cattell, 1976), but at present one must consider the possibility that an O-A factor measure, at any rate for anxiety, *involves some state as well as trait* measurement. As a final perspective, let us mention, however, that the recent work of Horn (1977) points to a "state" in general intelligence measures, too! So the difference of personality and ability traits in function fluctuation is relative, not categorical.

In leaving validity-consistency questions, let us refer the reader to the value of *utility and efficiency coefficients* (Cattell & Warburton, 1967; Cattell, 1973b). The unwary psychologist is often caught, e.g., in comparing repeated test indices, when reading Buros' *Mental Measurements Yearbook* (1972), by being presented with validities and reliabilities (consistencies) that are not adjusted to and referred to any *standard length* of test. Validity and, especially, reliability increase with the number of items in the test by the Spearman-Brown calculation, but since items are of different length in different tests, and time is proportional to items, we can apply the S-B formula to *time* length, the usual assumptions being granted. This should be remembered in any comparisons of the "information per minute" available from the O-A with what is offered by other personality test alternatives. Also, the user should be familiar with the general principle that if, say, 2 hours are available for testing, the psychologist can predict the typical criterion far better by measuring any four relevant independent factors, each with the reliability and validity possible with only half an hour for each, than by taking a single measure, raised to the highest validity by 2 hours being devoted to it. This is an argument in favor of factored tests, incidentally, where we can be sure that the "bits" of information are independent, not duplicative, as in some choices of test batteries.

Finally, a word is necessary in psychometric theory on the basic difference between (1) using tests to assign the subject to a *type* and (2) using them to assess, via the specification equation, a *criterion performance*. The O-A, yielding 10 profile scores (or 20 with the Extended Kit) can, of course, be used for both.

The concept of types and species-type classification can be studied in compact and up-to-date form in such writings as those of Bolz (1972), Cattell, Coulter, and Tsujioka (1966), Kleinmuntz (1967), and Mahrer (1970). These are concerned with taking profile scores on the basic factor dimensions and then using the *profile similarity coefficient*, r_p, to discover the groupings into which people naturally fall. As a variant on ways of finding the groups by objective methods, with r_p's, the Taxonome computer program (IPAT, 1970)[2] may be utilized.

Alternatively to such a radical objective advance in grouping, one can accept certain existing type groupings, e.g., psychiatrist's syndrome grouping or occupational groupings, and then find the best multiple discriminant function weights (Tatsuoka, 1972) on the O-A factors to assign persons by their trait-score profiles into their appropriate groups. The former—the application of the Taxonome program to O-A scores—is a basic research task yet to be done; but Schmidt (1974; also Cattell, Schmidt, & Bjerstedt, 1972) gives extensive results on multiple discriminant functions for the O-A scores applied to psychiatric diagnosis as discussed in Chapter 11. A special case of such diagnostic separation—which may or may not turn out to be typical in nature, but is of considerable importance in practice—is the separation of clients at clinics or, indeed, of children in school into those of essentially good mental health from those seriously in need of treatment. As Cattell points out (1973b), this is not a unidimensional difference on a single continuum, but involves differences on many personality traits. Consequently, it calls for use of a discriminant function involving most of the 10 O-A factors, as well as some source traits found in the Extended Kit.

---

[2] This first discovers the natural type groupings of the various profiles in an objective way. By the congruence coefficient it then gives an equally diagnostic assignment of an individual with respect to the types found.

The scope of this chapter cannot include expounding the general principles of psychometry any further. It must be assumed that the reader understands the general principles of estimation by various regression equations: of assigning probabilities of success on some all-or-nothing scale to various test scores; (see Schuerger & Watterson, 1977) of using discriminant functions weighting the discriminatory power efficiency of batteries; (see Cattell, 1973) of allowing for the effects of sampling and of moderator variables, for example, on predictions; and of using analysis of variance and covariance in detecting significant trait changes under therapy or environmental influences. It would be invidious to suggest particular psychometric texts from among the host of good books available today in the area, but to the extent that a multivariate emphasis is needed, we might mention Lawlis and Chatfield (1974) as a clear elementary introduction, Cooley and Lohnes (1971), Guion (1965), Guilford (1970), Kleinmuntz (1967), Nunnally (1967), and Chapters 9 and 10 in Cattell (1973b) as intermediate, and the *Handbook of Multivariate Experimental Psychology* (1966) and Tatsuoka's monographs (1969, 1970, 1971, 1974, 1975, 1976) for the highest technical levels.

While industrial and educational psychologists have advanced slowly but steadily toward an appropriate and effective use of structured trait test usage, clinical psychology (and to some extent counseling) has stood peculiarly in the doldrums, trimming its sails rather desperately now to a slant of wind from the "humanistic" intuitive direction and now from the reflexological "behavior therapy" direction, both of which have neglected measurement of the patient. The escape from the doldrums into a surging progress will occur only when the total dynamic and trait structures of the individual are assessed and heeded in both the diagnostic and therapeutic procedures.

Even apart from the debate over Eysenck's assertions of negligible gain from existing therapies, most realists recognize that the gain is, on the average, small and uncertain. For all but the most encapsulated therapists, the reign of nonstatistical, nonexperimental faith in the potency of clinical theories ended with the indisputable demonstrations of Meehl (1950), McNemar (1958), Eysenck (1952), Goldberg (1972), and others that "actuarial" (psychometric) predictions decidedly exceeded unaided, "intuitive" clinical judgments in their accuracy. Wiggins (1973, p. 183) sums up, "The impact of Meehl's review on clinical psychologists was nothing less than devastating," and adds, "Obviously from the practical standpoints of cost, efficiency, and utilization of clinical time, the statistical method of data combination would be preferable to clinical prediction [even] in cases where the two have been shown to be approximately equal in validity."

This conclusion may seem only to concern diagnosis, but diagnostic understanding and intelligent therapeutic action are an organic whole. Soon a social demand for accountability—which industrial and educational applications more frequently have to meet—will require clinicians to give a more thorough trial to the neglected structured model. And since measurement without theory is empty, this means studying personality theory which centers around objective observations and experiments. Substantial theoretical developments have quite recently been presented on this quantitative basis in the *Handbook of Modern Personality Theory* (Cattell & Dreger, 1977), *Personality and Learning Theory* (Cattell, 1978), and *Modern Psychotherapy and the Dynamic Calculus* (Cattell & Birkett, in press), *Handbook of Abnormal Psychology* (Eysenck, 1961), and several articles by Eber, Krug, Price, Schuerger, Sweney, Watterson, and others.

The reader who wishes a clinically sensitive but up-to-date introduction to what can be done in diagnosis and therapy by structured measurement would do well to study Cattell and Birkett's book above, Karson and O'Dell's *A Guide to the Clinical Use of the 16 PF* (1976), Kleinmuntz's *Personality Assessment* (1965), Krug, et al., *IPAT Anxiety Scale* (1963), Krug's *Psychological Assessment in Medicine* (1977), Pervin's *Personality Theory, Assessment and Research* (1975), Schuerger and Watterson's *Using Tests and Other Information in Counseling* (1977), and Wiggins' *Personality and Prediction* (1973). These books deal mainly with questionnaire scales such as the *16 PF, HSPQ, Eight State Questionnaire*, but also with objective tests such as the *Motivation Analysis Test* (MAT), the *School Motivation Analysis Test* (SMAT), and the *Culture Fair Intelligence Scale*. Inevitably, a few years must elapse before clinical experience with the O-A yields directly comparable information, but meanwhile the techniques and strategies that these writers report with structured measurement by Q-data are essentially the same as for measurement of the same trait and changing state levels by the O-A.

However, there is also much to be gleaned from several articles on criterion relations of these U.I. personality factors published before the O-A itself was made available to the general public.[3] As such criterion relations become confirmed, it will be increasingly possible to wed this information to the psychological natures of the source traits, to the obtained scores, and to invoke *psychological* laws, of a quantitative kind, for extension of the purely static psychometric-statistical prediction of relationships. Work with the O-A (as with the 16 PF and other theory-based instruments) is no longer a statistical procedure handling psychologically opaque, relatively meaningless scores on a set of "predictor variables." Knowledge of the natures of the traits renders us capable of

---

[3] The research demonstrating the structures in objective behavioral personality measures was summarized 12 years ago (Hundleby, Pawlik, & Cattell, 1965; Nesselroade & Delhees, 1966). Before that it lay in dozens of articles, requiring careful perusal either to evaluate the nature of the new structures or to replicate measures for them. For all but a few psychologists, therefore, the concepts and measures in this area of psychology have become *practically* available only with the present publication.

incorporating effects from changing environments, genetic information about the family, expected age-curve changes over time, etc.

First in this supplementary information is that on the relative genetic and environmental determination of traits levels (Cattell, Stice, & Kristy, 1957; Cattell & Klein, 1978). There is no point in expending much clinical effort on traits that are largely "given," such as intelligence, and neglecting to work on those such as U.I. 16, 23, 24, 30, 32, and 33, which investigation shows can be altered for the better. And knowledge of what is firmly given by constitution, i.e., of levels on traits of the former type, tells us where the firm fulcra exist within the personality upon which leverage can be dependably exerted.

Secondly, it is important to take stock of the known age trends. Regardless of whether they follow maturational curves, as in the genetic traits U.I. 19, 20, etc., or express the average effect of learning experience in our culture, as in U.I. 16, 23, and 24, these trends have to be taken into account in projecting an individual's behavior into the future, or understanding, in diagnosis, how deviant he actually is in terms of his own age group.

The full use of personality theory, however, requires, beyond the above genetic and age change principles, an understanding of what trait changes are likely to follow from exposure to different learning environments, conflict situations, physiological trauma, and therapeutic treatments. Here the theoretical models of *Path Learning Analysis* and *Adjustment Process Analysis* (Cattell, 1978b) permit matrix calculations to handle the combined impact of several life situations. Unfortunately, at the moment, empirical research lags in determining the necessary coefficients. Our store of knowledge about changes in the 20 O-A source traits and the required coefficients for major situations is small—but precious. We know that psychotherapy and tranquilizers will significantly lower the level of U.I. 24, anxiety, U.I. 23—, regression (Cattell, Rickels, et al., 1966), and probably that of the exvia-invia (U.I. 32) balance. If non-manipulative results such as those of Reuterman, Howard, and Cartwright (in press) can be included, we may conclude that U.I. 16, ego standards, U.I. 32, exvia, and U.I. 33—, sanguineness, rise through the influence of a higher social status and more favorable environment.

We know also of physiological influences on fluid intelligence, defined as g_f (Cattell, 1930, 1971), and education influences on crystallized intelligence, g_c (Baltes & Nesselroade, 1973; Jensen, 1969). If we are prepared to accept evidence from questionnaire second-order equivalents to the O-A primaries, e.g., on Q I as U.I. 32, Q II as U.I. 24, Q IV as U.I. 19, and Q VIII as U.I. 17, then we can draw on a wider field of past work recording personality factor responses to and effects upon environment (Krug & Cattell, 1971). The excellent alignment of Q and T in certain cases clearly permits this referral of findings to instrument-transcending trait measures.[4]

Whether the practitioner should feel free to carry over theory from the premetric, clinical, and literary phases of psychology to the traits here designated ego strength standards (U.I. 16), regression (U.I. 23—), anxiety (U.I. 24), etc., is a more difficult question. A comment thereon is our designating the precisely defined U.I. 32 as exvia-invia, instead of using the journalistically battered remnants of Jung's terms extraversion-introversion.[5] Unquestionably, much that goes under the latter popular terminology, and even under Jung's secondary theoretical elaboration of extraversion, is *not* sustained by the correlational analysis of the pattern and criterion associations of U.I. 32. Yet where psychometric relevance figures do not yet exist, one must surely agree that the practicing psychologist should accept the probability that the present measures will predict as clinical theory presently indicates for comparable concepts, rather than fail to use the information that past general experience has gained. This is not to deny that the quality and properties of knowledge in the new domain of multivariate experimental personality and learning theory are not fundamentally different in scientific status. They constitute, in fact, an entirely new and independent foundation for personality theory,

---

[4] A more precise discussion of the issue of how far we may use theory developed by experiment with *questionnaire* measures of the same source traits to apply to *objective* (O-A) measures of them, when the direct proof of criterion relations in T-data has not yet been given, is offered in *personality traits* (Cattell, 1973b; Cattell, Pierson, & Finkbeiner, 1976). An example would be the relation of anxiety (U.I. 24, Q II) and exvia (U.I. 32, Q I) to certain group dynamics behaviors when it has not yet been shown in T-data measures, but where there is already substantial Q-data evidence. The well-supported theory of instrument-transcending personality factors does not say that there will be a near perfect correlation of measures of the same trait in the two different media. Imperfect validities and reliabilities, and a difference in the two instrument factor contributions, would reduce straight mutual test correlation, though factor analysis could check and demonstrate the existence of a true alignment. In the above account of factor ''validities'' (actually *relevances*), age trends, inheritances, etc., *we have depended almost entirely on evidence found with the actual T-data batteries*, indicating in the perhaps 10% of findings taken from questionnaire equivalents that it is so taken. However, one may properly expect that as the cross-media matches become more established, measurement findings in either medium will add to the theory, and the common theory will implement prediction and monitoring of behavior in both media. In translation, only the usualy allowances for different validities and specific factors and (in questionnaires) the susceptibility to motivational distortion will need to be made.

[5] Eysenck has made a good deal of use of ideas from the Jungian extraversion-introversion concept, but, somewhat strangely, has denied that any recognition is possible in multivariate experimental work of Freudian concepts. Cattell has incurred virtually perennial criticism for failing to include in bibliographies of findings in, say, anxiety or exvia, presented as uniquely defined factors, the far more extensive literature on anxiety and extraversion defined only as anyone pleases to define them. The fact is that as far as experimental conclusions are concerned, nothing but contamination, confusion, contradiction (and its child disillusion) spread from, say, including in statements about anxiety, as a factor, a variety of results from some scale that is 50 percent anxiety, 30 percent neuroticism, and 20 percent introversion. The clinical and experimental methodologies must be recognized and respected, but seen as distinct as oil and water. On the other hand, an historical *conceptual* development, as from the Freudian ego and superego, to the C and G factors (in questionnaires such as the 16 PF) which now define them, should be denied no more than the *historical* continuity of exvia-invia (U.I. 24) with Jung's extraversion and introversion. And while the psychologist is waiting for the firm statistical findings relating a given factor to this or that criterion, surely he may—though with explicit reservations—use expectations from older clinical observations.

and there is nothing for it but to have the practitioner in the personality realm learn it afresh, as the change from astrology to astronomy and from alchemy to the weighing and measuring of Lavoisier, Dalton, and Priestley required a fresh start in chemistry. The practicing psychologist can be thankful, in view of the very questionable reputation of existing clinical procedures exposed by the work of Meehl, Eysenck, and others above, that this firmer platform has been provided for his advance. If the practitioner complains that the new principles are as scant as they are rigorous, he is free to contribute by his own work with the O-A and other structured batteries to the growth of firm developmental and clinical knowledge which—if he is not to be a charlatan—he desperately needs.

Meanwhile, let us not overlook that we have available a remarkable growth of principles and criterion relations in a comparatively short time, as a careful perusal of Chapters 3, 10, and 11 will show. As mentioned above, we know, for example, that psychotherapy and chemotherapy produce significant reductions in U.I. 23— and U.I. 24, and that the former may also raise U.I. 32. These deal with central concepts in psychotherapy and personality theory. For other relations we depend most, at present, on the New Zealand study (Barton & Cattell, 1972a) following up 1,000 young men for 4 years after leaving high school, which stands as a classical centerpiece in research on life change in personality factors.

As the analysis of Barton and Cattell (1972a, 1972b) reveals, significant changes on factor scores can be shown to occur with marriage, divorce, illness, success in career, frequency of job change, etc. However, what we now know is fragmentary compared to what can soon be established with the release of the O-A Kit in a form practical for general psychological use. In the meantime, the information in Chapters 3, 10, and 11 should permit the psychologist at least a number of shrewd guesses on the action of these traits in new situations. For example, one sees a broad importance in all kinds of controlled and realistic behavior of U.I. 25, realism. Where reliability either in the sense of nondelinquency or lack of proneness to neurosis or psychosis is concerned, U.I. 25 (probably as frontal lobe functionality) is going to be diagnostic.

The general sense of U.I. 23—, inability to mobilize, is that of some long-term fatigue such as one would suspect arises from prolonged mental conflict or overwork, or even some physiological dysfunction. A shrewd hunch would be that since this is fairly sensitive to change, it could be used as a "clinical thermometer" monitoring the general recovery under rest or therapy.

Depressives are known to recover spontaneously, with little behavior change to foretell the recovery. Is it possible that measures on U.I. 23 would yield a rise foreshadowing this change? And is it possible that examination of depressions in terms of U.I. 23, U.I. 21, U.I. 20, and U.I. 30 as begun by Patrick and Price (1978) would yield profiles permitting separation of suicidal from other depressions?

In studying proneness to delinquency, U.I. 20 is apparently of central importance, and one can see it as probably a temperamental component urging the individual to sociability and overactivity, with little depth of character. If it is combined with rejection of superego values, which seems to characterize U.I. 28, and with the exuberance of U.I. 21, one would guess that delinquency of a particularly difficult type would be met.

Although occupational evidence is scant outside military fields, one is perhaps entitled to infer from the nature of U.I. 16, U.I. 19, U.I. 23, and U.I. 25 that these are needed in occupations requiring ability to face stress, as in air pilots, executives, and others.

A feature of the empirical results which is at present a little puzzling is the joint action of several distinct factors in producing a certain effect. This is evident on the positive side in the action of U.I. 16, 19, and 25 in producing successful achievement in school or occupation, and on the negative side in low U.I. 16, 19, 21, 23, and 24 being involved in schizophrenia and some other pathologies. Since there is no question of their distinctness as factors and of the different subtest performances which they affect, we can only safely assume that their several contributions to, say, pathology are of different kinds, and that they may well have importance at different stages in the pathological process.

A considerable domain of precision research thus opens up in the use of the O-A source-trait measures. In this section we have ventured to speculate in terms of, at present, dimly perceived properties, and have done so briefly because the practitioner gaining experience with the test is likely soon to gain fruitful hypotheses beyond the hunches on such restricted evidence as is presently available. Two things only can be stated with certainty at present: (1) that the source traits predict a considerable array of real-life behaviors significantly, and (2) that since psychometric research shows them to be unitary and distinct, their causal actions must be of a psychologically distinct and meaningful kind.

A broader issue of theory that will soon come up in O-A practice concerns the possible interaction of O-A personality factor measures with other measures. There is every evidence that the O-A Kit stands largely in the modality of general personality and temperament, and that the ability and motivation-interest modalities are outside it. If it spans adequately the general personality-temperament space, *there is no reason to use any other personality measures along with the O-A.* But there *is* something to be gained in prediction by adding factor measures of the *ability* modality, on the one hand, and the *dynamic structure* modality, on the other.

As to the first issue, it must be remembered that the T-data personality factors are derived, one step removed, from the basis provided by the *personality sphere* (Cattell, 1946, 1972, 1975; Norman, 1967) in L- and Q-data, which claims, methodologically, to sample the totality of human trait behavior. It also represents a factoring of virtually every objective T-data test device that has been invented. Furthermore, if the proof of the pudding is the eating, it proceeds to justify this claim to catholicity by *demonstrating a 20-dimensional space* (in the 20 factors of the combined Main and Extended Kit). It is highly *unlikely*, therefore, that any *ad hoc* questionnaire scale or new objective test will lie outside this space, though it just may do so. Psychologists unfamiliar with the cogency of the dimensionality principle will quite often be found in practice throwing into some applied study all kinds of tests—"everything but the kitchen sink"— in the belief that they are thereby increasing their chances of good prediction. Frequently, there is already evidence in the literature that these superfluous tests are covered by existing dimensions. For example, Eysenck's extraversion, E, and neuroticism, N, are already more than covered as secondaries in the 16 PF, tests of vocabulary add virtually nothing to an intelligence measure, and, as Pieszko's (1967) analysis shows, "sensitivity" measures add nothing to a standard, defined anxiety factor measure. The virtue of well-chosen, factor-pure, source-trait scales is that they maximally, and without overlap, cover a broad domain. Yet, even when pushed for time, psychologists uncertain of these principles may be seen cluttering up a battery with unquestionably overlapping tests in the interest of "safety" in coverage.

Although there is very rarely any point in bringing in various questionnaire scales or other batteries along with the O-A to cover the personality sphere, there is, of course, a real point in adding factored ability tests, such as the Culture Fair Intelligence Test (Cattell, 1960; Cattell & Cattell, 1973*a*, 1973*b*) or the Comprehensive Ability Battery, CAB (Hakstian & Cattell, 1975, 1976), and factored dynamic trait (motivation) measures, like the Motivation Analysis Test, MAT (Cattell, Horn, Sweney, & Radcliffe, 1975), in certain diagnoses and predictions. For example, in predicting scholarship achievement or diagnosing underachievement at high school or college level, both ability and dynamic trait measures are practically certain to improve the prediction. The psychologist may at first recoil from the impracticality of 3 hours of the O-A Battery, a half hour of the Culture Fair Intelligence Test, and 1 hour of the MAT (Motivation Analysis Test) or SMAT (School Motivation Analysis Test). But, as Chapter 11 indicates, it is quite unlikely that more than two to four personality factors will have substantial weights for school achievement, and cutting down to these and the intelligence and motivation factors may thus leave one with demand for little more than 2 hours of testing. The essentials of personality theory remind one at every turn that the total personality enters most performances and needs to be viewed in most diagnoses; so that source traits from the three modalities will generally give the best result—though after preliminary investigation one may not need all factorial dimensions from each modality.

As pointed out earlier, comprehensive personality theory requires one to think not only of ability and dynamic traits that flank the general personality traits in the specification equation, but also the diagnostic and predicted use of *states*. Levels on the states of depression, anxiety, fatigue, etc., in the Eight State Questionnaire (8SQ) by Curran and Cattell (1971, 1974, 1976) are demonstrably determiners of performance (and especially of displays of symptoms) over and above the traits. This is shown beyond cavil in the P-technique studies of Cattell and Birkett (1978) and of Cattell and Cross (1952). The practical problem here, of course, is that when predicting some future behavior, the state level at that time will not be known. However, this can be handled by modulator action and state proneness calculations (Cattell, 1973*b*, 1977*a*). Incidentally, the reader should realize, if his understanding and calculations are to be insightful, that state scales cannot be arbitrarily set up for "anxiety," "depression," "arousal," "excitation," etc., but must also be structured, i.e., based on factor-analytic evidence by P- and dR-techniques about the number and nature of dimensions along which human behavior changes with time.

Already the use of state measures in clinical and therapeutic work, either in the objective state batteries of Nesselroade (1966) or the Q-measures of Curran (1968), is beginning to show that state measures, particulatly in relation to incidents in the course of therapy, can give the skilled clinician as much guidance as a medical doctor gets from a temperature or blood count test.

Equally, if not more important, is the combination of the general personality structure measures in the O-A with dynamic trait and state measures. As far as factored interest and dynamic traits are concerned, the available batteries are the MAT (Cattell, Horn, Radcliffe, & Sweney, 1964), or the SMAT (Krug, Sweney & Cattell, 1976). Combining these with the O-A presents no problem and has been shown to substantially enhance educational achievement and other predictions (Cattell & Butcher, 1968).

Psychologically, it is easy to understand that persons of the *same* personality can have acquired very different interests and motivations—and vice versa, that persons of the same interests and beliefs may have different personalities. Furthermore, in a personality theory that properly incorporates the environment, it is clear that given personality traits will operate with different effects when the situation raises various degrees of motivation and ergic tension. What the psychologist needs to keep in mind, if the above analysis is complete, can be compactly stated in one further extension of the comprehensive specification equation as follows:

$$a_{ijk} = \sum_{a=1}^{p} b_{ja}A_{ai} + \sum_{t=1}^{q} b_{jt}T_{ti} + \sum_{d=1}^{r} b_{jd}D_{di} + \sum_{s=1}^{y} b_{js}S_{ksi} \qquad (12.1)$$

where the A_i's are the person's score on p ability factors, as measurable in the CAB; the T_i's on q personality traits, as in the O-A; the D_i's on r

275

dynamic traits, as in the MAT; and the S_i's are y state factors, as in the 8-State Questionnaire (1974, 1975). The Σ's, of course, indicate the sum across the product pairs. The b's are behavioral indices (weights or loadings) found by research and peculiar to the performance or act, a_j, and to the trait. Note that only S and the act have the subscript k which betokens a particular occasion and situation, since traits retain levels (but not effects) across situations. It is assumed in (12.1) that all variance is taken care of by broad traits, i.e., no specifics are introduced, which is appropriate to practice, where one cannot measure specifics.

In practice one might have about a dozen primary abilities, A's, 10 T's from the O-A, and 10 dynamic traits, D's, from the MAT. However, the great majority of O-A users will probably confine themselves to situations where the O-A source traits are themselves essentially sufficient. Indeed, in most cases the psychologist will be able to cut down his O-A testing to two to four factors and a time of 1 to 2 hours. For the advance of theoretical understanding and criterion correlation information will soon lead to a discriminating selection of the particular source traits most relevant to this task.

In retrospect, one sees that the message of this chapter is directed to two divergent flanks of the would-be advancing march of psychology. On the one hand, it calls to the psychometrist not to be too static and too exclusively statistical in his development of measurement. Measurement must be organically related to natural psychological structures, and must extend far beyond scholastic and ability measures into personality, dynamics, and transient states and processes. On the other hand, it calls to the clinician who has depended too much on a crystal ball to look up and recognize that structured measurement advances have been made that supply him, as parallel instruments do the domain of physical medicine, with means of predicting, by computer and systems theory, the probable nature and causes of a disorder. The *art of therapy is not thereby reduced, but raised to a new level of capacity to handle complexities.*[6]

Admittedly, the theoretical framework for getting the most of the new objective measures in the O-A Kit is in its infancy, but it is a lusty infancy, likely to lead, as it grows up, to an altogether more effective science and art of psychological practice.

---

[6]One of the main obstacles to the growth of a mutual enrichment of clinical practice and multivariate experimental personality theory has been a mutual exclusion of clinical ideas from the training of the experimentalist and of sophisticated multivariate statistico-experimental concepts from the required training of clinicians. Actually, there is no need for the clinician to be fully *au fait* with the sometimes complex procedures by which factor analysis, for example, established the existence of unique trait and state structures and relations. He needs only a clear *logical* understanding of what factorial research and applied calculations are saying. The rest can be left to technicians. The logic—that symptoms and behaviors are multiply determined, and that unitary structures and forces in persons and situations are the determiners—is no different from that of psychoanalysis.

Appendix A
The Extended Source Trait Kit

As indicated earlier, the Extended Battery defines the best tests presently known for the *remaining* factors that have been discovered and replicated to date: these are U.I. 17, 18, 22, 26, 27, 29, 30, 31, 34, and 35, making 20 dimensions in all when added to those in the present battery.

For full information about the present stage of replication and understanding of these factors, the reader is referred to Hundleby, Pawlik, and Cattell (1965), the articles in its bibliography, and a few articles that have appeared since 1966 and are found in the O-A Handbook bibliography.

The list below gives the U.I. numbers and tentative titles and the Master Index numbers and titles of the tests. With these M.I. numbers, the reader can enter the Cattell and Warburton compendium (1967), find the T (test) numbers, and look at the actual test designs. In most cases, he will need to make up more items on the models given, in order to work with sufficient test length. He is also advised to bring the five subtests set out for each up to eight, as in the Main O-A Kit, by studying tables of replicated test loadings in Hundleby, Pawlik, and Cattell (1965). Such extended batteries may alternatively be found in several cases in the articles, e.g., Cattell, Schuerger, and Klein (1976) and Cattell, Schmidt, and Pawlik (1973), and the reports of Reuterman, Howard, and Cartwright (1978), Tatro (1967), Wardell and Yeudall (1976), Schmidt, Hacker, and Cattell (1975), and others have used and presented more complete batteries for various of these factors.

In what follows, the Master Index Number (M.I.), as in Cattell and Warburton (1967) and numerous publications, defines the variable to be scored, and the direction of scoring is indicated by the verbal title—"more," "faster," "slower," etc.

U.I. 17. Control; or Inhibition by Good Upbringing

This factor was called *general inhibition* until it was shown by Wardell and Yeudall (1976) to be apparently identical with Q VIII, "restraining upbringing," or control in Q-data (second order in 16 PF; see Cattell, Eber, & Tatsuoka, 1970). The latter loads high superego, G; high self-sentiment, Q3; and desurgency, F—, suggesting exposure to an environment teaching control and inhibition. It correlates with high dependability and carefulness, negatively with military pilot performance, and to some extent with neurosis, as discussed in Chapter 11. The fact that U.I. 17 has a fairly strong genetic determination, nevertheless tells us that the good control is as much due to a receptive, docile, inhibitable temperament as to the family or school cultural influences.

M.I. 21 Fewer questionable reading preferences
7 Slower speed of closure in gestalt completion
43 Larger GSR deflection in response to threatening stimuli
336 More threatening objects seen in unstructured drawings
117 More responses indicative of "highbrow," educated taste

U.I. 18. Hypomanic Temperament

This almost certainly represents a manic-depressive axis, and high scores on it have been shown by Tatro (1968) to be very closely related to manic diagnosis in mental hospital patients.

M.I. 153 Faster speed of decision on the Cursive Miniature Situation (CMS) test
15 More use of excess circles on the CMS (rule breaking)
39 Higher ratio of color to form dependence in color-form sorting
193a More shifting of attitudes to those of people designated successful
269 Faster leg-circling tempo (and other tempos)

U.I. 22. Cortertia-vs-Pathemia

This has been hypothesized to be high cortical alertness and cognitive activity relative to a predominance of feeling (pathemia) expression, such as might arise from hypothalamic action. It significantly separates (in the pathemic direction) neurotics from non-neurotics, and is potent also in job prediction. It is omitted from the primary O-A only because it demands individual tests.

M.I. 5 Higher ratio of regularly to irregularly warned reaction time
40 More responses to irrelevantly introduced reaction time stimuli
8 High frequency of alternating perspective
83 Higher fidgetometer frequency
9 Better ideomotor performance (cancellation)

U.I. 26. Narcism; or Concern with Self-Sentiment Development and Self-Command

Persistence, attempts at pre-eminent performance, better educational background, but also narcistic interest and rejection of society, as in delinquency, characterize this factor; but as yet little is known about criteria other than delinquency and school achievement (both positive!). It has only slight genetic determination and is very largely the product of environment (Cattell & Klein, in press).

M.I. 273　Higher proportion of fluency on self
　　　　2a　Lower motor rigidity
　　　167　Better immediate memory performance
　　　24a　Higher ratio of final to initial performance in novel task
　　　　71　Fewer errors in reaction time under complex instructions

U.I. 27. Apathetic Temperament

This seems to be a temperament factor of apathy, with some indifference to and disregard of society. It correlates negatively with sociometric popularity ratings by peers, with low regard for social demands, with low motivation, and a tendency to emotional drift (as seen by adult supervisors). The level in an individual is largely environmentally determined.

M.I.　42　More body sway suggestibility
　　　13a　More oscillation of performance
　　　194　More shift of attitudes from those designated as neurotic
　　　108　Less confident assumption of skill in untried performance
　　　101a　Less excess of aspiration level over performance level

U.I. 29. Overreactivity; or Greater Self-Performance Demand

This is an important factor, clinically, which might well have been included in the O-A but for some difficulty in getting subtests sufficiently high in validity. Interpretative hypotheses have varied rather widely. On first appearance its high performance standards suggested superego strength, but more recently Wardell and Yeudall (1975) have suggested "ego strength." It has a large environmental determination and associations with a close parental concern. It also has associations (moderate) with pathological depressions and with delinquency. It suggests some hard-driving need for ego-expression such as could derive from a sense of inferiority.

M.I.　2a　Low motor rigidity
　　　143　Higher total CMS score
　　　268　Faster tempo of tapping (and leg circling)
　　　152　More tendency to agree
　　　116b　More critical severity in moral standards

U.I. 30. Somindence-vs-Dissofrustance

The high-U.I. 30 individual is stolid, aloof, apathetic, and desurgent, but less given than the dissofrustant individual to delinquent behavior. The name of the negative pole arises from a theoretical interpretation that individuals there have a tendency to *dissociative rejection* of *frustrating ideas*, and in accordance with this there are other signs of some hysteric behavior and instability.

M.I. 269, 270   Slower leg and arm circling tempos
        42   Higher body sway suggestibility
     282   Fewer objects seen in unstructured drawings
      31   Less fluctuation of attitudes
   1414   Slower speed of letter cancellation

U.I. 31. *Wariness-vs-Impulsivity-variability*

This is a factor of cautiousness, steadiness, and self-control, but not good or accurate performance. So far no very definite life criteria associations have been found for it.

M.I. 192   More considered possible in given time for self
    203   Less confidence in correctness of one's own exact results in computations, etc.
    67b   Less extremity of viewpoint in judging aphorisms
    280   Higher accuracy of time interval estimates
    106   Less unreflective acceptance of unqualified statements

U.I. 34. *Inconautia-vs-Practicalness*

The negative pole of U.I. 34, judging by ratings, is perhaps what psychiatrists have called "bound anxiety," representing a high concern with orderliness and practicality. The "incontinent autism" (condensed to "inconautia") of the positive bond, with its happy-go-lucky, casual, indifferent unconcern, is perhaps no more than the absence of bound anxiety.

M.I. 120a   Lower ratio of accuracy to speed
    282   Greater number of objects reported in unstructured drawings
    83   Lower fidgetometer frequency
    33   Larger size of myokinetic movements
   732   More readiness to commit oneself to a course of action

U.I. 35. *Stolparsomnia-vs-Proneness to Excitement*

The novel title is an acronym for the best present description: "stolid, parasympathetic-dominated, somnolent temperament." Behavior is sluggish, self-disillusioned, not well organized, but with a stolid, realistic outlook on the world. The lower systolic blood pressure and higher skin resistance suggest a temperamental involvement of the parasympathetic autonomic system. Strangely, it has some relation to talkativeness (surgency) (Dickens' Micawber fits it tolerably) and to long-term views, but a negative relation to school and other achievement, as might be expected.

M.I. 458   More remote, long-term life goals
     199   Lower numerical ability
     460   Preference for the strange over the familiar
     464   Lower average handwriting pressure
      43   Larger GSR response to threat

A 21st factor, U.I. 36, is well replicable in objective motivation test terms and is recognizable as *self-sentiment strength.* However, it is already most appropriately measured by the instrumentality of the Motivation Analysis Test (MAT: Cattell, Horn, Radcliffe, & Sweney, 1964).

The above lists of subtests are chosen to combine highest loadings with least overlap of subtests between one factor and another. In adding to these subtests as proposed, by use of Hundleby, Pawlik, and Cattell (1965), the reader will find, in addition to records of replicated tests, more extensive discussion of the theoretical interpretations of these factors, their nature-nurture values, and criterion relations. There will undoubtedly be found other, less replicated factors beyond the above 10 and the 10 in the O-A, and the psychologist interested in exploring a more extensive map is referred to the studies of Brengelmann (1954), Brogden (1940), Connor (1952), Crutcher (1934), Darling (1940), Eysenck (1947, 1952, 1960, 1972), Hargreaves (1927), Knapp (1961a, 1962), Pawlik (1968), Rethlingshafer (1942), Reuterman, Howard, and Cartwright (in press), Rimoldi (1951), Ryans (1938), Schmidt, Hacker, and Cattell (1975), Wardell and Royce (1975), Wardell and Yeudall (1976), besides the 20 or so studies by Cattell and coworkers in the bibliography of Cattell and Warburton (1967) and the more recent studies by Cattell and Klein (1975), Cattell, Schmidt, and Pawlik (1973), and Cattell, Schuerger, Klein, and Finkbeiner (1976).

It should be noted that some of these less replicated factors have nevertheless recently shown a promise in criterion relations that is as great as for factors in the published, standardized series. Certainly U.I. 17, 18, 22, and 29 in the Extended Kit are at the same general level of life significance, if not of reliable testability, as those in the Main Kit.

In the interests of research advance, the authors would appreciate receiving at the earliest opportunity the results of experiments with traits either in the Main or the Extended Kit, relating them to criterion, to developmental evidence, to structural change with age, etc.

Appendix B
Supplementary Tests, Individual in Administration, for the Main Battery

There are occasions, notably in the intensive study of a particular source trait, when an investigator is prepared to give more time, and the care required in individual testing, to raise a measure to a truly high validity. The validities reached by group testing and less than 20 minutes of actual testing time per factor, satisfactory though they are for general testing, can undoubtedly be exceeded if it is important to do so.

With eight subtests of low mutual correlation and a correlation with the factor of 0.4 to 0.5, the ensuing validities of 0.7 to 0.85 can be brought to 0.85 to 0.95 by the addition of only three or four more subtests having the same psychometric properties. It will be noted, also, that if one goes to more subtests, the measure is not only more valid but less biased toward a narrow sample of specific factors. However, despite nearly 40 years of experiment, and the more than 400 subtests invented and tried, as set out in the Cattell and Warburton compendium (1967), it is still not easy to find more than seven to nine subtests per factor that are of sufficient validity and sufficiently free of correlation with other factors. The extra tests can, in fact, be provided in sufficient numbers only by reverting to individually administered tests and tests requiring laboratory apparatus.

Supplementary Tests for the Main Kit

Four or five supplementary tests are provided for each of the 10 factors, and with one unavoidable exception, no subtest is shared by two factors. The particulars of these tests, their apparatus, and their scoring, can be located by the T numbers and M.I. numbers below, in Cattell and Warburton (1967), and their loadings can be traced in Hundleby, Pawlik, and Cattell (1965) and in the articles mentioned therein or appearing later.

U.I. 16. Ego Standards

T 138	M.I. 270	Faster arm-shoulder circling tempo (Individual)
T 304	M.I. 444	Higher systolic blood pressure (Individual)
T 230	M.I. 346	Less decrease in muscular endurance over time (leg raising) (Individual)

U.I. 19. Independence

T 122	M.I.	176	Faster irregularly warned reaction time (Individual)
T 128(a)	M.I.	80	Less rapid GSR upward drift in skin resistance (Individual)
T 128(b)	M.I.	469	More rapid GSR conditioning (Individual)

U.I. 20. Evasiveness

T 127	M.I.	42	More body sway suggestibility (Individual)
T 121	M.I.	78	Less involuntary muscle tension (Individual)

U.I. 21. Exuberance

T 124	M.I.	33	Larger size of myokinetic movement (Group or Individual)
T 296	M.I.	428b	More attention to disturbing relative to non-disturbing pictures (Group or Individual)
T 106	M.I.	466	Higher magnitude of hand tremor (Individual)
T 209	M.I.	75	More increase of metabolic rate with stimulation (Individual)

U.I. 23. Mobilization

T 126	M.I.	41	Better two-hand coordination performance (Individual)
T 108	M.I.	84b	Less increase in pulse rate due to startle (Individual)
T 109	M.I.	510	More articulatory efficiency under delayed feedback (Individual)

U.I. 24. Anxiety

T 211	M.I.	464	Lower average handwriting pressure (Group or Individual)
T 313	M.I.	657	Fewer push-ups before failure (Group or Individual)
T 233	M.I.	455a	Greater volume of saliva in 30 seconds (Individual)
Not yet indexed			Faster respiration rate (Individual)
"	"	"	Greater trapeziums muscle tension (on myograph) (Individual)
"	"	"	Shorter lag in pulse response to cold pressor test (Individual)
"	"	"	Higher 17 OH ketosteroid excretion (Individual)
T 314	M.I.	566	Fewer dips in EKG (Individual)

U.I. 25. Realism

T 122	M.I. 263	Less variability in simple reaction times (Individual)
T 242	M.I. 691	Much "regression to the real" in figure perception (Individual)
T 68	M.I.1107	Less hesitancy in shuffle board game (Individual)

U.I. 28. Asthenia

T 122	M.I. 71	Greater number of R. T. response errors with complex instructions (Individual)
T 299	M.I. 96a	Less impairment of reading speed by frustrated preference (Group or Individual)
T 301	M.I. 491	Larger area under EKG pulse wave (Individual)
T 128	M.I. 443	Lower absolute level of skin resistance (Individual)

U.I. 32. Exvia-vs-Invia

T 182	M.I. 422	Lower height of child's block tower construction (or carelessness in adult equivalent task) (Individual)
T 125	M.I. 492	Shorter endurance time on treadmill run (or equivalent) (Individual)
T 180	M.I. 423	Less planfulness in bridge construction (Individual)

U.I. 33. Discouragement-vs-Sanguineness

T 235	M.I. 46a	Less impairment of maze performance by shock punishment (Individual)
T 128	M.I. 305	Lower ratio of GSR deflections to mental than physical threats (Individual)
T 119	M.I. 166	Less impairment of classification performance by shock (Individual)

Supplementary Tests for the Extended Battery

The psychologist wishing maximally to augment validities in the Extended Kit can find suitable tests in the factor tables in Hundleby, Pawlik, and Cattell (1965), with about equal frequencies to the above, except in the last three or four factors.

Appendix C
Instructions and Illustrations for Scoring
of a Trait Battery

Those psychologists who have followed basic psychometric research on personality over the last 30 years can have little doubt that the future of structured personality assessment, i.e., assessment in terms of dependable and predictive functionally unitary concepts, lies with objective behavioral batteries. But it is equally certain that many potential users will be dismayed by the apparent difficulties of scoring the batteries. "Apparent" is the correct word, because the psychologist who is prepared to give the study to this Handbook that he would to any serious textbook will find the rationale for the apparently complex weighting tables clear enough. And if the reasons for the procedures with single batteries, on the one hand, and computer synthesis on the whole Kit, on the other, are clear, it is only a matter of good mechanical arrangement to make sure that neither shall become a time-consuming chore.

Since the responses, except for a small minority of tests, go on answer sheets, the user of the batteries on samples of appreciable size can be depended upon to use ingenuity and experience, with scanner and suitable computer programs, to proceed the whole way from the subjects' responses to finished standard score profiles without personal labor. It is the clinical user, scoring only two or three profiles a day, and needing diagnostic results too immediately to allow time to send away to a scoring service, who most needs help at this point. Procedures are set out here, but our hope is that two or three years of practical experience by various users will result in improved devices to be offered to test users in due course.

Meanwhile, in this Appendix (Table A.1, next page), it is proposed to take a typical completed score sheet for any factor—actually the first battery in the Kit—U.I. 16, ego standards—and follow the recommended scoring process in Chapter 8, step-by-step, to a finished standard score. However, even though we take a single battery, hand-scored, the alert user will recognize that such scoring can be aided by a simple hand calculator and by writing out, for clerical help, a simple routine, which experience will render automatic.

Referring to Chapter 8, the reader will see that Test 1 is scored as number done, and that John Smith has done 8 (score sheet, Table A.1). From this value, 8, which he will enter in the first column (Table A.2, p. 290), he then subtracts the mean score, written in the second column, and records the value for the difference (plus or minus and to the number of decimal places possible) in the third column as shown.

Keeping to the same labeled Test 1, he then multiplies the column (3) value by column (4) to get (5), which is —.06. In the second test, the derived raw score is again the number done, which is 25, and treating

Table A.1*

*Note that columns 1 through 6 on the lower right are left blank here. They are for coding—by the psychologist, not the subject—of data, e.g., social class, patient-vs-control subject, rating in profession, etc., relevant to research and certain routine records.

Referring to Chapter 8, the reader will see that Test 1 is scored as number done, and that John Smith has done 8. From this, which he will enter in the first column, he then subtracts the mean score, written in the second column, and records the value for the difference (plus or minus and to the number of decimal places possible) in the third column as shown.

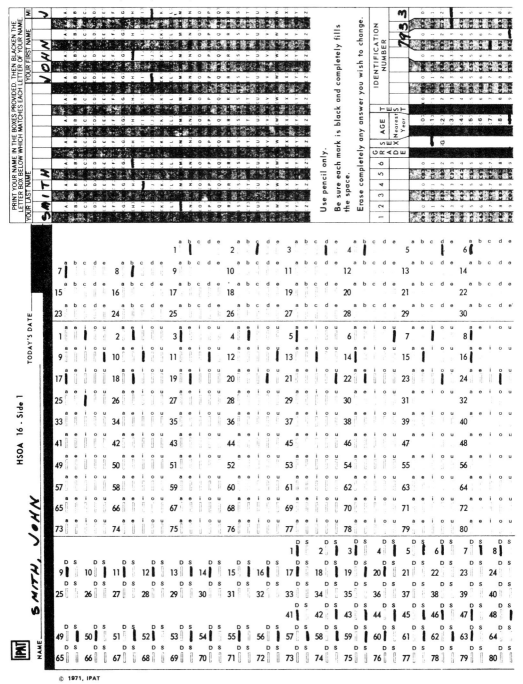

288

Use pencil only.

Be sure each mark is black and completely fills the space.

Erase completely any answer you wish to change.

IDENTIFICATION NUMBER

TODAY'S DATE

NAME — SMITH, JOHN

HSOA 16 - Side 2

Table A.2

Test	(1) Raw Score	(2) Mean of Raw Scores	(3) (1) Minus (2)	(4) Weight	(5) Special Subtest Standard Score, (3) x (4)
1	8	11	−3	.02	−.06
2	25	29	−4	.03	−.12
3	43	38	5	.04	.20
4	7	10	−3	.07	−.21
5	12	13	−1	.02	−.02
6	23	20	3	.01	.03
7	18	27	−9	.04	−.36
8	33	34	−1	.03	−.03
					−.57

this now as for the first test, we finish with −.12. The minus values on standard scores mean, of course, that John Smith is below the population average on that test.

The next test consists of two equivalent parts, and he scores 20 on one and 23 on the other, so the total sum, 43, is entered in the first column and the final standard score is .2. It should not surprise us that one or two scores, belonging as here to one-and-the-same factor, work out a bit above average, even though the majority are somewhat below, for the correlations among the eight subtests are, of course, not perfect. The need to note, in this case, that there are two parts in Test 3 is a good reminder that the scorer, unless he is already familiar with the test booklets, is well advised to have a specimen of the booklet lying alongside the answer sheet. At any rate, in the early stages he needs this help in order not to miss indications that the new score comes from two or more parts or that there are other peculiarities.

Tests 4, 5, 6, and 8 need no further comment and are entered as shown. Test 7 is a case using number right rather than number done and exemplifies the kind of test for which a key is needed. The key is always given (in this Handbook but not to the client) on the answer sheet itself and in this case is written babb, etc., indicating the right answer in the first row is b, in the second, a, and so on. As a result of applying this key, one finds that out of 27 attempted, 9 are wrong and 18 are right, so the last figure is entered.

To obtain John Smith's final standard score on U.I. 16, one simply adds these eight subtest scores, yielding a value of −.57, which is already correct to two decimal places. In short, he is well over half a standard deviation below average on ego standards, and that value has implications in light of our knowledge of this source trait.

It will be seen that, although the statistical rationale that has gone into the preparation of the summary sheet values, as explained in Chapter 7, may seem complex, it has succeeded in making the actual scoring procedure very simple. Essentially, there is nothing to do but make one subtraction for each subtest. The principal care required in the clerical scoring help is to put down the *right signs* after the subtraction and to get the *decimal point* right in the multiplication.

As suggested above, additional devices for speed and accuracy can be provided for clerical help. They are not set out here in order not to obscure the essential process and because each office situation has special facilities. But one can see advantages in such practices as multiplying the weights (column 4 above) by 100 in this battery to avoid decimal points (this would have to be followed by dividing the final answer by 100). Also, it would help avoid sign slips if one sets up one adding column for positive and one for negative values. Obviously, a small desk calculator is almost indispensable here.

Bibliography

Anastasi, A. *Psychological testing.* (3rd ed.) New York: Macmillan, 1975.

Anderson, H. H., & Anderson, M. *Projective techniques.* New York: Prentice-Hall, 1950.

Anderson, J. C., & Cattell, R. B. The measurement of personality and behavior disorders by the IPAT musical preference test. *Journal of Applied Psychology,* 1953, *37,* 446-454.

Arndt, W. B. *Theories of personality.* New York: Macmillan, 1974.

Baehr, M. *A factorial study of temperament.* Chicago: University of Chicago Press, 1951.

Baggaley, A. R., & Cattell, R. B. A comparison of exact and approximate linear function estimates of oblique factor scores. *British Journal of Statistical Psychology,* 1956, *9,* 83-86.

Baggaley, A. R., & Cattell, R. B. The objective measurement and evaluation of principles and devices. *Journal of Personality,* 1956, *24,* 401-423.

Baltes, P. B., & Nesselroade, J. R. The developmental analysis of individual differences on multiple measures. In J. R. Nesselroade & H. W. Reese (Eds), *Life span developmental psychology.* New York: Academic Press, 1973.

Barton, K., & Cattell, R. B. Personality factors related to job promotion and turnover. *Journal of Counseling Psychology,* 1972, *19*(5), 430-435.

Barton, K., & Cattell, R. B. Changes in personality over a five-year period: Relationship of change to life events. *JSAS Catalog of Selected Documents in Psychology,* 1975, *5,* 283-284.

Barton, K., Cattell, R. B., & Conner, D. V. The identification of "state" factors through p-technique factor analysis. *Journal of Clinical Psychology,* 1972, *28*(4), 459-463.

Barton, K., Dielman, T. E., & Cattell, R. B. The prediction of school grades from personality and IQ measures. *Personality,* 1971, *2*(4), 325-333.

Barton, K., Dielman, T. E., & Cattell, R. B. Personality and IQ measures as predictors of school achievement. *Journal of Educational Psychology,* 1972, *63*(4), 398-404.

Bass, A. Multivariate model of quantitative, structural and quantitative-structural ontogenetic change. *Developmental Psychology,* 1974, *10,* 190-203.

Baughman, E. E. *Personality.* New York: Prentice-Hall, 1972.

Beloff, J. R., Cattell, R. B., & Blewett, D. B. The inheritance of personality: A multiple variance analysis determination of approximate nature-nurture ratios for primary personality factors in Q-data. *American Journal of Human Genetics,* 1955, *7,* 122-146.

Beyme, R., & Fahrenberg, J. Zur deutschen bearbeitung der Anxiety-Test von R. B. Cattell. *Diagnostica,* 1968, *14,* 39-44.

Bischof, L. J. *Interpreting personality theories.* (2nd ed.) New York: Harper, 1970.

Birkett, H., & Cattell, R. B. Diagnosis by P-technique of the dynamic roots of a clinical symptom. *Multivariate Experimental Clinical Research,* 1978, in press.

Bock, R. D. Contributions of multivariate experimental designs to educational research. In R. B. Cattell (Ed.), *Handbook of multivariate experimental psychology.* Chicago: Rand McNally, 1966. Ch. 28, pp. 820-840.

Breen, J. L. Anxiety factors related to physical fitness variables. Doctoral dissertation, University of Illinois, 1959.

Brengelmann, J. C. Spaltungsfaehigkeit als Persoenlichkeits-merkmal. *Zeitschrift fur Experimentelle und Angewandte Psychologie,* 1954, *2,* 454-494.

Brody, N. *Personality research and theory.* New York: Academic Press, 1972.

Brogden, H. E. A factor analysis of forty character tests. *Psychological Monographs,* 1940, *234,* 35-55.

Buros, O. K. *The seventh mental measurements yearbook.* Highland Park, N.J.: Gryphon Press, 1972.

Burt, C. L. The factorial analysis of emotional traits. *Character and Personality,* 1939, *7,* 238-254, 285-299.

Burt, C. L. The factorial study of temperamental traits. *British Journal of Psychology, Statistical Section,* 1948, *1,* 178-203.

Buss, A. R., A general developmental model for inter-individual differences, intra-individual differences, and intra-individual changes. *Developmental Psychology,* 1974, *10,* 70-78.

Buss, A. R. Interface of Alston's conceptual analysis of trait theory and Cattell's multi-trait theory of personality. *Multivariate Experimental Psychology,* 1977, *3,* 21-29.

Byrne, D. *An introduction to personality.* New York: Prentice-Hall, 1974.

Carrigan, P. M. Extraversion-introversion as a dimension of personality: A re-appraisal. *Psychological Bulletin,* 1960, *57,* 329-360.

Cartwright, D. S. Personality. In K. Schlesinger & P. M. Groves, *Psychology: A dynamic science.* Dubuque, Iowa: W. C. Brown, 1976.

Cartwright, D. S. *Theories of personality.* Dubuque, Iowa: W. C. Brown, 1977, Ch. 11.

Cartwright, D. S., Tomson, B., & Schwartz, H. *Gang delinquency.* Monterey, Calif.: Brooks/Cole, 1975. Pp. 11-12.

Cattell, R. B. The effects of alcohol and caffeine on intelligent and associative performance. *British Journal of Medical Psychology,* 1930, *13,* 20-23.

Cattell, R. B. *The description and measurement of personality.* New York: Harcourt, Brace, & World, 1946.

Cattell, R. B. Primary personality factors in the realm of objective tests. *Journal of Personality,* 1948, *16,* 459-487.

Cattell, R. B. *Personality: A systematic theoretical and factual study.* New York: McGraw-Hill, 1950.

Cattell, R. B. A factorization of tests of personality source traits. *British Journal of Psychology, Statistical Section,* 1951, *4,* 165-178.

Cattell, R. B. The principal replicated factors discovered in objective personality tests. *Journal of Abnormal and Social Psychology,* 1955, *50,* 291-314. (a)

Cattell, R. B. Psychiatric screening of flying personnel: Personality structure in objective tests—a study of 1,000 Air Force students in basic pilot training. Report No. 9, Project No. 21-0202-007. Randolph Field, Texas: U.S.A.F. School of Aviation Medicine, 1955. (b)

Cattell, R. B. *Personality and motivation structure and measurement.* New York: World Book, 1957. (a)

Cattell, R. B. A universal index for psychological factors. *Psychologia,* 1957, *1,* 74-85. (b)

Cattell, R. B. What is "objective" in "objective personality tests"? *Journal of Counseling Psychology,* 1958, *5,* 285-289.

Cattell, R. B. *Handbook for the Culture Fair Intelligence Test, Scale 1.* Champaign, Ill.: Institute for Personality and Ability Testing, 1960.

Cattell, R. B. Theory of situational, instrument, second-order, and refraction factors in personality structure research. *Psychological Bulletin,* 1961, *58,* 160-174.

Cattell, R. B. The basis of recognition and interpretation of factors. *Educational and Psychological Measurement,* 1962, *22,* 667-697.

Cattell, R. B. Concepts of personality growing from multivariate experiments. In J. M. Wepman & R. W. Heine (Eds), *Concepts of personality.* Chicago: Aldine, 1963. Pp. 413-448. (a)

Cattell, R. B. The interaction of hereditary and environmental influences. *British Journal of Mathematical & Statistical Psychology,* 1963, *16,* 191-210. (b)

Cattell, R. B. Objective personality tests: A reply to Dr. Eysenck. *Occupational Psychology,* 1964, *38,* 69-86. (a)

Cattell, R. B. The parental early repressiveness hypothesis for the "authoritarian" personality factor U.I. 28. *Journal of Genetic Psychology,* 1964, *106,* 333-349. (b)

Cattell, R. B. Factor theory psychology: A statistical approach to personality. In W. S. Sahakian (Ed.), *Psychology of personality: Readings in theory.* Chicago: Rand McNally, 1965.

Cattell, R. B. Evaluating therapy as total personality change: Theory and available instruments. *American Journal of Psychotherapy,* 1966, *20,* 69-88. (a)

Cattell, R. B. (Ed.) *Handbook of multivariate experimental psychology.* Chicago: Rand McNally, 1966. (b)

Cattell, R. B. Patterns of change: Measurement in relation to state dimension, trait change, lability and process concepts. In R. B. Cattell (Ed.), *Handbook of multivariate experimental psychology.* Chicago: Rand McNally, 1966. Ch. 11, pp. 355-402. (c)

Cattell, R. B. Personality structure: The larger dimensions. In B. Semeonoff (Ed.), *Personality assessment*. Baltimore: Penguin, 1966. (d)

Cattell, R. B. Progress in clinical psychology through multivariate experimental designs. *Multivariate Behavioral Research*, 1968, *75*, 96-113.

Cattell, R. B. The diagnosis of schizophrenia by questionnaires and objective personality tests. In D. V. Siva Sankar (Ed.), *Schizophrenia, current concepts and research*. Hicksville, N.Y.: PDJ Publications, 1969. (a)

Cattell, R. B. Is field independence an expression of the general personality source trait of independence, U.I. 19? *Perceptual and Motor Skills*, 1969, *28*, 865-866. (b)

Cattell, R. B. A factor analytic system for clinicians. 1. The integration of functional and psychometric requirements in a quantitative and computerized diagnostic system. In A. R. Mahrer (Ed.), *New approaches to personality classification*. New York: Columbia University Press, 1970. (a)

Cattell, R. B. The isopodic and equipotent principles for comparing factor scores across different populations. *British Journal of Mathematical and Statistical Psychology*, 1970, *23*, 23-41. (b)

Cattell, R. B. Separating endogenous, exogenous, ecogenic, and epogenic component curves in developmental data. *Developmental Psychology*, 1970, *3*, 151-162. (c)

Cattell, R. B. *Abilities: Their structure, growth, and action*. Boston: Houghton Mifflin, 1971.

Cattell, R. B. The interpretation of Pavlov's typology and the arousal concept, in replicated trait and state factors. In J. A. Gray (Ed.), *Biological bases of individual behavior*. New York: Academic Press, 1972.

Cattell, R. B. The measurement of the healthy personality and the healthy society. *Psychiatry & Society*, 1973, *40*, 1-10. (a)

Cattell, R. B. *Personality and mood by questionnaire*. San Francisco: Jossey-Bass, 1973. (b)

Cattell, R. B. Personality theory derived from quantitative experiment. In A. M. Freedman, H. I. Kaplan, & B. J. Sadock (Eds), *Comprehensive textbook of psychiatry. Vol. 1*. (2nd ed.) Baltimore: Williams & Wilkins, 1975.

Cattell, R. B. Lernfahigkeit, Personlichkeitsstruktur und Theorie des struktuierten Lernens. In G. Nissen, *Intelligentz und Lernstorungen*. Berlin: Springer, 1977.

Cattell, R. B. Adolescent age trends in primary personality factors, measured in T-data: A contribution to standardized measures. In press, 1978. (a)

Cattell, R. B. *Personality and learning theory*. New York: Springer, 1978. (b)

Cattell, R. B. *The scientific use of factor analysis*. New York: Plenum, 1978. (c)

Cattell, R. B. Journalism, commercial publication and the education of psychologists. *Multivariate Experimental Clinical Research*, in press. (d)

Cattell, R. B., et al. *Handbook for the objective-analytic [O-A] personality factor batteries*. Champaign, Ill.: Institute for Personality and Ability Testing, 1955. [Although there are references to the actual test, it is assumed that the reader would understand that to reference each and every subtest would be beyond the scope of this bibliography.—Editor]

Cattell, R. B., & Bartlett, H. W. An R-dR-technique operational distinction of the states of anxiety, stress, fear, etc. *Australian Journal of Psychology*, 1971, *23*, 105-123.

Cattell, R. B., & Beloff, H. La structure factorielle de la personalite des enfants de onze ans á travers trois types d'epreuves. *Revue de Psychologie Appliquée*, 1956, *6*(2), 65-89.

Cattell, R. B., & Birkett, H. *Modern psychotherapy and the dynamic calculus.* In press.

Cattell, R. B., & Butcher, H. J. *The prediction of achievement and creativity.* Indianapolis: Bobbs-Merrill, 1968.

Cattell, R. B., & Cattell, A. K. S. *Measuring Intelligence with the Culture Fair Intelligence tests. Manual for Scales 2 and 3.* Champaign, Ill.: Institute for Personality and Ability Testing, 1973. (a)

Cattell, R. B., & Cattell, A. K. S. *Tabular Supplement for the Culture Fair Intelligence Test, Scales 2 and 3.* Champaign, Ill.: Institute for Personality and Aility Testing, 1973. (b)

Cattell, R. B., Cattell, A. K. S., & Rhymer, R. M. P-technique demonstrated in determining psycho-physiological source traits in a normal individual. *Psychometrika*, 1947, *12*, 267-288.

Cattell, R. B., & Child, D. *Motivation and dynamic structure.* New York: Halsted, 1975.

Cattell, R. B., & Coan, R. W. Objective-test assessment of the primary personality dimensions in middle childhood. *British Journal of Psychology*, 1959, *50*, 235-252.

Cattell, R. B., & Coulter, M. A. Principles of behavioral taxonomy and the mathematical basis of the taxonome computer program. *British Journal of Mathematical & Statistical Psychology*, 1966, *19*, 237-269.

Cattell, R. B., Coulter, M. A., & Tsujioka, B. The taxonomic recognition of types and functional emergents. In R. B. Cattell (Ed.), *Handbook of multivariate experimental psychology.* Chicago: Rand McNally, 1966.

Cattell, R. B., & Cross, P. Comparison of the ergic and self-sentiment structures found in dynamic traits by R- and P-techniques. *Journal of Personality*, 1952, *21*, 250-271.

Cattell, R. B., & Damarin, F. L., Jr. Personality factors in early childhood and their relation to intelligence. *Monographs of the Society for Research in Child Development*, 1968, *33*(6, Whole No. 122), 1-95.

Cattell, R. B., Delhees, K. H., Tatro, D. F., & Nesselroade, J. R. Personality structure checked in primary objective test factors for a mixed normal and psychotic sample. *Multivariate Behavioral Research*, 1971, *6*(2), 187-214.

Cattell, R. B., & Dreger, R. M. (Eds). *Handbook of modern personality theory.* New York: Hemisphere; Halsted, 1977.

Cattell, R. B., & Drevdahl, J. E. A comparison of the personality profile (16 PF) of eminent researchers with that of eminent teachers and administrators. *British Journal of Psychology*, 1955, *46*(4), 248-261.

Cattell, R. B., Dubin, S. S., & Saunders, D. R. Personality structure in psychotics by factorization of objective clinical tests. *Journal of Mental Science*, 1954, *100*, 154-187. (a)

Cattell, R. B., Dubin, S. S., & Saunders, D. R. Verification of hypothesized factors in one hundred objective personality test designs. *Psychometrika*, 1954, *3*, 209-230. (b)

Cattell, R. B., Eber, H. W., & Tatsuoka, M. M. *Handbook for the sixteen personality factor questionnaire.* Champaign, Ill.: Institute for Personality and Ability Testing, 1970.

Cattell, R. B., & Gruen, W. The primary personality factors in 11-year-old children by objective tests. *Journal of Personality*, 1955, *23*, 460-478.

Cattell, R. B., Horn, J. L., Radcliffe, J., & Sweney, A. B. *The motivation analysis test: MAT.* Champaign, Ill.: Institute for Personality and Ability Testing, 1964, Revised Edition, 1975.

Cattell, R. B., Horn, J. L., Sweney, A. B., & Radcliffe, J. *Handbook for the motivation analysis test "MAT."* Champaign, Ill.: Institute for Personality and Ability Testing, 1964.

Cattell, R. B., & Howarth, E. Verification of objective test personality factor patterns in middle childhood. *Journal of Genetic Psychology*, 1964, *104*, 331-349.

Cattell, R. B., & Hundleby, J. H. Conceptual and experimental requirements in relating independence (U.I. 19) and field independence in L- and Q-data media: A comment on Dr. Ohnmacht's research. *Perceptual and Motor Skills*, 1968, *27*, 733-734.

Cattell, R. B., & Jaspars, J. A general plasmode (No. 30-10-5-2) for factor analytic exercises and research. *Multivariate Behavioral Research Monograph*, 1967, *67*(3), 1-212.

Cattell, R. B., & Killian, L. R. The pattern of objective test personality factor differences in schizophrenia and the character disorders. *Journal of Clinical Psychology*, 1967, *23*(3), 343-348.

Cattell, R. B., & Klein, T. M. A check on hypothetical personality structures and their theoretical interpretation at 14-16 years in T-data. *British Journal of Psychology*, 1973, *66*(2), 131-151.

Cattell, R. B., & Klein, T. M. An estimation by MAVA of heritabilities and environmental variances for source traits U.I. 16, ego standards, U.I. 17, inhibitory control, and U.I. 19, independence, from 589 families. 1979, in preparation. (a)

Cattell, R. B., & Klein, T. M. An estimation by MAVA of heritabilities for source traits U.I. 20, evasiveness, U.I. 21, exuberance, U.I. 23, mobilization-vs-regression, and U.I. 24, anxiety. 1979, in preparation. (b)

Cattell, R. B., & Klein, T. M. Heritabilities and environmental variances for source traits U.I. 25, realism-vs-psychoticism, U.I. 26, narcistic ego, U.I. 28, asthenia, U.I. 32, extraversion, and U.I. 33, dismay-vs-sangineness, based on 589 families. 1979, in preparation. (c)

Cattell, R. B., & Kline, P. *The scientific analysis of personality and motivation.* New York: Academic Press, 1977.

Cattell, R. B., Knapp, R. R., & Scheier, I. H. Second-order personality factor structure in the objective test realm. *Journal of Consulting Psychology*, 1961, *25*(4), 345-352.

Cattell, R. B., & Nesselroade, J. R. The discovery of the anxiety state pattern in Q-data, and its distinction, in the LM model, from depression, effort stress, and fatigue. *Multivariate Behavioral Research*, 1976, *11*, 27-46.

Cattell, R. B., & Peterson, D. R. Personality structure in four and five year olds in terms of objective tests. *Journal of Clinical Psychology*, 1959, *15*, 355-369.

Cattell, R. B., Pierson, G., & Finkbeiner, C. Proof of alignment of personality source trait factors from questionnaires and observer ratings: The theory of instrument-free patterns. *Multivariate Experimental Clinical Research*, 1976, *2*(2), 63-88.

Cattell, R. B., Price, P. L., & Patrick, S. V. The diagnostic power of the O-A Kit source traits U.I. 19, 20, 25, and 30 in differentiating depressive disorders. *Multivariate Experimental Clinical Research*, in press, 1978.

Cattell, R. B., Radcliffe, J. A., & Sweney, A. B. The nature and measurement of components of motivation. *Genetic Psychology Monographs*, 1963, *68*, 49-211.

Cattell, R. B., & Rickels, K. Diagnostic power of IPAT objective anxiety neuroticism tests. *Archives of General Psychiatry*, 1964, *11*, 459-465.

Cattell, R. B., & Rickels, K. The relationship of clinical symptoms and IPAT factored tests of anxiety, regression and asthenia: A factor analytic study. *Journal of Nervous and Mental Disease*, 1968, *146*, 147-160.

Cattell, R. B., Rickels, K., Weise, C., Gray, B., & Yee, R. The effects of psychotherapy upon measured anxiety and regression. *American Journal of Psychotherapy*, 1966, *20*, 261-269.

Cattell, R. B., & Saunders, D. R. Beitrage zur Faktoren-Analyse der Personlichkeit. *Zeitschrift fur experimentelle und angewandte Psychologie*, 1954, *2*, 325-357.

Cattell, R. B., & Scheier, I. H. The nature of anxiety: A review of thirteen multivariate analyses comprising 814 variables. *Psychological Reports*, 1958, *4*, 351-388. (a)

Cattell, R. B., & Scheier, I. H. The objective test measurement of neuroticism, U.I. 23(—): A review of eight factor analytic studies. *Journal of Indian Psychology*, 1958, *33*, 217-236. (b)

Cattell, R. B., & Scheier, I. H. Extension of meaning of objective test personality factors: Especially into anxiety, neuroticism, questionnaire, and physical factors. *Journal of General Psychology*, 1959, *61*, 287-315.

Cattell, R. B., & Scheier, I. H. *The meaning and measurement of neuroticism and anxiety.* New York: Ronald, 1961.

Cattell, R. B., Schiff, H., et al. Psychiatric screening of flying personnel: Prediction of training criteria by objective personality factors and development of the seven factor personality test. Report No. 10, Contract No. AF 33(038)-19569, Project No. 21-0202-0007, Randolph Field, Texas: USAF School of Aviation Medicine, 1953.

Cattell, R. B., Schmidt, L. R., & Bjerstedt, A. Clinical diagnosis by the objective-analytic personality batteries. *Journal of Clinical Psychology Monograph Supplements*, 1972, No. 34, 239-312. Brandon, Vermont: Clinical Psychology Publishing Company, 1972.

Cattell, R. B., Schmidt, L. R., & Pawlik, K. Cross-cultural comparison (U.S.A., Japan, Austria) of the personality factor structures of 10 to 14 year olds in objective tests. *Social Behavior and Personality*, 1973, *1*(2), 182-211.

Cattell, R. B., Schuerger, J. M., Klein, T., & Finkbeiner, C. A definitive large-sample factoring of personality structure in objective measures, as a basis for the high school objective analytic battery. *Journal of Research in Personality*, 1976, *10*, 22-41.

Cattell, R. B., Sealy, A. P., & Sweney, A. B. What can personality and motivation source trait measurements add to the prediction of school achievement? *British Journal of Educational Psychology*, 1966, *36*, 280-295.

Cattell, R. B., Stice, G. F., & Kristy, N. F. A first approximation to nature-nurture ratios for eleven primary personality factors in objective tests. *Journal of Abnormal and Social Psychology*, 1957, *54*, 143-159.

Cattell, R. B., & Tsujioka, B. The importance of factor-trueness and validity versus homogeneity and orthogonality, in test scales. *Educational and Psychological Measurement*, 1964, *24*, 3-30.

Cattell, R. B., & Warburton, F. W. *Objective personality and motivation tests: A theoretical introduction and practical compendium.* Champaign, Ill.: University of Illinois Press, 1967.

Coan, R. W. Child psychology and developmental psychology. In R. B. Cattell (Ed.), *Handbook of multivariate experimental psychology.* Chicago: Rand McNally, 1966. Ch. 24.

Coan, R. W. The changing personality. In R. M. Dreger (Ed), *Multivariate personality research.* Baton Rouge: Claitor, 1972.

Cohen, J. The impact of multivariate research in clinical psychology. In R. B. Cattell (Ed.), *Handbook of multivariate experimental psychology.* Chicago: Rand McNally, 1966. Ch. 30, pp. 856-877.

Conner, D. V. The effect of temperamental traits upon the group intelligence test performance of children. Unpublished doctoral dissertation, University of London Library, 1952.

Cooley, W. W., & Lohnes, P. R. *Multivariate data analysis.* New York: Wiley, 1971.

Cronbach, L. J. Response sets and test validity. *Educational and Psychological Measurement*, 1946, *6*, 487-494.

Cronbach, L. J. *Essentials of psychological testing.* New York: Harper, 1960.

Crutcher, R. An experimental study of persistence. *Journal of Applied Psychology*, 1934, *18*, 409-417.

Cureton, T. K. Improvement of psychological states by means of exercise-fitness programs. *Journal of the Association for Physical & Mental Rehabilitation*, 1963, *17*, 1-6.

Curran, J. P. Dimensions of state change in Q-data, by chain P-technique. Master's Thesis, University of Illinois Library, 1968.

Curran, J. P., & Cattell, R. B. *The eight-state questionnaire battery.* Champaign, Ill.: Institute for Personality and Ability Testing, 1974.

Curran, J. P., & Cattell, R. B. *Manual for the eight state questionnaire [8SQ].* Champaign, Ill.: Institute for Personality and Ability Testing, 1975.

Damarin, F. L. A special review of Buros' personality test reviews. *Educational and Psychological Measurement*, 1971, *31*, 215-241.

Damarin, F. L., & Cattell, R. B. Personality factors in early childhood and their relation to intelligence. *Monographs of the Society for Research in Child Development*, 1968, *33*(6, Whole No. 122), 1-95.

Darling, R. P. Autonomic action in relation to personality traits in children. *Journal of Abnormal and Social Psychology*, 1940, *35*, 246-260.

Delhees, K. H. The abnormal personality: Neurosis and delinquency. In R. B. Cattell & R. M. Dreger (Eds), *Handbook of modern personality theory*. New York: Halsted, 1977. Ch. 27.

Delhees, K. H., & Cattell, R. B. Differences of personality factors, by the O-A battery, in paranoid and non-paranoid schizophrenics, manic-depressives, psychoneurotics, and the personality disorders. *Archiv fur Psychologie*, 1971, *123*, 35-48.

Delhees, K. H., & Nesselroade, J. R. Methods and findings in experimentally based personality theory. In R. B. Cattell (Ed.), *Handbook of multivariate experimental psychology*. Chicago: Rand McNally, 1966.

Dielman, T. E., Barton, K., & Cattell, R. B. The prediction of junior high school achievement from objective motivation tests. *Personality*, 1971, *2*(4), 279-287.

Dielman, T. E., Schuerger, J. M., & Cattell, R. B. Prediction of junior high school achievement from IQ and the objective-analytic personality factors U.I. 21, U.I. 23, U.I. 24, and U.I. 25. *Personality*, 1970, *1*(2), 145-152.

Digman, J. M. Interaction and linearity in multivariate experiment. Ch. 15 in R. B. Cattell (Ed.), *Handbook of multivariate experimental psychology*. Chicago: Rand McNally, 1966. Pp. 459-475.

Dreger, R. M. (Ed.) *Multivariate personality research*. Baton Rouge: Claitor, 1972.

Drevdahl, J. E. A study of the etiology and development of the creative personality. Cooperative Research Program Study, Office of Education, U.S. DHEW, 1961.

Drevdahl, J. E., & Cattell, R. B. Personality and creativity in artists and writers. *Journal of Clinical Psychology*, 1958, *14*, 107-111.

Dubin, S. S., & Cattell, R. B. Objective determination of the incidence and degree of neuroticism. *Journal of Insurance Medicine*, 1951, *6*, 44-47.

Duffy, E. *Activation and behavior*. New York: Wiley, 1962.

Eysenck, H. J. *The dimensions of personality*. London: Kegan Paul, 1947.

Eysenck, H. J. *The scientific study of personality*. London: Routledge and Kegan Paul, 1952.

Eysenck, H. J. *The structure of human personality*. London: Methuen, 1960.

Eysenck, H. J. *Handbook of abnormal psychology*. New York: Basic Books, 1961.

Eysenck, H. J. *Readings in introversion and extraversion*. London: Staples Press, 1970.

301

Eysenck, H. J. Multivariate analysis and experimental psychology. In R. M. Dreger (Ed.), *Contributions to the understanding of personality*. Baton Rouge: Claitor, 1972. Ch. 5.

Eysenck, H. J. Extraversion and scholastic achievement. In G. Nissen (Ed.), *Intelligentz und Lernstorungen*. Berlin: Springer, 1977.

Eysenck, S. B. G., & Eysenck, H. J. The measurement of psychoticism: A study of factor stability and reliability. *British Journal of Social and Clinical Psychology*, 1968, *7*, 286-294.

Eysenck, H. J., & Prell, D. B. The inheritance of neuroticism. *Journal of Mental Science*, 1951, *97*, 441-465.

Fahrenberg, J. Objective tests zur messung der personlichkeit. In R. Heiss (Ed.), *Handbuch der psychologie*. Gottingen: Hogrefe, 1964. Pp. 488-532.

Freedman, A. M., Kaplan, H. I., & Sadock, B. J. *Comprehensive textbook of psychiatry*. Baltimore: Williams & Wilkins, 1975.

French, J. W. *The description of personality measurements in terms of rotated factors*. Princeton, N.J.: ETS, 1953.

Getzels, J. W., & Jackson, P. W. *Creativity and intelligence: Explorations with gifted students*. New York: Wiley, 1962.

Gibb, C. A. Personality traits by factorial analysis. III. *Australian Journal of Psychology and Philosophy*, 1942, *22*, 1-27.

Goldberg, L. R. Explorer on the run: A review of *Objective personality and motivation tests* by Cattell and Warburton. *Contemporary Psychology*, 1968, *13*, 617-619.

Goldberg, L. R. Parameters of personality inventory construction and utilization: A comparison of prediction strategies and tactics. *Multivariate Behavioral Research Monographs*, 1972, *72*, 1-59.

Goldberg, L. R. Objective diagnostic tests and measurements. *Annual Review of Psychology*, 1974, *25*, 343-366.

Goldberg, L. R. Language and personality; toward a taxonomy of trait descriptive teams. Paper at Annual Meeting of the Society for Multivariate Experimental Psychology, Oregon, Nov., 1975.

Goldberg, L. R., Norman, W. F., & Schwartz, E. The comparative validity of questionnaire data (16 P.F. scales) and objective test data (O-A Battery) in predicting five peer rating criteria. *ORI Research Bulletin*, 1972, *12*, 1-18.

Gorsuch, R. L. The clarification of some superego factors. Doctoral dissertation. University of Illinois (Urbana), 1965.

Gorsuch, R. L., & Cattell, R. B. Second-stratum personality factors defined in the questionnaire realm by the 16 PF. *Multivariate Behavioral Research*, 1967, *2*, 211-224.

Gray, J. A. Strength of the nervous system, introversion-extraversion, conditionability and arousal. *Behavior Research & Therapy*, 1967, *5*, 151-169.

Gray, J. A. *Biological bases of individual behavior*. New York: Academic Press, 1972.

Guilford, J. P. *Psychometric methods.* (4th ed.) New York: McGraw-Hill, 1970.

Guion, R. M. *Personnel testing.* New York: McGraw-Hill, 1965.

Häcker, H., & Schmidt, L. R. Entwicklungsstand einer deutschsprachigen objectiven Testbatterie nach Cattell. *Diagnostica,* 1976.

Hakstian, A. R., & Cattell, R. B. *The comprehensive ability battery : CAB.* Champaign, Ill.: Institute for Personality and Ability Testing, 1975.

Hakstian, A. R., & Cattell, R. B. *Manual for the comprehensive ability battery [CAB].* Champaign, Ill.: Institute for Personality and Ability Testing, 1976.

Hall, C. W., & Lindzey, G. *Theories of personality: Primary sources and research.* New York: Wiley, 1965, 1974.

Hammond, D. C., & Stanfield, K. *Multidimensional psychotherapy: A counselors' guide for the MAP form.* Champaign, Ill.: Institute for Personality and Ability Testing, 1977.

Hargreaves, H. L. The "faculty" of imagination. *British Journal of Psychology Monograph Supplement,* 1927, *3,* 10.

Hartshorne, M., & May, M. *Studies in deceit.* New York: Macmillan, 1930.

Haverland, E. M. The application of an analytical solution for proportional profiles rotation to a box problem and to the drive structure in rats. Doctoral dissertation, University of Illinois, 1954.

Hendrickson, A. L., & White, P. O. A method for the rotation of higher-order factors. *British Journal of Mathematical and Statistical Psychology,* 1966, *19,* 97-103.

Herrman, T. *Lehrbuch der empirischen Persönlichkeitsforschung.* Gottingen: Hogrefe, 1969.

Hildebrand, E. P. A factorial study of introversion-extraversion. *British Journal of Psychology,* 1958, *49,* 1-11.

Horn, J. L. Structure in measures of self-sentiment, ego and super-ego concepts. Unpublished Master's thesis, University of Illinois, 1961.

Horn, J. L. A note on the estimation of factor scores. *Educational and Psychological Measurement,* 1964, *24,* 525-527.

Horn, J. L. Organization of abilities and the development of intelligence. *Psychological Review,* 1968, *75,* 242-259.

Horn, J. L. Personality and ability theory. In R. B. Cattell & R. M. Dreger (Eds), *Handbook of modern personality theory.* New York: Halsted, 1977.

Horn, J. L., & Cattell, R. B. Refinement and test of the theory of fluid and crystallized intelligence. *Journal of Educational Psychology,* 1966, *57,* 253-270.

Horn, J. L., & Cattell, R. B. Age differences in fluid and crystallized intelligence. *Acta Psychologica,* 1967, *26,* 107-129.

Horn, J. L., & Sweney, A. B. The dynamic calculus model for motivation and its use in understanding the individual case. In A. R. Mahrer (Ed.), *New approaches to personality classification.* New York: Columbia University Press, 1970. Pp. 53-97.

Horowitz, J., & Cattell, R. B. Objective personality tests investigating the structure of altruism in relation to the source traits A, N, and L. *Journal of Personality*, 1952, *21*, 103-117.

Hundleby, J. D. The trait of anxiety as defined by objective performance and indices of emotional disturbance, in middle childhood. *Multivariate Behavioral Research*, 1968, *Special Issue*, 7-14.

Hundleby, J. D. The structure of personality surface and source traits. In R. M. Dreger (Ed.), *Multivariate personality research.* Contributions in honor of Raymond B. Cattell. Baton Rouge: Claitor, 1972. Pp. 261-275.

Hundleby, J. D. The measurement of personality by objective tests. In P. Kline (Ed.), *New approaches in psychological measurement.* London: Wiley, 1973. (a)

Hundleby, J. D. Personality constructs and adjustment in the middle childhood years. Research Report, University of Guelph, Canada, 1973. (b)

Hundleby, J. D., & Cattell, R. B. The improvement of the measurement of objective test personality factors U.I. 18 and U.I. 21. Champaign, Ill.: Laboratory of Personality and Group Analysis Publication No. 11, 1967.

Hundleby, J. D., & Cattell, R. B. Personality structure in middle childhood and the prediction of school achievement and adjustment. *Monographs of the Society for Research in Child Development*, 1968, *33*(5, Whole No. 121), 1-61.

Hundleby, J. D., Horn, J. L., & Cattell, R. B. An investigation of objective factors U.I. 23, U.I. 24, U.I. 27, and U.I. 35. Champaign, Ill.: Laboratory of Personality and Group Analysis Publication No. 4, 1967.

Hundleby, J. D., & Loucks, A. Personal communication on unpublished thesis, 1974.

Hundleby, J. D., Pawlik, K., & Cattell, R. B. *Personality factors in objective test devices.* San Diego: R. R. Knapp, 1965.

Hunt, J. McV., Ewing, T. N., LaForge, R., & Gilbert, W. M. An integrated approach to research on therapeutic counseling with samples of results. *Journal of Counseling Psychology*, 1959, *6*(1), 46-54.

Ismail, A. H., & Young, J. The effects of chronic exercise on the multivariate relationships between selected biochemical and personality variables. *Multivariate Behavioral Research*, 1977, *12*, 49-67.

Ishikawa, A. Trait description and measurement through discovered structure in objective tests. Ch. 4 in R. B. Cattell & R. M. Dreger (Eds), *Handbook of modern personality theory.* New York: Halsted, 1977.

Jackson, D. N., & Messick, S. Response styles and the assessment of psychopathology. In S. Messick & J. Ross (Eds), *Measurement in personality and cognition.* New York: Wiley, 1962.

Jensen, A. R. How much can we boost I.Q. and scholastic achievement? *Harvard Educational Review*, 1969, *39*, 1-123.

Kagan, J. Developmental studies in reflection and analysis. In A. H. Kidd & J. L. Rivoire (Eds), *Perceptual development in children.* London: University of London Press, 1966. Pp. 487-505; 517-522.

Karson, S. Second-order personality factors in positive mental health. *Journal of Clinical Psychology*, 1961, *17*(1), 14-19.

Karson, S., & O'Dell, J. W. *A guide to the clinical use of the 16 PF*. Champaign, Ill.: Institute for Personality and Ability Testing, 1976.

Killian, L. R. The utility of objective test personality factors in diagnosing schizophrenia and the character disorders. Master's thesis, University of Illinois Library (Urbana), 1960.

King, L. D. The correlation of 10 HSOA factor scores to school-related criteria and personality data from HSPQ. Unpublished Master's thesis, Cleveland State University, 1976.

Kleinmuntz, B. *Personality measurement*. Homewood, Ill.: Dorsey, 1967.

Knapp, R. R. The nature of primary personality dimensions as shown by relations of Cattell's objective personality test factors to questionnaire scales. Mimeographed report, 1960.

Knapp, R. R. Criterion predictions in the navy from the objective analytic personality test battery. Paper read at Annual Meeting of APA, New York, September 4, 1961. (a)

Knapp, R. R. Objective personality test and sociometric correlates of frequency of sick bay visits. *Journal of Applied Psychology*, 1961, *45*(2), 104-110. (b)

Knapp, R. R. The validity of the objective-analytic personality test battery in navy settings. *Educational and Psychological Measurement*, 1962, *22*(2), 379-387.

Knapp, R. R. Personality correlates of delinquency rate in a navy sample. *Journal of Applied Psychology*, 1963, *47*, 68-71.

Knapp, R. R. Delinquency and objective personality test factors. *Journal of Applied Psychology*, 1965, *49*, 8-10.

Knapp, R. R., & Most, J. A. Personality correlates of marine corps helicopter pilot performance. *U.S.N. Medical Field Research Laboratory Report*, 1960, No. MR 005.15-1001.1.3.

Koch, S. *Psychology, the study of a science*. New York: McGraw-Hill, 1959.

Krawiec, T. S. (Ed.) *The psychologists, II*. New York: Oxford University Press, 1974.

Krug, S. E. An examination of experimentally induced changes in ergic tension. Doctoral dissertation, University of Illinois (Urbana), 1971.

Krug, S. E., & Cattell, R. B. A test of the trait-view theory of distortion in measurement of personality by questionnaire. *Educational and Psychological Measurement*, 1971, *31*, 721-734.

Krug, S. E. (Ed.) *Psychological assessment in medicine*. Champaign, Ill.: Institute for Personality and Ability Testing, 1977.

Krug, S. Reliability and scope in personality assessment: A comparison of the Cattell and Eysenck inventories. *Multivariate Experimental Clinical Research*, 1978, *3*, 1-10.

Kuhn, T. S. *The structure of scientific revolutions.* Chicago: University of Chicago Press, 1962.

Lawlis, G. F., & Chatfield, D. *Multivariate approaches for the behavioral sciences: A brief text.* Lubbock: Texas Tech Press, 1974.

Levy, L. H. *Conceptions of personality: Theories and research.* New York: Random House, 1970.

Liebert, R. M., & Spiegler, M. D. *Personality strategies for the study of man.* Homewood, Ill.: Dorsey, 1970.

Lindzey, G. *A history of psychology in autobiography.* Englewood Cliffs, N.J.: Prentice-Hall, 1974.

Loehlin, J. C. Psychological genetics from the study of human behavior. Ch. 13 in R. B. Cattell & R. M. Dreger (Eds), *Handbook of modern personality theory.* New York: Halsted, 1977.

Maddi, S. R. *Personality theories.* Homewood, Ill.: Dorsey, 1976.

Mahrer, A. H. *New approaches to personality classification.* New York: Columbia University Press, 1970.

May, D. R. Psychiatric syndrome classifications checked by taxonome and discriminant functions on the clinical analysis questionnaire. Doctoral dissertation, University of Illinois (Urbana), 1971.

Mayeske, G. W. Some associations of musical preferences with dimensions of personality. Doctoral dissertation, University of Illinois (Urbana), 1962.

McMichael, R. E., & Cattell, R. B. Clinical diagnosis by the IPAT musical preference test. *Journal of Consulting Psychology*, 1960, *24*, 333-341.

McNemar, Q. On growth measurement. *Educational and Psychological Measurement*, 1958, *18*, 47-55.

Meehl, P. E. *Clinical versus statistical prediction.* Minneapolis: University of Minnesota Press, 1950.

Meeland, T. An investigation of hypotheses for distinguishing personality factors A, F, and H. Doctoral dissertation, University of Illinois (Urbana), 1952.

Meredith, G. M. Contending hypotheses of ontogenesis for the exuberance-restraint personality factor U.I. 21. *Journal of Genetic Psychology*, 1966, *108*, 89-104.

Meredith, G. M. Observations on the origins and current status of the ego assertive personality factor U.I. 16. *Journal of Genetic Psychology*, 1967, *110*, 269-286.

Messick, S. J., & Ross, G. (Eds), *Measurement in personality and cognition.* New York: Wiley, 1962.

Mischel, W. *Personality and assessment.* New York: Wiley, 1968.

Nesselroade, J. R. The separation of state and trait factors by dR technique with special reference to anxiety, effort stress, and cortertia. Master's thesis, University of Illinois (Urbana), 1966.

Nesselroade, J. R., & Bartsch, T. W. Multivariate experimental perspectives on the construct validity of the trait-state distinction. In J. R. Nesselroade & H. W. Reese (Eds), *Life span developmental psychology: Research and theory.* New York: Academic Press, 1973.

Nesselroade, J. R., & Cattell, R. B. The discovery of the anxiety state pattern in Q-data and its distinction in the LM model from depression, effort stress, and fatigue. *Multivariate Behavioral Research,* 1976, *11,* 27-40.

Nesselroade, J. R., & Delhees, K. H. Methods and findings in experimentally based personality theory. In R. B. Cattell (Ed.), *Handbook of multivariate experimental psychology.* Chicago: Rand McNally, 1966. Ch. 19, pp. 563-610.

Nesselroade, J. R., & Reese, H. W. *Life span developmental psychology: Research and theory.* New York: Academic Press, 1973.

Norman, W. T. 2800 personality trait descriptors: Normative operating characteristics for a university population. NIMH Grant No. MH 07195, Ann Arbor, University of Michigan, 1967.

Nunnally, J. *Psychometric theory.* New York: McGraw-Hill, 1967.

Patrick, S., Cattell, R. B., & Price, P. The diagnostic power of the O-A battery in regard to hospitalized depressives. *Multivariate Experimental Clinical Research,* in press.

Patrick, S., Price, P., & Cattell, R. B. The clinical psychological interpretation of personality source traits U.I. 19, independence, U.I. 20, evasiveness, U.I. 25, realism, and U.I. 30, somindence. 1978, in preparation.

Pawlik, K. *Dimensionen des Verhaltens.* Bern: Huber, 1968.

Pawlik, K. Ansatze fur ein eigenschaftsfreie Interpretation von Persönlichkeits factoren. In J. H. G. & U. S. Eckensberger (Eds), Ber 28 *Kgr Dtsch Ges Psychol.* Bd. 3. Gottingen: Hogrefe, 1974. Pp. 248-250.

Pawlik, K. Faktorenanalytische Persönlichkeits-Forschung. In G. Strube (Ed.), *Die Psychologie des 20 jahrhundets.* Zurich: Kindler Verlag, 1978. Pp. 617-712.

Pawlik, K., & Cattell, R. B. Third-order factors in objective personality tests. *British Journal of Psychology,* 1964, *55,* 1-18.

Pawlik, K., & Cattell, R. B. The relationship between certain personality factors and measures of cortical arousal. *Neuropsychologia,* 1965, *3,* 129-151.

Pervin, L. A. *Personality theory, assessment and research.* (3rd ed.) New York: Wiley, 1975.

Pieszko, H. A. Global perceptiveness and the factors of independence, comention and asthenia. Master's thesis, University of Illinois (Urbana), 1967.

Price, P. L., Patrick, S. V., & Cattell, R. B. A confirmation of the factor structure of personality traits U.I. 19, independence, U.I. 20, evasiveness, U.I. 25, realism, and U.I. 30, somindence. 1978, in press.

Rethlingshafer, D. The relation of tests of persistence to other measures of continuance of action. *Journal of Abnormal and Social Psychology,* 1942, *37,* 71-82.

Reuterman, N. A., Howard, K. I., & Cartwright, D. S. Multivariate analysis of gang delinquency IV: Personality variables. *Multivariate Behavioral Research*, in press.

Rickels, K., & Cattell, R. B. The clinical factor validity and trueness of the IPAT verbal and objective batteries for anxiety and regression. *Journal of Clinical Psychology*, 1965, *21*, 257-264.

Rimoldi, H. J. A. Personal tempo. *Journal of Abnormal and Social Psychology*, 1951, *46*, 283-303.

Royce, J. R. Factors as theoretical constructs. *American Psychologist*, 1963, *18*, 522-528.

Royce, J. R. (Ed.) *Multivariate analysis and psychological theory*. New York: Academic Press, 1973.

Ryans, D. G. An experimental attempt to analyze persistent behavior. *Journal of General Psychology*, 1938, *19*, 333-353.

Sahakian, W. S. *Psychology of personality*. Chicago: Rand McNally, 1965.

Sankar, S. *Schizophrenia, current concepts and research*. Chapter on The diagnosis of schizophrenia by questionnaire and objective personality tests. Hicksville, N.Y.: PJD Publications, 1969.

Sarason, S. B. *Personality: An objective approach*. New York: Wiley, 1966.

Schaie, K. W. A test of behavioral rigidity. *Journal of Abnormal and Social Psychology*, 1955, *51*, 604-610.

Scheier, I. H. What is an "objective test"? *Psychological Reports*, 1958, *4*, 147-157.

Scheier, I. H., & Cattell, R. B. Confirmation of objective test factors and assessment of their relation to questionnaire factors: A factor analysis of 113 rating, questionnaire and objective test measurements of personality. *Journal of Mental Science*, 1958, *104*, 608-624.

Scheier, I. H., & Cattell, R. B. *Handbook and test kit for the IPAT eight-parallel-form anxiety battery*. Champaign, Ill.: Institute for Personality and Ability Testing, 1960.

Scheier, I. H., Cattell, R. B., & Horn, J. L. Objective test factor U.I. 23: Its measurement and its relation to clinically judged neuroticism. *Journal of Clinical Psychology*, 1960, *16*, 135-145.

Scheier, I. H., Cattell, R. B., & Mayeske, G. W. The objective-test factors of imaginative tension (U.I. 25), introversion (U.I. 32), anxiety (U.I. 24) and autistic nonconformity (U.I. 34): (1) Data on new factor-measuring tests, and (2) relation of factors to clinically judged psychosis. Laboratory of Pesonality Assessment and Group Behavior Advance Publication No. 10, 1960.

Schlesinger, K., & Groves, P. M. *Psychology: A dynamic science*. Dubuque, Iowa: Brown, 1976.

Schmidt, L. R. Zur Frage der Verfalschbarkeit von objectiven Persönlichkeitstests im Vergleichzen Fragebogen. *Psychol. Praxis*, 1972, *16*, 77-85.

Schmidt, L. R. Type analyses with U.I. scores in clinical psychology: Some data and some problems. Bad Homburg, Paper presented to SMEP Conference, 1974.

Schmidt, L. R. *Objective Personlichkeits-messung in diagnostischer und klinischer Psychologie.* Weinheim u Basel: Beltz, 1975.

Schmidt, L. R., & Cattell, R. B. Differentialdiagnosen mit Hilfe objektiver Persönlichkeitstests: Diskriminantzanalytische Untersuchungen auf Depression, Manie, Schizophrenie und Neurose. *Sonderdruck aus Diagnostica,* 1972, *18,* 61-86.

Schmidt, L. R., Häcker, H. O., & Cattell, R. B. *Objective Testbatterie OA-TB, 75. Testheft.* Weinheim: Beltz, 1975.

Schneewind, K. R. Wie universel sind Cattell's objektive Personlichkeitsfaktoren? *Diagnostica,* 1970, *16,* 94-97.

Schneewind, K. R. Personality and perception. Ch. 23 in R. B. Cattell & R. M. Dreger (Eds), *Handbook of modern personality theory.* New York: Halsted, 1977.

Schuerger, J. M., & Cattell, R. B. Questionnaire scales produced to align with objective test factors in the O-A Personality Kit. In preparation.

Schuerger, J. M., Dielman, T. E., & Cattell, R. B. Objective personality factors U.I. 16, 17, 19, and 20 as correlates of school achievement. *Personality,* 1970, *1,* 95-101.

Schuerger, J. M., & Watterson, D. G. *Using tests and other information in counseling: A decision model for practitioners.* Champaign, Ill.: Institute for Personality and Ability Testing, 1977.

Sells, S. B. (Ed.) Psychiatric screening of flying personnel. *U.S.A.F. School of Aviation Medicine Report No. 9.* Cattell, R. B. Personality structure in objective tests—a study of 1,000 Air Force students in basic pilot training. Fort Worth, Texas, 1955. Project No. 21-0202-0007. Pp. 1-50.

Sells, S. B. *Essentials of psychology.* New York: Ronald, 1962.

Short, J. F., Jr., & Strodtbeck, F. L. *Group process and gang delinquency.* (2nd ed.) Chicago: University of Chicago Press, 1974. Esp. Ch. 10.

Sixtl, F. Faktoreninvarianz u Faktoreninterpretation. *Psychol. Beitrage,* 1967, *10,* 99-111.

Spielberger, C. D. *Anxiety and behavior.* New York: Academic Press, 1966.

Spielberger, C. D. *Anxiety: Current trends in research and theory.* New York: Academic Press, 1972.

Stagner, R. *Psychology of personality.* New York: McGraw-Hill, 1974.

Stricker, H. J. *Response styles and 16 P.F. higher order factors. Bulletin RB-73-8.* Princeton, N.J.: ETS, 1973.

Sweney, A. B. Objective measurement of the strength of dynamic structure factors. In R. B. Cattell & F. W. Warburton (Eds), *Objective personality and motivation tests.* Champaign, Ill.: University of Illinois Press, 1967.

Sweney, A. B. *Individual assessment with the motivation analysis test: MAT.* Champaign, Ill.: Institute for Personality and Ability Testing, 1968.

Sweney, A. B., & Cattell, R. B. Relationships between integrated and unintegrated motivation structure examined by objective tests. *Journal of Social Psychology*, 1962, *57*, 217-226.

Tatro, D. F. The interpretation of objectively measured personality factors in terms of clinical data and concepts. Doctoral dissertation, University of Illinois (Urbana), 1967.

Tatro, D. F. The utility of source traits measured by the O-A (objective-analytic) battery in mental hospital diagnosis. *Multivariate Behavioral Research*, 1968. *Special Issue.*

Tatsuoka, M. M. *Selected topics in advanced statistics: II. Standardized scales: Linear and area transformations.* Champaign, Ill.: Institute for Personality and Ability Testing, 1969.

Tatsuoka, M. M. *Selected topics in advanced statistics: VI. Discriminant analysis: The study of group differences.* Champaign, Ill.: Institute for Personality and Ability Testing, 1970.

Tatsuoka, M. M. *Selected topics in advanced statistics: IV. Significance tests: Univariate and multivariate.* Champaign, Ill.: Institute for Personality and Ability Testing, 1971.

Tatsuoka, M. M. *Selected topics in advanced statistics: III. Classification procedures: Profile similarity.* Champaign, Ill.: Institute for Personality and Ability Testing, 1974.

Tatsuoka, M. M. *Selected topics in advanced statistics: VII. The general linear model: A "new" trend in analysis of variance.* Champaign, Ill.: Institute for Personality and Ability Testing, 1975.

Tatsuoka, M. M. *Selected topics in advanced statistics: V. Validation studies: The use of multiple regression equations.* Champaign, Ill.: Institute for Personalit and Ability Testing, 1976.

Tatsuoka, M. M., & Cattell, R. B. Linear equations for estimating a person's occupational adjustment, based on information on occupational profiles. *British Journal of Educational Psychology*, 1970, *40*, 324-334.

Taylor, J. A. The relations of anxiety to conditional eyelid response. *Journal of Experimental Psychology*, 1951, *41*, 81-92.

Thompson, D. C. The effective use of personality constructs in applied situations. Ch. 30 in R. B. Cattell & R. M. Dreger (Eds), *Handbook of modern personality theory*. New York: Halsted, 1977.

Thornton, G. R. A factor analysis of tests designed to measure persistence. *Psychology Monographs*, 1939, *51*, 1-42.

Thurstone, L. L. *A factorial study of perception*. Chicago: University of Chicago Press, 1944.

Ustrzycki, G. J. Personality assessment and indices of delinquent behavior. Master's thesis, University of Guelph (Canada), 1974.

Van Egeren, L. F. Multivariate research on the psychoses. Ch. 28 in R. B. Cattell & R. M. Dreger (Eds), *Handbook of modern personality theory*. New York: Halsted, 1977.

Vernon, P. E. *Personality tests and assessments*. London: Methuen, 1953.

Wardell, D. M. A multivariate study of extraversion. Doctoral dissertation, University of Alberta (Edmonton, Canada), 1976.

Wardell, D., & Royce, J. R. Relationships between cognitive and temperament traits and the concept of style. *Journal of Multivariate Experimental Personality and Clinical Psychology*, 1975, *1*, 244-266.

Wardell, D., & Yeudall, L. T. A multidimensional approach to criminal disorders. I. The factor analysis of impulsivity. *Journal of Clinical Psychology*, 1976, *32*, 12-31.

Wardell, D., Yeudall, L. T., Bannister, G., Lind, J., Gerrard, B., & Utendale, B. A multidimensional approach to criminal disorders: The factors and types of impulsivity and their relation to crime. In preparation.

Wells, H. P. Relationship between physical fitness and psychological variables. Doctoral dissertation, University of Illinois (Urbana), 1958.

Wenger, M. A. Studies of autonomic imbalance in army air force personnel. *Comparative Psychology Monographs*, 1948, *101*, 1-111.

Wenig, P. The relative roles of naive, autistic, cognitive, and press compatibility misperception and ego defense operations in tests of misperception. Master's thesis, University of Illinois (Urbana), 1952.

Wepman, J. M., & Heine, R. W. *Concepts of personality*. Chicago: Aldine, 1963.

Wessman, A. E., & Ricks, D. F. *Mood and personality*. New York: Holt, Rinehart, & Winston, 1966.

Wiggins, J. S. *Personality and prediction: Principles of personality assessment*. London: Addison Wesley, 1973.

Wilde, G. J. S. Trait description and measurement by personality questionnaires. In R. B. Cattell & R. M. Dreger (Eds), *Handbook of modern personality theory*. New York: Halsted, 1977.

Williams, H. V. A determination of psychosomatic functional unities in personality by means of P-techniques. *Journal of Social Psychology*, 1954, 25-45.

Witkin, H. A. *Psychological differentiation: Studies of development*. New York: Wiley, 1962.

Wolman, B. *Personality*. New York: Prentice-Hall, 1973.

Dicks-Nireaux, M. J. Extraversion-introversion in experimental psychology. *Journal of Analytical Psychology*, 1968, *13*, 117-127.

Marshall, N. I. Extraversion and libido—Jung and Cattell. *Journal of Analytical Psychology*, 1967, *12*, 115-135.

Author Index

Adcock, C. J., 6
Anastasi, A., 165
Anderson, J. C., 6
Arndt, W. B., 15
Arnold, W., 6

Baehr, M., 6
Baggaley, A. R., 6
Baltes, P. B., 6, 270
Bartlett, H. W., 6, 234
Barton, K., 6, 22, 23, 223, 237, 272
Bartsch, T. W., 6, 49
Bass, A., 49
Baughman, E. E., 15
Beloff, J. R., 6
Binet, A., 4
Birkett, H., 269, 275
Bischof, L. F., 15
Bjerstedt, A., 3, 6, 22, 23, 30, 49, 56, 229, 232, 248, 249, 250, 251, 252, 256, 267
Blewett, D. B., 6
Bolz, C., 6, 267
Brengelmann, J. C., 6, 248, 281
Brody, N., 15
Brogden, H. E., 6, 233, 281
Brown, W., 50
Bucell, A., 6
Burdsal, C., 6
Buros, O. K., 165
Buss, A. R., 6
Butcher, H. J., 6, 22, 233, 237, 244, 245, 275
Byrne, D., 15

Cable, D., 6
Cartwright, D. S., 3, 5, 10, 15, 56, 228, 230, 231, 233, 236, 238, 248, 257, 258, 259, 260, 270, 277, 281

Cattell, A. K. S., 6, 274
Chatfield, D., 253, 268
Child, D., 10, 11
Churchill, W., 29, 231
Coan, R. W., 4, 6
Cogan, J., 6
Conner, D. V., 6, 22, 281
Cooley, W. W., 268
Copernicus, N., 1
Coulter, M. A., 6, 267
Cronbach, L. J., 2, 184
Cross, K., 6, 275
Crutcher, R., 6, 281
Cureton, T. K., 234
Curran, J. P., 6, 275

Dalton, J., 272
Damarin, F. L., 3, 4, 6, 56, 237
Darling, R. P., 281
Das, R., 6
Delhees, K. H., 3, 6, 16, 56, 165, 214, 257, 259, 269
Dermen, D., 6
DeYoung, G., 6
Dickens, C., 29, 280
Dickman, K., 6
Dielman, T. E., 6, 22, 23, 56, 228, 231, 232, 237
Digman, J. M., 6
Downey, J., 12
Dreger, R. M., 6, 10, 15, 269
Drevdahl, J. E., 6, 237, 246
Dubin, S. S., 6, 56
Duffy, E., 6, 237

Eber, H. W., 15, 50, 129, 247, 256, 269, 277
Eysenck, H. J., 3, 5, 6, 10, 15, 16, 22, 23, 30, 31, 32, 223, 231, 234, 235, 236, 237, 238, 244, 248, 251, 252, 259, 268, 269, 271, 272, 274, 281

Fahrenberg, J., 6
Faraday, M., 4

Finkbeiner, D., 6, 12, 16, 17, 55, 56, 136, 137, 170, 212, 214, 215, 222, 257, 271, 281
Fiske, D., 6
Freedman, A. M., 5
French, J. W., 6, 13
Ford, J., 6
Freud, S., 25, 26, 28, 222, 233, 235, 251, 271

Getzels, J. W., 230, 246
Gibb, C. A., 6
Gibbons, B. D., 6
Goldberg, L. R., 6, 212, 213, 268
Gorsuch, R. L., 6
Gray, J. A., 6
Gruen, W., 4, 6, 184, 231, 233, 237
Guilford, J. P., 10, 246, 268
Guion, R. M., 268

Häcker, H., 3, 6, 12, 27, 277, 281
Hakstian, A. R., 2, 6, 274
Hall, C. W., 3, 5, 10, 15
Hammond, D. C., 6
Hargreaves, H. L., 6, 281
Hartshorne, M., 12
Harvey, W., 1
Haverland, E. M., 6
Herrington, L. P., 6
Hildebrand, E. P., 6
Horn, J. L., 2, 6, 23, 130, 148, 165, 236, 274, 275, 281
Horowitz, J., 6
Howard, K. I., 56, 228, 230, 238, 248, 257, 259, 270, 277, 281

Howarth, E., 6, 56, 237
Hundleby, J. D., 3, 4, 6, 11, 12, 17, 22, 23, 26, 27, 29, 33, 46, 56, 165, 229, 230, 231, 237, 252, 269, 277, 281, 283, 285
Hunt, J. McV., 234
Husek, E., 6

Ishikawa, A., 6
Ismail, A. H., 234

Jackson, D. N., 2
Jackson, P. W., 230, 246
Jaspars, J., 6
Jensen, A. R., 270
Jung, C. G., 25, 26, 238, 271

Kagan, J., 234
Kaplan, H. I., 5
Karson, S., 6, 10, 247, 269
Kawash, G., 6
Killian, L. R., 3, 6, 22, 23, 56, 228, 232, 235, 248, 250, 251, 255, 259
King, L. D., 23, 243, 244, 245, 246
Klein, T. M., 6, 22, 33, 53, 54, 56, 135, 136, 137, 170, 214, 215, 222, 228, 234, 236, 238, 270, 277, 278, 281
Kleinmuntz, B., 267, 268, 269
Kline, P., 3, 5, 6, 10, 15, 17
Knapp, R. R., 3, 6, 22, 23, 56, 214, 218, 228, 229, 230, 231, 232, 233, 234, 235, 236, 237, 238, 247, 248, 257, 258, 259, 260, 281
Koch, S., 5, 10
Korth, B., 6
Krawiec, T. S., 3
Kristy, N. F., 6, 22, 58, 228, 229, 270
Krug, S. E., 6, 10, 16, 269, 270, 275

Kuder, G. F., 232, 237, 238, 247
Kuhn, T. S., 4

La Rochefoucauld, F., 264
Laughlin, J., 6, 16
Lavoisier, A. L., 272
Lawlis, G. F., 253, 268
Le Bon, G., 235
Leiman, J. M., 224, 225
Levy, L. H., 15
Liebert, R. M., 15
Lily, J., 6
Lindzey, G., 3, 5, 10, 15
Lohnes, P. R., 268
Loucks, A., 229
Luborsky, L., 6
Lushene, R. E., 6

McDougall, W., 235
McMichael, R. E., 6
McNemar, Q., 268

Maddi, S. R., 15
Madsen, D., 6
Mahrer, A. H., 5, 267
May, M., 12
Mayeske, G. W., 6, 56, 236
Meehl, P. E., 268, 272
Meeland, T., 6
Meredith, G. M., 3, 6, 231
Meschieri, L., 6
Messick, S. J., 2, 184
Mitchell, B., 5
Most, J. A., 3, 228, 230, 247

Nesselroade, J. R., 3, 6, 10, 49, 56, 58, 165, 214, 257, 269, 270, 275
Nichols, K., 6
Norman, W. F., 212, 213, 273
Nunnally, J., 268

O'Dell, J. W., 10, 247, 269

Patrick, S., 6, 228, 229, 235, 238, 248, 256, 272

Pawlik, K., 3, 4, 6, 10, 11, 12, 17, 22, 26, 29, 33, 46, 51, 56, 222, 228, 229, 230, 233, 236, 237, 238, 265, 269, 277, 281, 283, 285
Pervin, L. A., 5, 10, 15, 269
Peterson, D. R., 6, 229
Pichot, P., 6
Pierson, G., 6, 12, 16, 55, 212, 257, 271
Pieszko, H. A., 274
Porter, R. B., 6
Prell, D. B., 234, 238
Price, P. L., 6, 228, 229, 235, 238, 248, 256, 269, 272
Priestley, J., 272

Quay, H., 229

Radcliffe, J., 6, 274, 275, 281
Reese, H. W., 10, 49
Rethlingshafer, D., 6, 281
Reuterman, N. A., 56, 228, 230, 238, 248, 257, 259, 270, 277, 281
Rhymer, R. M., 6
Rican, P., 6
Rickels, K., 6, 23, 56, 234, 248, 270
Rimoldi, H. J., 281
Rorschach, H., 1, 9, 12, 129, 166, 265
Ross, G., 184
Royce, J. R., 6, 10, 23, 165, 184, 229, 230, 281
Ryans, D. G., 6, 281

Sahakian, W. S., 15
Sankar, S., 5
Sarason, S. B., 15, 233
Saunders, D. R., 6, 56, 212
Schaie, K. W., 6
Scheier, I. H., 3, 6, 22, 23, 30, 55, 56, 58, 155, 165, 214, 218, 228, 229, 230, 231, 232, 233, 234, 236, 248, 249, 250, 251, 259

Schiff, H., 56

Schmid, J., 224, 225

Schmidt, L. R., 3, 4, 6, 10, 12, 17, 22, 23, 27, 30, 33, 49, 51, 56, 58, 165, 227, 228, 229, 230, 231, 232, 235, 236, 238, 248, 249, 250, 251, 252, 255, 256, 261, 265, 267, 277, 281

Schneewind, K. R., 6

Schoenemann, P., 6

Schuerger, J. M., 3, 6, 10, 17, 23, 27, 56, 58, 136, 137, 170, 214, 215, 222, 228, 229, 231, 232, 248, 257, 268, 269, 277, 281

Schwartz, E., 212

Schwartz, H., 228, 231, 233, 235, 260

Sealy, A. P., 6

Sells, S. B., 6, 10, 15, 228, 234

Spearman, C., 1, 50

Spiegler, M. D., 15

Spielberger, C. D., 5, 10, 30

Stagner, R., 15

Stice, G. F., 6, 22, 58, 228, 229, 270

Sullivan, W. P., 6

Sweney, A. B., 6, 269, 274, 275, 281

Swenson, A., 23

Szondi, 1

Tatro, D. F., 3, 6, 23, 34, 56, 227, 228, 229, 231, 232, 235, 236, 238, 248, 250, 251, 255, 277, 278

Tatsuoka, M. M., 15, 50, 129, 234, 237, 256, 267, 268, 277

Taylor, J. A., 233

Thornton, G. R., 6

Thurstone, L. L., 2, 6

Tiner, L. G., 6

Tollefson, D., 6

Tomson, B., 228, 231, 233, 235, 260

Tsujioka, B., 51, 267

Tsushima, T., 233, 234

Uberla, K., 6

Ustrzycki, G. J., 229, 230, 234, 259

Valley, J., 6

Vaughan, D., 6

Vaughan, G., 6

Vernon, P. E., 2, 265

Vidal, A., 6

Wagner, A., 6

Warburton, F. W., 1, 3, 6, 33, 46, 264, 277, 281, 283

Wardell, D. M., 3, 6, 16, 23, 33, 34, 56, 57, 58, 165, 184, 212, 229, 230, 231, 233, 234, 235, 248, 257, 277, 279, 281

Watterson, D. G., 6, 10, 11, 268, 269

Wenger, M. A., 6

Wenig, P., 6

Wepman, J. M., 15

White, P. O. 6, 222

Wiggins, J. S., 6, 10, 15, 268, 269

Wilde, G. J. S., 6

Williams, H. V., 6

Winder, A. E., 6

Wispe, L., 6

Witkin, H. A., 6, 28, 229, 245

Wolman, B., 5

Yee, R., 6, 23

Yeudall, L. T., 3, 16, 23, 33, 34, 56, 57, 58, 212, 233, 234, 235, 248, 277, 279, 281

Young, F., 234

Subject Index

Ad hoc tests
  unprofitableness in relation to theory, 241
Affective psychoses
  depressives, trait distinctions, 254-255
  manics, trait distinctions, 254-256
Age corrections of scores
  age curve for U.I. 16, 149
  age curve for U.I. 17, 150
  age curve for U.I. 19, 151
  age curve for U.I. 20, 152
  age curve for U.I. 21, 153
  age curve for U.I. 23, 154
  age curve for U.I. 24, 155
  age curve for U.I. 25, 156
  age curve for U.I. 26, 157
  age curve for U.I. 28, 158
  age curve for U.I. 32, 159
  age curve for U.I. 33, 160
ANOVA
  role as a research design, 5, 26
Answer sheets
  keys to, 172-208
  mechanical aids in scoring, 166
  OpScan use, 166
  use in O-A battery, 47, 166
Anxiety, U.I. 24
  age curve for, 155
  criterion correlations with clinical, occupational, educational, social, and physiological variables, 232
  description of, 30
  eight subtests and timing in, 41
Apathetic temperament, U.I. 27
  description, 279
  subtests in battery, 279
Asthenia-vs.-self-assurance, U.I. 28
  age curve for, 158
  criterion correlations in clinical, educational, occupational, and other areas, 236
  description of, 31
  seven subtests and timing in, 43

Basic research
  utility of O-A Kit in, 22
Behavioral indices, b's, 11
Behavior (or symptom) specification equation. See Specification equation
"Bound anxiety"
  possible interpretation as U.I. 34, 280

Capacity to mobilize-vs.-regression, U.I. 23
  age curve for, 154
  criterion correlations in clinical, occupational, educational, social, and physiological areas, 231
  description of, 30
  early criterion relations, 9
  eight subtests and timing in, 40
CAQ (Clinical Analysis Questionnaire), 211
Character disorders
  profile of source trait deviations, 259
Clinical, pathological areas
  chief source traits operative, 249
  clinical diagnosis of six syndromes: power of O-A Kit to separate, 262
  utility of O-A Kit in, 28
Computer synthesis scoring
  background of, 34
  rationale of calculations in, 140-143
  table of weights for, 144-147
  values of concept validities attained by it for 10 source traits, 54
Concrete "validity" or relevance
  as basis for trait choice, 33
Concrete relevances
  and concrete validity concept, 55
Consistency of tests
  defined, 49
  values for 10 trait batteries, 51
Conspective tests
  coefficient of conspection, 166
  value of, 166
Control (or Inhibition), U.I. 17
  age curve for, 150
  description of, 277
  subtests in, 278

Cortertia-vs.-Pathemia, U.I. 22
    reason for absence from main battery, 34
    subtests in battery, 278
    theory of, 278
CORAN
    research use contrasted with ANOVA, 5
Creativity
    source traits in real life creativity, 246
Cross-cultural O-A measures
    constancy of personality structure, 265
Culture fair intelligence tests
    appropriate time in relation to O-A Kit, 264
    their integration with personality measurement, 245

Delinquency and crime
    main differences from normals, 260
    main trait difference from neurotic and psychotic, 258
    personality researches in, 248, 257
    specification equation for probability of delinquency, 261
Dependability coefficient
    considering test length, 50
    defined, 49
    for 10 source traits corrected to standard length, 52
    for 10 source trait batteries, 51
Depth psychometry
    relation to factor strata structure, 210
    space shared by T, L, and Q-data factors, 212
    utility in predictions, 223
Diagnosis
    clinical; by O-A Kit, 248
    educational, 242
    by types, 267
Discouragement-vs.-Sanguineness, U.I. 33
    age curve for, 160
    criterion correlations in clinical, educational, social, and other areas, 238
    description of, 32
    seven subtests and timing in, 45
Dynamic traits
    measured to extend O-A predictions, 273-274

Educational prediction and selection
    utility of O-A Kit in, 22
Educational psychology
    O-A contribution to understanding the individual case, 245
    predictions of different school performance areas from the full O-A battery, 244
    the source traits of highest predictive value, 243
    the source traits of lesser predictive value, 243-244
Ego standards (Competitiveness), U.I. 16
    age curve for, 149
    criterion relations, clinical, occupational, educational and physiological, 227
    description of, 28
    eight subtests and timing in, 36
Eight State Questionnaire
    as adjunct to the O-A Kit, 276
Evasiveness, U.I. 20
    age curve for, 152
    criterion correlations, clinical, occupational, educational, 229
    description of, 27
    seven subtests and timing in, 38
Extended O-A Kit
    design of, 33
    factors in, 14, 277
    high criterion relations in some traits, 58, 281
    validities in, 56
Exuberance, U.I. 21
    age curve for, 153
    criterion correlations in clinical, occupational, educational, and physiological areas, 230
    description of, 29
    eight subtests and timing in, 39
Exvia-vs.-Invia, U.I. 32
    age curve for, 159
    criterion relations in clinical, occupational, educational, social, and physiological areas, 236
    description of, 32
    eight subtests and timing in, 44

Factor analysis
    logic of, 5

Fluctuation of traits
    need to recognize magnitude of in source
        traits, 266
    See also Trait constancy coefficient
Functional testing
    and structured tests, 9

Genetic and environmental components
    value of source trait knowledge of, in
        personality theory and therapy, 270
    See separate source trait descriptions
        beginning page 28

Handbook
    principles in designing, 15
    connections with theory, 15
HSPQ (High School Personality Question-
    naire), 211
Homogeneity coefficient
    defined, 49
Hypomanic temperament, U.I. 18
    description, 278
    subtests in battery, 278

Inconautia-vs.-Practicalness, U.I. 34
    subtests in battery for, 280
    theory of, 280
Independence-vs.-Subduedness, U.I. 19
    age curve for, 151
    criterion correlations in clinical, occupa-
        tional, educational, etc., areas, 228
    description of, 28
    seven subtests and timing in, 37
Individual test supplement to Kit, 33
Inductive-hypothetico-deductive spiral in
    source trait definition, 3
Instructions to subjects. *See* Test adminis-
    tration
Intelligence
    as the 11th O-A Kit battery, 264
    its interaction with personality in school
        performance, 246
    See also Culture fair intelligence tests
Instrument-transcending, "instrument
    free" trait measures
    and concept validity, 55
    and inferences across media, 257
    and matchings across media, 212
    See also Principle of indifference of indi-
    cator

Interpretation of source traits
    difficulties in, 26
    neologisms necessary, 26
    previously recognized vs. new traits, 27
    role of criterion relations in, 27

Keys to answer sheets, arranged by
    individual factors
    for U.I. 16, 172
    for U.I. 19, 176
    for U.I. 20, 179
    for U.I. 21 (Expendable booklets), 186
    for U.I. 23, 188
    for U.I. 24, 192
    for U.I. 25, 197
    for U.I. 28, 200
    for U.I. 32, 204-205
    for U.I. 33, 208

Master Index numbers
    meaning of, 36
    numbers in the Extended O-A Kit, 277-
    281
Mental health gain
    in personality theory not a change on
        one factor only, 267
Mobilization-vs.-Regression. *See* Capacity
    to Mobilize
Motivation measures (the MAT) in relation
    to O-A Kit
    in specification equation, 241
    as to time allowance, 265
Multivariate experimental methods
    shortage of teaching in, 5

Narcism or Narcistic Ego, U.I. 26
    age curve for, 157
    description of, 278
    subtests in battery, 279
Neurosis
    discriminant function separation from
        psychosis, 252-254
    significances of differences from con-
        trols, 250
    as a trait pattern, 249

O-A Kit, Main Battery
    administration. *See also* Instructions, 59
    areas of utility, 21, 22
    choice of factors in, 33

construction principles, 14, 17, 33, 35
first publication of, 13
general reliability and validity in practical time, 58
power to separate six clinical syndrome groups, 262
relations to Q-data factors, 56, 57
its spanning of the personality sphere, 273
special properties of, 11
as a teaching aid, 6
Objective tests and T-data
absence of "inherent theory in the media," 26
advantages over questionnaires, 214
definition and history of, 12
obstacles to development of, 2
skills and time expenditures in, 24
Occupational psychology
main predictive source traits in, 247
Over-reactivity, U.I. 29
subtests in battery, 279
theory of, 279

Paranoia
pattern of distinction from other psychoses, 255
Personality sphere concept
as basis of L-, Q-, and T-media factors, 213
Personality theory
central role of behavioral equation in, 241
and clinical psychology, 249
concept of "general pathology," 249
concept of predisposing, process, and residual trait associations, 249
its dependence on psychometry, 263
on distinction of anxiety and neuroticism, 251-252
on exvia and delinquency, 259
on genetics and delinquency, 260
historical stages in theory growth, 4
on the inclusion of states in the specification equation, 275
on interaction of mathematical model and psychological concepts, 263
and manic-depressive psychoses, 256
in prediction of delinquency, 273

problems in blending present theory with pre-metric clinical theory, 271
on psychosis-neurosis distinction, 251
and psychotherapy, 253
quantitative theory, recent, of rapid growth, 272
regarding traits effective in groups, 248
role in educational psychology, 243
theory of inability to mobilize, 272
Popularity
source traits predictive of, 248
Principle of indifference of indicator
in source trait measurement, 11
as transcendance of instrument factors, 16
Psychological insights and the mathematical model of personality theory
gain from knowing natural history of source traits, 263
Psychometry
conspection coefficient, 166
efficiency coefficient, 266
general principles in, 265-268
knowledge assumed in reader, 268
and personality theory, 265
standard length coefficients, 50
varieties of consistency coefficients, 49
varieties of validity coefficients, 50
utility coefficient, 266
Psychosis
discriminant function for separating from neurotics and controls, 253-254
pattern of differences from controls, 251
Psychotherapy
and general personality theory, 269
O-A Kit as a monitoring device, 23
therapeutic gain measured on U.I. 23 and 24, 257-258
training of the therapist, 276
uncertainty of gain when not measured on traits, 268

Qualifications required in the O-A user, 5
Questionnaire (Q-data) factors
in the case of anxiety, U.I. 24
in the case of exvia, U.I. 32; independence, U.I. 19; cortertia, U.I. 22; and control, U.I. 17, 56

factorial evidence for identity in U.I. 17, U.I. 24, and U.I. 32, 56
   in relation to T-data traits, 55
Realism-vs.-Tensidia, U.I. 25
   age curve for, 156
   criterion correlations in clinical, educational, occupational, and genetic areas, 235
   description of, 31
   seven subtests and timing in, 42
Reflexological therapy
   its need for psychometric enlargement, 268
Reliability coefficient
   defined, 49
Retesting
   reliability as dependability coefficients for 10 traits, 51, 52
   time interval for repeat, 47
Rorschach test, 1

Schizophrenia
   distinctions from normals, 255
   placed on discriminant functions, 254
   as a trait pattern, 249
Scoring. See Test scoring
Second-stratum T-data (O-A) traits
   criterion relations of, 224, 225
   estimation of scores on, 211, 217
   nature and scoring elements for O-A secondaries, 218
   predictive power of secondaries (formulae for), 225
   relative importance of primaries and secondaries, 223
   Schmid-Leiman equation for joint prediction from primaries and secondaries, 224
   second-stratum Q factors matched with T primaries, 213
   table of second-stratum factor loadings in the O-A, 216
Self-sentiment strength, U.I. 36
   described, 281
16 PF Questionnaire, 211
Social currents in scientific advance, 2
Somindence-vs.-Dissofrustance, U.I. 30
   subtests in battery for, 280
   theory of, 279

Source traits
   best replicated examples, 4
   definition of, 16
   correlation table for primary source traits, 215
   cross-cultural constancy of, 27
   "natural history" of, 17
   number now discovered, 3
   problems in descriptions of, 25
   relation of T- and Q-factors, 16
   testable theories about, 3
   theoretical starkness of, 10
Specification equation
   with abilities and dynamic traits included, 241
   as a basis for analyzing the individual case, 242
   general form of, 10
   for probability of delinquency, 261
   with states and error of measurement included, 18
Stability coefficient
   defined, 49
   for 10 source trait batteries, 51
Step-wise regression
   of trait prediction in school performance, 245
Stolparsomnia-vs.-Proneness to Excitement, U.I. 35
   subtests in battery for, 281
   theory of, 280
Stratified uncorrelated determiner (SUD)
   model for personality structure, 223
Structured tests
   meaning of, 9
Subtests
   number required per factor, 35
   psychologists' title and subjects' title, 36, 167
   scoring keys for, 171-208
   set out for traits U.I. 16 - U.I. 33, 36-46
Supplementary O-A Battery
   design of, 33
   general nature of validities, 56
   use of individual testing in, 56
Score Summary Sheets, by factors
   for U.I. 16, 174
   for U.I. 19, 177
   for U.I. 20, 181-184
   for U.I. 21, 186

for U.I. 23, 189-190
for U.I. 24, 193-194
for U.I. 25, 198
for U.I. 28, 201-202
for U.I. 32, 205-206
for U.I. 33, 209
practical illustration of scoring use, on U.I. 16, 290
Suppressor action
in battery design, 34
Surface traits
contrasted with source traits, 26
Szondi test, 1

Test administration instructions
for U.I. 16, Ego standards, 62-68
for U.I. 19, Independence, 69-75
for U.I. 20, Evasiveness, 76-80
for U.I. 21, Exuberance, 81-88
for U.I. 23, Mobilization-vs.-Regression, 89-94
for U.I. 24, Anxiety, 95-100
for U.I. 25, Realism-vs.-Tensidia, 101-107
for U.I. 28, Asthenia-vs.-Self-assurance, 108-113
for U.I. 32, Exvia-Invia, 114-122
for U.I. 33, Discouragement-vs.-Sanguineness, 123-127
general requirements, 59-61
Test booklets
reusable and expendable, 60
Test scoring practice
age correction table, 162
devices suggested for speeding scoring, 291
keys to answer sheets, 172-208
See also keys by factors
practical illustration of scoring, on U.I. 16, 287
score summary sheets, 134, 167, 174-209
score summary sheets derivation of, 134
See also score summary sheets by factors
score summary sheet; practical illustration of use, 290
translations among stens, standard scores, and centiles, 163

Test scoring principles
age development curve, U.I. 16, 149
age development curve, U.I. 17, 150
age development curve, U.I. 19, 151
age development curve, U.I. 20, 152
age development curve, U.I. 21, 153
age development curve, U.I. 23, 154
age development curve, U.I. 24, 155
age development curve, U.I. 25, 156
age development curve, U.I. 26, 157
age development curve, U.I. 28, 158
age development curve, U.I. 32, 159
age development curve, U.I. 33, 160
approximate and exact procedures, 132
computer synthesis: rationale of calculations, 143
principles of age corrections, 148
principles of age correction tables, 161-162
psychometry of factor measurement, 129
rationale of derivation of subtest weights, 135
single factor matrix score estimation, 130-131
sten scores and their relations to centiles and standard scores, 161-164
table showing use of e, m, s, and w values on U.I. 16 score, 133
table showing use of e, m, s, and w values on U.I. 19 score, 134
table showing use of e, m, s, and w values on U.I. 20 score, 135
table showing use of e, m, s, and w values on U.I. 21 score, 136
table showing use of e, m, s, and w values on U.I. 23 score, 137
table showing use of e, m, s, and w values on U.I. 24 score, 138
table showing use of e, m, s, and w values on U.I. 25 score, 139
table showing use of e, m, s, and w values on U.I. 28 score, 140
table showing use of e, m, s, and w values on U.I. 32 score, 141
table showing use of e, m, s, and w values on U.I. 33 score, 142
weights tabulated for computer synthesis, 144-147

Testing strategy, in relation to personality theory, 264
Testing time
  wise allocation of, 267
Third-stratum T-data (O-A) traits
  correlations among tertiaries, 221
  derivation of structure from primaries, 211
  loadings of tertiaries on secondaries, 221
  utility of higher strata in depth psychometry, 222
Titles of source traits
  list of 10 in main battery, 26
  neologisms superior to popular terms, 25
  rationale for, 25
Trait constancy and fluctuation indices
  defined, 49
  values for 10 source traits, 51
Transferability coefficient
  defined, 51
Type (species type) placement
  rationale of, 267
  relation to APA diagnostic categories, 262

Universal Index, U.I.
  numbers for source traits, 25

Vocational guidance and industry
  utility of O-A Kit in, 22
Validity of test
  concept validity, 50
  concept validity for computer synthesis scoring, 54
  concept validity for 10 source trait batteries, 53
  concrete validity, 50
  defined, 49
  and proposed standard test length, 50
Variance allocation scoring. *See* computer synthesis

WAIS, scoring comparison, 130
WISC, scoring comparison, 130
Wariness-vs.-Impulsivity-variability, U.I. 31
  description of, 280
  subtests in battery, 280